The Road to Cooperstown

THE ROAD TO COOPERSTOWN

A Critical History of Baseball's Hall of Fame Selection Process

by James F. Vail

McFarland & Company, Inc., Publishers
Jefferson, North Carolina, and London

Library of Congress Cataloguing-in-Publication Data

Vail, James F., 1948–
    The road to Cooperstown : a critical history of baseball's Hall
of Fame selection process / by James F. Vail.
        p.   cm.
    Includes index.
    ISBN 0-7864-1012-4 (softcover : 50# alkaline paper) ∞
    1. National Baseball Hall of Fame and Museum.   I. Title.
GV863.A1V35   2001
796.357'64'07474774 — dc21   2001037060

British Library cataloguing data are available

Manufactured in the United States of America

*McFarland & Company, Inc., Publishers
    Box 611, Jefferson, North Carolina 28640
    www.mcfarlandpub.com*

For Patti,
whose heart exceeds any imaginable expectation

Contents

Acknowledgments

I would like to thank Bill Deane, former Senior Research Associate for the National Baseball Library and Archive at Cooperstown, for his patience and kind assistance in answering my questions, especially regarding the voting rules and procedures of the Veterans Committee. Thanks also to archivist Steve Gietschier and *The Sporting News* for their aid in locating and providing the photos in the text, and to Bruce Koon for his generous contribution to their acquisition. I also owe a note of appreciation to Allen A. Gwinnell for his helpful commentary about many players from the 1940s, who I was not privileged to see play — especially Vern Stephens and other shortstops of that era. Thanks also to Frank Domiano for asking many pertinent questions and listening to far more in response than he ever wished to hear, and to Tom Crooks, who knows more about the game itself than anyone I've ever met.

Finally, my deepest gratitude goes to my wife, Patti, who has been nothing less than soul mate, intellectual confidante, statistical co-analyst, constructive literary critic and proofreader; whose loving patience surpasses that of Job; and whose ceaseless positive support deserves as much credit for the completion of this book as does stubborn perseverance on my part.

Introduction

The Baseball Hall of Fame at Cooperstown, New York, has two sets of electors, both of which vote each year. One group, the Baseball Writers Association of America (BBWAA), votes by mail, using a preordained list of retired players that meet the writers' current eligibility requirements. Results of that balloting are announced in mid–January. Their counterpart, the Veterans Committee (VC), comprises former players who are Hall of Fame members plus retired baseball executives and sportswriters. They meet annually in Florida during spring training (usually in March), where the members vote in person after debating the merits of the candidates, all of whom are no longer eligible for the writers' voting. The VC's mandate is to select deserving men who have somehow slipped through the BBWAA process without being honored. Given that, the panel serves as the Hall of Fame's court of last resort and is widely perceived as its "back-door" method of election.

In 2000 the two groups chose five new members for Cooperstown. Prior to their elections, each of those men —catcher Carlton Fisk and first baseman Tony Perez (chosen by the writers) plus nineteenth-century second baseman John "Bid" McPhee, ex-manager George "Sparky" Anderson and former Negro-league outfielder Norman "Turkey" Stearnes (all tabbed by the VC)— had been victims of at least one of many problems which have plagued the Hall of Fame selection process since its beginning in 1936.

Fisk, whose career spanned 1969–93, played more games at catcher (2226) than anyone else in major-league history (he appeared in 2499 overall). At the time of his election, Carlton also had more runs scored (1276) and total bases (3999) than any man who played primarily at his position; his 376 career home runs ranked second among catchers, behind Hall of Famer Johnny Bench (389); his 2356 hits were more than any other backstop except Ted Simmons (2472); and his 1330 runs batted in were the fourth-best total among the men who played behind the plate (Cooperstown member Yogi Berra was the leader with 1430). Beyond all that, while playing for Boston, Fisk hit what probably was the second or third most dramatic home run in baseball history — his extra-inning solo shot that won game six of the 1975 World Series against Cincinnati (Bobby Thomson's playoff-winning homer for the New York Giants against Brooklyn in 1951 is usually placed on the top of that list; and, beyond it, only Bill Mazeroski's World Series–ending tater of 1960 rivals Fisk's for number two).

With those statistical and subjective credentials, by all rights Fisk should've been elected to Cooperstown in his first year of eligibility, which came in 1999. Instead, he placed only fourth on the BBWAA ballot that year, earning 330 of a possible 497 votes for 66.4 percent support that fell forty-three votes shy of the 75 percent approval required for election. Fisk was passed over in 1999 because three other men who were also new to the ballot — pitcher Nolan Ryan (324 career victories), third baseman George Brett (3154 hits) and shortstop Robin Yount (3142 safeties) — all had met one of Cooperstown's three unofficial but de facto standards for election (300 pitching wins, 3000 hits or 500 home runs). As a result, these men commanded the attention of most voters (Ryan earned 98.8 percent support, Brett received 98.2 percent and Yount got 77.5), and their attainment of these de facto totals made Carlton's achievements appear relatively humdrum in comparison.

Perez had been a victim of a different problem. At the time of his election, Tony ranked eighteenth among the career leaders in runs batted in; and, for several years, his 1652 RBI — more than those accumulated by 112 Hall of Famers elected as batters including Tris Speaker, Joe DiMaggio and Mickey Mantle — easily represented the highest total among eligible players not yet elected to the Hall (Dave Parker's 1493 were the most in 2000). Also, his 379 home runs ranked fortieth among the leaders in that category, although there were seven Cooperstown-eligible men above him who had not been elected (topped by Dave Kingman with 442). But, unlike hits and homers, there is no de facto standard for runs batted in, and the voters have a decided preference for sluggers with high batting averages. As a result, among the fifteen Cooperstown members ahead of Perez on the career RBI list, twelve of them had batting averages above .300, and the three who didn't — Carl Yastrzemski (3419 hits), Frank Robinson (586 home runs) and Reggie Jackson (563 four-baggers) — each had achieved one of the de facto criteria. Among that group, only Jackson (.262) had a lower batting average than Tony's .279. So Perez, who became eligible for election in 1992, waited nine years—in which his support ranged between 50.0 and 67.9 percent—to gain election; and, when Tony did, he just barely made it with 77.2 percent approval.

McPhee's election was delayed by at least three factors. Bid played during the period 1882–99, and died in 1943. For much of Cooperstown's voting history, and for reasons which varied over time, the electors have had difficulty choosing players from the nineteenth century. Among the non-pitchers from that era who have gained election, almost all of them were men with batting averages above .300. McPhee batted .271 for his career, the lowest figure for any non-pitcher from that period elected to date (although his 2250 career hits were the highest total for any eligible second baseman not yet elected through 1999). In contrast, Bid was probably the greatest fielder of the nineteenth century. He led his league in double plays at his position eleven times and topped his circuit in fielding on nine occasions, in putouts eight times, in chances-per-game seven and in assists six times. But, as must be obvious from the discussion to this point, Cooperstown glory is usually reserved for great hitters. There are only a handful of Hall of Famers whose fielding prowess was arguably instrumental in their elections, and the selections of each of those has drawn considerable criticism over the years. Finally, McPhee also spent eight of his eighteen big-league seasons in the defunct American Association (AA). The association, which operated for a decade (1882–91), was the first and longest lasting nineteenth-century rival to the still existent National League, which—formed in 1876—is generally regarded as baseball's first "major" circuit. For inexplicable reasons, the electors have shied away from AA players; and, before McPhee's election, only one man on the Cooperstown roster (outfielder Tommy McCarthy) had spent as many as four seasons in the association.

When the Hall of Fame was established in the late 1930s, there was little or no thought given to honoring anyone for a non-playing capacity. But, because of the absence of any meaningful guidelines, at least two men—John McGraw and Connie Mack—received support in the first BBWAA election of 1936 that was based, in part, on their lengthy and successful careers as managers, and both of those men were elected the following year by a forerunner to the current Veterans Committee. Over the next three decades, a handful of pilots continued to receive sporadic support from the writers, but only one—former Yankees skipper Miller Huggins—ever came relatively close to election by the scribes. By the late 1960s, the VC possessed exclusive authority to select managers; but, until the 1990s—when five of the Hall's first fifteen skippers were chosen by the panel — their election remained a low priority. Upon his selection in 2000, Sparky Anderson became number sixteen. At the time, his 2194 regular-season victories were the third-best total in history, and — because he didn't retire until after the 1995 season — he was the last of baseball's seven pilots with 2000 wins or more to be chosen.

Stearnes, who played from 1923 to 1942 and died in 1979, was a victim of baseball's early segregation and the absence of complete statistical records for the Negro leagues. Men of color were barred from the Show from the late 1880s until Jackie Robinson joined the Brooklyn Dodgers in 1947; and, in the absence of big-league opportunity, several "major" Negro circuits operated after 1919. Robinson was elected to Cooperstown in 1962, but it was not until a decade later that the Hall — with much reluctance — opened its doors to players from those leagues. Since then, the men elected have been chosen primarily for their subjective reputations (even more so than most other Hall of Famers), in large part because the economics of Negro-league operation — which dictated limited personnel, a relatively small number of official league games and much barnstorming exhibition — precluded copious recording of the players' statistical performances. As a result, although Stearnes batted .352 in the 910 league games for which his statistics are available and is the recognized career leader for home runs in those contests (182), his reputation was never as glorious as those of other sluggers like Josh Gibson (whose known homer total is 155, but who some historians estimate hit over 800 four-baggers) or Buck Leonard (who is officially credited with 77). In turn, Stearnes became one of many great players from the Negro majors who were overlooked in the first three decades of their Cooperstown inclusion.

Because it depends entirely upon subjective impressions which inevitably derive from individual bias, the Hall of Fame selection process has always been captive of political exigencies that often outweigh the testimony of individual performance statistics. The procedure is also infected by a rivalry between Cooperstown's two elective organs, which often have worked at cross purposes. All of this has prompted widespread criticism of the institution and its roster, most of it from baseball's most avid fans. By the late 1990s members of the Society for American Baseball Research (SABR), a group of more than six thousand of the game's most ardent and knowledgeable followers, had become so exasperated by perceived injustices among the Cooperstown roster that the organization seriously discussed establishing its own rival hall of fame. But, even if they do so, the SABR version would have great difficulty achieving the same recognition and significance among the public at large as that accorded to the established predecessor.

In 1994 baseball historian Bill James published *The Politics of Glory* (paperback title, *Whatever Happened to the Hall of Fame?*), which exposed much of the institutional bumbling that led to Cooperstown's political quagmire. But, although that effort explained many of the human reasons why some men are elected and others are not, it did little to examine the actual numbers of Hall of Fame voting — either the voting patterns of the electors or the precedents set by the performance statistics of the men who've been elected. This book attempts to fill that gap; and, by necessity, it focuses mainly on process. In most instances, for reasons of space, it also is written with the assumption that the reader has some knowledge of the players discussed.

1

The Tainted Shrine

I believe in the Church of Baseball. I've tried all of the major religions, and most of the minor ones. I've worshipped Buddha, Allah, Brahma, Vishnu, Shiva, trees, mushrooms and Isadora Duncan. I know things. For instance, there are 108 beads in a Catholic Rosary, and 108 stitches in a baseball. When I learned that, I gave Jesus a chance. But, it just didn't work out between us. The Lord laid too much guilt on me. I prefer metaphysics to theology. You see, there's no guilt in baseball. ... I've tried 'em all. I really have. And, the only church that truly feeds the soul, day-in, day-out, is the Church of Baseball.—Annie Savoy

To some baseball fans—casual ones who might think that Fred Merkle was Ricky and Lucy Ricardo's bald, cigar-chewing neighbor, and maybe even a few students of the game who know that Merkle was an old-time player whose failure to touch second base on a key late-season play supposedly cost the New York Giants a pennant early in the twentieth century—the Hall of Fame at Cooperstown, New York, is just a museum that houses artifacts celebrating the careers of the sport's most legendary personalities. Many of these people perceive that a man's election to Cooperstown is, on face value, inviolate evidence of his stature among the greats of the game; and, unless some player they idolize has been denied membership to date, they have no reason to question the roster of men honored there.

But, for others who are more obsessed with the national pastime—those who are tithing members of the Church of Baseball defined by fictional A-ball groupie Annie Savoy in the opening scene of the 1988 film *Bull Durham*, who can describe the roles played in "Merkle's Boner" by Al Bridwell, Moose McCormick, Johnny Evers and Iron Man McGinnity and can tell you that Merkle's baserunning gaffe didn't hurt the Giants' pennant chances in 1908 nearly as much as the club's three losses later that same week to Phillies pitcher Harry Coveleski (who won only one other game that season)— the edifice at Cooperstown is their temple, a holy site like the Grand Mosque at Mecca. To these true believers, the baseball adage "take a pitch, then hit to right" is one of their Ten Commandments, Ernest Lawrence Thayer's "Casey at the Bat" is their Twenty-third Psalm, the Macmillan *Baseball Encyclopedia* is their Bible and Pete Palmer and John Thorn's *Total Baseball* its official concordance. For them, the museum is the "Shrine," to which each is compelled to make at least one pilgrimage in a lifetime in order to attain eternal horsehide salvation, and every Hall of Fame induction is a sacred rite in which players are not merely honored, but "enshrined"— as though membership is tantamount to Roman Catholic sainthood or being among the twenty-eight anointed prophets of Islam.

In the six decades since the Hall of Fame (HOF) was established in the late 1930s, this reverential nomenclature has also become ingrained in the language of America's print and electronic media, extending the sense of Cooperstown's hallowed status into the nation's vernacular so that whether people take the Shrine seriously or not they are nonetheless aware of its exalted importance to the game's most avid followers. As a result, although virtually every sport played in America — from billiards to volleyball — has its own Hall of Fame, none of them, not even the football or basketball counterparts, generate the same level of interest and awareness as baseball's among the general population. So, when the annual announcements of new inductees into the pigskin and roundball halls are made, unless you live in Canton, Ohio, or Springfield, Massachusetts, the items appear as filler in the back of newspaper sports sections. But, every January when results of the Baseball Writers Association of America balloting for Cooperstown are released, the story merits a front-page teaser in *USA Today* and almost always can be found above the fold on the first page of the sports section in the nation's big-city dailies. Take a random poll of ten people at a grocery store or shopping mall and it's guaranteed that, whether or not they follow sports at all, eight or nine of them will be able to name more members of the Baseball Hall of Fame than those of any other game.

The annual selections for Cooperstown also generate much more debate and controversy than those for any other sport's Hall of Fame. When a John Mackey or Connie Hawkins is tabbed for his game's highest honor, you rarely hear some hard-core football or basketball fan grouse that Fred Arbanas or Mel Daniels should've been chosen instead, and no one who is already a member of either hall makes public statements that the selection somehow cheapened that institution's membership standards. But, when the Cooperstown Veterans Committee elected former New York Yankees shortstop Phil Rizzuto in 1994, many older fans across the country would've told you that either Vern Stephens, Marty Marion or Johnny Pesky was more deserving, and after second baseman Nellie Fox was chosen by the same committee in 1997, even Hall of Famer Reggie Jackson felt compelled to criticize the selection.

In that light, Annie Savoy was wrong about one thing. There is *some* guilt in baseball. Anyone who has a religious interest in the game is well aware that Cooperstown is, and probably always has been, a flawed institution — because, due to errors of selection and omission, the roster of men honored there is not perfect. To baseball's most pious faithful, these errors are sacrilege, grave heresies that defile their Shrine and must be recanted or corrected. So as a whole, the flaws among Cooperstown's membership constitute the Church of Baseball's great shame.

Unfortunately, there is little agreement among the faithful regarding these errors. In part, that's because, unlike most religions, conversion to the Church of Baseball grants each member an absolute right to question the faith's doctrine without fear of excommunication — the same way that the purchase of a ticket to a ball game imparts the privilege to boo. As a result, baseball's faithful are a contentious lot who endlessly debate the potential heresy of artificial turf, the designated hitter and wild-card playoff teams, and no church authority, not even the baseball commissioner — the sport's version of the pope — is ever perceived as infallible. In turn, the church is rife with sectarianism, much of it based upon subjective and often provincial loyalties.

So, many church members' personal lists of erroneously enshrined or unfairly excluded players are dependent upon their allegiance to a given team and (by association) league, and the level of heresy perceived in these errors is often relative to the member's distance from a given major-league city. Fans in Detroit or Philadelphia are unlikely to criticize the Hall of Fame status of former Tigers and A's third baseman George Kell and probably will not bemoan the omissions of hot-corner heroes like Ken Boyer, Stan Hack and Ron Santo. But, the faithful in St. Louis will decry Boyer's omission from Cooperstown, and the patrons in any tavern on Addision Street in Chicago will give you an earful about the injustice of both former Cubs being denied a place there.

But, the mistakes among the Hall of Fame's membership are not just false sightings of the Virgin Mary or mere figments of the provincial preferences among the Church of Baseball's members. The national pastime's most zealous converts may be disputatious about who, specifically, belongs in Cooperstown and who doesn't, but they agree almost universally that the Hall of Fame roster as presently constituted is rife with errors.

Through the year 2000, 249 men — excluding writers and announcers — had been elected to Cooperstown, including 185 chosen for their performance as major-league players, sixteen managers, seventeen executives, eight umpires, six pioneer contributors to the game, and seventeen men who were stars in the Negro leagues prior to baseball's integration in 1947. The 185 players chosen represent about 1.3 percent of the roughly fourteen thousand men who appeared in at least one big-league game in the years between the National League's formation in 1876 and 1994 (the last season a player could be active and still be eligible for HOF election by the year 2000). That number is also equal to an average of about 1.5 new Hall of Fame players entering the majors each year.

Most of the debate regarding errors of selection involves the men chosen for their playing careers. A substantial number of the faithful believe that the Shrine has been tainted by the admission of too many players who are undeserving of the honor. So, for every Babe Ruth, Hank Aaron or Walter Johnson, whose worthiness for baseball sainthood is undisputed, there is also a Tommy McCarthy, Fred Lindstrom, Chick Hafey or Jesse Haines, whose Cooperstown membership seems blasphemous to many.

But, to many diamond-obsessed believers — including some who argue that the Hall is already overstocked with mediocrity — errors of omission are also legion. As a result, there is also an army of players whose individual omissions as a whole absolutely debase the sacred temple. They include, but are nowhere close to being limited to, well-known names like Spud Chandler, Joe Gordon, Charlie Grimm, Mel Harder, Babe Herman, Gil Hodges, Roger Maris, Carl Mays, Lefty O'Doul, Al Oliver, Wally Schang, Ted Simmons, Maury Wills and — of course — the scandal-tainted Pete Rose and Joe Jackson, along with more obscure old-timers like Harlond Clift and Harry Stovey.

Those who believe that the Hall is tainted by mediocrity would no doubt prefer a current Cooperstown membership of around 140, which would approximate 1 percent of all players in history and equate with the 99th percentile that is the highest, traditional measure of excellence applied by statistical science. Others, who feel that too many deserving players have been overlooked in the selection process, might favor as much as a 2 percent standard instead, which would boost the Hall of Fame's current roster to about 280 players.

Regardless of the representational percentile applied, there is only one reason for these errors of selection and omission: meaningful standards for election to Cooperstown are virtually nonexistent. In the six decades since the first Hall of Fame voting was held in 1936, the only objective criterion ever established for membership is a requirement that candidates have at least ten years of service in the major leagues—and even that rule was circumvented on one occasion. Beyond that, in what has passed as ongoing refinement of the selection process, the only other guidelines ever provided to assist Hall of Fame electors in choosing new members are (1) a vague dictum, enacted in 1945, equating HOF qualification with undefined terms like "playing ability," "sportsmanship" and "character"; (2) a 1991 ruling that men placed on baseball's ineligible list for gambling or other indiscretions cannot be considered for membership; and (3) over the years, a series of changes in the voting rules that have defined the period of a candidate's eligibility for election. As a result, except for the ten-year service requirement, no measurable performance standard has ever been adopted for judgment of a man's credentials, and all determinations about the significance of a player's achievement have remained entirely dependent upon the subjective whims of the Hall of Fame electors.

As the only objective criterion established for Hall of Fame election, ten years of major-league service is hardly a standard of excellence. The National Association (NA) operated as America's first professional baseball circuit during 1871–75. But, although many of its players joined the modern National League (NL) upon its formation in 1876, the association is rarely given "major" status by the game's historians. During the years from the National League's formation through 1994, almost 2300 players, or about 16 percent of the overall total, appeared on some big-league roster in at least ten different seasons. Technically, all of those men have been, are, or will be eligible for Cooperstown. But, as will be demonstrated in a later chapter, many of them are not credible candidates for baseball's highest honor, and there are others who played less than ten seasons with far better credentials for enshrinement.

What's more, additional objective standards are unlikely to be adopted in the future. By mutual agreement between the Cooperstown museum's trustees and major-league baseball's administrative hierarchy, the Hall of Fame has been granted sole institutional authority to control the selection of its honorees. In turn, the board of trustees has anointed two separate groups as its only elective functionaries: the Baseball Writers Association of America (BBWAA), whose voting members currently include nearly five hundred journalists who cover the sport for the media, and the Veterans Committee (VC), a panel of about fifteen retired players, team executives and journalists, who are empowered — after the fact — to correct oversights in the BBWAA voting. Both groups vote annually, with successful candidates required to achieve 75 percent support in either election.

Members of the writers panel are entitled to vote for no more than ten men, all former players, among a list of about forty who are eligible each year. The Veterans Committee cannot choose anyone who is currently eligible for BBWAA election and in 2000 could select no more than one man from each of four separate categories—modern players overlooked by the BBWAA, major leaguers from the nineteenth century, former Negro leaguers, and (combined) former managers, executives or umpires.

Given the exclusivity of their separate powers, it's predictable that both elective parties would equate their respective privileges with the Divine Right of Kings, and that they would resist any impetus to curb their power as forcefully, or more so, than Britain's King John fought signing the Magna Carta. Since each of these groups has resisted adoption of any objective standards to date, and the use of any measurable criteria would inevitably reduce their current level of subjective authority, there is no reason to expect any change in the status quo—even if it would help to correct the errors among Hall of Fame membership.

Beyond the electors' urge to preserve the exclusivity of their powers, there is also much resistance among the Church of Baseball as a whole to the concept that there should be any objective standards for Cooperstown. Rooted in the romance of baseball, this opposition attempts to preserve the notions that greatness is subjectively obvious to anyone who is sufficiently knowledgeable and that it supersedes the ability to measure it statistically. So, although many members criticize the composition of the Hall of Fame roster, an equal or larger number staunchly defend the subjective foundation upon which the institution's selection process is based. That's because, generally, the faithful—electors and fans alike—are all prideful, at times even arrogant, about the righteousness of their individual, subjective perceptions regarding players' relative skills. Church members will cite any statistic that supports their own opinion about a player's ability or career achievement but are loathe to accept any data that subverts or contradicts the impressions that are the foundation for their own pantheon of great players. So, once a given believer has hoisted Babe Ruth, Ted Williams, or even Johnny Bench to the top of that pedestal, subjective opinion becomes righteous Truth, and no amount of evidence is sufficient to dislodge that player from his exalted position in that hierarchy or to elevate another man previously deemed unworthy.

As is natural to human nature, these pecking orders are almost always built upon a foundation of emotional memory. Most Church of Baseball faithful hold in highest reverence those players who displayed their skills during the formative years of the believer's youth. So it follows that those who now qualify for social security regard men like Bob Feller (who threw thunderbolts), Ted Williams (who served his country in time of war) and Joe DiMaggio (whose handsome features inspired poetry, song and a sex symbol) as the Jupiter, Mars and Apollo of their individual pantheons. It's also a rare baby boomer who does not perceive that either Willie Mays, Hank Aaron, Mickey Mantle or Sandy Koufax was the greatest player ever, and those Generation Xers who belong to the Church are far more likely to have Mike Schmidt, Reggie Jackson or Tom Seaver atop their sacred pyramids.

Unavoidably, this time-dependent bias also manifests among the Hall of Fame electorate, and who gets elected when is always dependent, in part, upon the age-related demography of the voters. Doubtless, no one has bothered to record the individual ages of BBWAA voters over the years. But during the early 1940s, when virtually everyone who had ever played the game was eligible for Hall of Fame consideration (and with the exception of Rogers Hornsby, who was elected in 1942), Dead-Ball-Era players (Frank Chance, Rube Waddell and Ed Walsh, to name a few) consistently outpolled better qualified men of a later time (like Lefty Grove, Carl Hubbell and Mickey Cochrane) in the BBWAA voting, and it's obvious that the HOF electorate of the early forties was dominated by sportswriters who had reached adulthood by the end of World War I. From 1947 to 1954 — after which a time delay was imposed upon a candidate's period of eligibility — the trend was reversed: Grove, Hubbell and Cochrane were elected in 1947 (along with contemporary Frankie Frisch); although many were still eligible, the only true Dead-Ball player to crack the BBWAA top-ten in that period was pitcher Charley Bender. It's evident that the majority of voters were scribes of a later generation than their early-forties counterparts. Post-1954 restrictions on a candidate's window of eligibility make it more difficult to identify later examples of this bias and may have lessened its impact. But, it's likely that most of the BBWAA voters over the years have been afflicted by the same subjective impulse, and it's certain that the Veterans Committee, which has always comprised older men, cannot avoid its influence.

Despite the effects of time-related bias, there are some good reasons to oppose any *absolute* numerical standards for Cooperstown. The history of major-league baseball has included much statistical ebb and flow, and the value of a given player's career performance must always be judged in the context of his era. For example, a career batting average of .300 or better is far more impressive if it was compiled during the game's Dead-Ball Era — the first two decades of this century when just one or two increasingly scuffed, yellowing, misshapen and hard-to-hit baseballs were used per game and, as a result, pitching reigned supreme — than it is in the context of the late 1920s or early thirties when a livelier ball was used, replaced more often during the game by new, clean ones, and players' batting averages soared in response. Similarly, a career earned run average of 2.50 might be run-of-the-mill among pitchers who played in the decade or so before the end of World War I, but may stand as one of the all-time best among hurlers of the 1930s. As a result, the validity of using absolute numbers to compare the performance of players from different eras is negated by the variations in normal performance over time. Any use of statistics for cross-generational comparisons must somehow account for, and neutralize, these differences to be valid, and these variations in statistical norms add to the difficulty of determining who is worthy of HOF selection.

The same ebb and flow also imposes that the adoption of any minimum statistical standards for enshrinement could eventually cheapen the honor of Cooperstown membership, and defenders of the subjective process argue that their application would be a floodgate assuring further mediocrity among the HOF roster. Evidence to support that argument can be seen among the list of baseball's career home-run leaders, the most glamorous statistic among baseball's myriad numbers. When the first Hall of Fame voting was held in 1936, just four men — Babe Ruth, Lou Gehrig, Jimmie Foxx and Rogers Hornsby — had amassed a total of three hundred career homers or more over the first six decades of major-league play. By 1951, all four had been elected to the Hall, deservedly, for their all-around abilities. But, eighty other players equaled or surpassed three hundred four-baggers in the years 1937–99, including thirty others who have since been elected to Cooperstown and six more who were retired but not yet eligible for the 2000 voting (three of whose eventual selections are virtually certain). Among the remaining forty-four, seventeen were still active as players in 1999 and also ineligible for consideration in 2000. So, if three hundred home runs— an astronomical total in 1936 — had been established from the beginning as an absolute minimum for automatic election, then the remaining twenty-seven from that list would also be enshrined now, and their inclusion would swell the ranks of Hall of Fame membership by about 15 percent above the total of 185 men elected as players through the latter date. Such an increase would add Joe Adcock, Willie Horton, Dave Kingman and Greg Luzinski, among others, to the HOF roster. They were good, even above-average, players who merited thoughtful consideration. Regardless, their skills were relatively one dimensional, and their presence in Cooperstown would be intolerable to the many who believe that the Shrine is already overstocked with less-than-deserving members.

But argument against the use of any statistical criteria is really just a smoke screen that obfuscates the fact that viable objective standards can be relative rather than absolute. It also ignores the fact that it's impossible to discuss—let alone judge—a player's abilities without examining his performance statistics. If someone claims that Babe Ruth was the greatest player ever, there is bound to be a skeptic who will demand proof. At that point, almost everyone will reply that Ruth's stats show he ranked among the very best pitchers *and* hitters of his time (or any era) or cite his 714 career home runs hit during a period when most players were lucky to get fifty, and absolutely no one will justify their perception of his superiority on the premise that he was more agile in the field, more graceful at the plate, or swifter afoot than anyone else who ever played the game. After all, it's laughable to make such claims about a man who—the available film clips seem to indicate—may have regularly waddled like a duck about the basepaths; and, if the Babe's relative greatness hinges on a measurement of his stats, then it's certain that everyone else's claims to fame are even more dependent upon their performance numbers.

So it follows that, with no formal performance guidelines, the Hall of Fame selection process inevitably has become a prisoner of what, over time, have evolved as de facto standards for election. Everyone within the Church of Baseball is well aware that 300 wins for pitchers and 3000 hits or 500 home runs for batters have emerged as levels of career achievement that guarantee a player's eventual entree to Cooperstown (as have 2000 victories for managers). Yet, consistent with their insistence upon subjective evaluation, neither the Hall of Fame trustees nor the electors (as a group) ever formally acknowledge that these de facto standards exist; and, over the years, there has been occasional resistance among some BBWAA voters to their application in the selection process. So two of the most recent three hundred-win pitchers eligible for election, Phil Niekro and Don Sutton, were both on the writers' ballot for five years each before they were chosen for the Hall—although everyone moderately knowledgeable about the selection process knew that they were certain of eventual election. But through the 2000 voting, despite those and earlier examples of resistance, every man who had ever achieved at least one of those career totals and was eligible for HOF consideration by that date had been elected to the Shrine, and the significance of those de facto standards was evident in 1999, when three-thousand-hit batters George Brett and Robin Yount, plus three hundred-win pitcher Nolan Ryan, all were elected in their very first year of BBWAA eligibility.

Regardless, because they are based on cumulative career achievement, de facto standards create the same problems for Hall of Fame selection as would the existence of any formal minimum statistical criteria. The possibility always exists that some player(s) with above average but not truly great ability will reach or surpass one of those standards by the grace of longevity alone and slip into Cooperstown based on accomplishments that are less significant than those of others with careers of shorter duration. The prospect can reduce HOF election to an award for mere endurance (or the good fortune not to suffer a career-ending injury) rather than superior performance.

Given the five-year delay in his election, some BBWAA voters of the 1990s obviously felt that was the case with Don Sutton. Sutton's career lasted twenty-three seasons (1966–88). Only six other pitchers in major-league history played longer, all of whom were his contemporaries— Nolan Ryan (1966–93), Tommy John (1963–89), Charlie Hough (1970–94), Jim Kaat (1959–83), Phil Niekro (1964–87) and Steve Carlton (1965–88). When Sutton was elected in 1998 his 324 career wins ranked twelfth best, all-time; his 3574 strikeouts were the fifth-best total ever; his 5282 innings pitched ranked seventh; and his 58 shutouts were tenth. Also, Sutton's final career numbers were very similar to those of Carlton, another Hall of Famer, who had 329 wins, 4136 strikeouts, 5217 innings and 55 shutouts.

But, Sutton won twenty games or more in a season only once during his career (21 wins in 1976); he never topped his league in victories in a year; he never won the Cy Young Award, given annually to the men judged the best pitchers in each league; and except for his league-best nine shutouts in 1972 and a 2.20 earned run average in 1980, he never led his circuit for a season in any of the major statistical categories for starting pitchers— games won, earned run average (ERA), winning percentage, innings pitched, strikeouts or shutouts. In fact, based solely on games won in a season, Sutton was rarely the best pitcher on his team, having topped the clubs he played for in victories only four times in twenty-three years (1973, 1976, 1981 and 1984). In contrast, Carlton won twenty or more games on six occasions and led his league in victories four times, in innings pitched and strikeouts five times apiece, and in earned run average, shut-outs and winning percentage once each. He also won four Cy Young Awards, and he led his team in games won during a season on eleven different occasions. Clearly, Carlton's peak performance was better than Sutton's; and, as a result, when both men became eligible for HOF consideration in 1994, "Lefty" was elected on his first try, while Sutton — despite his similar career numbers— had to wait to be enshrined.

Much of Sutton's statistical accomplishment obviously resulted from longevity; and, during his period of eligibility for Cooperstown, there were other pitchers on the HOF ballot, with careers of shorter duration, whose achievements were more significant in some ways. Among them was Ron Guidry, who compiled only 170 wins in a fourteen-year career, but won twenty or more games three times, topped his league in victories, winning percentage and earned run average twice each, led in shutouts once, and won a Cy Young trophy in 1978 (when he was also a close runner-up for his league's Most Valuable Player award). Guidry led his team in victories six times. He also had a career earned run average of 3.29 that was the virtual equal of Sutton's 3.26, although Guidry spent his entire career in the American League, where the presence of the designated hitter inflated pitchers' ERAs significantly above that of the National, where Sutton pitched most of his games. And, Guidry's overall winning percentage of .651 was almost one hundred points better than Sutton's career mark of .559, despite the fact that both men often played for pennant contenders. So, statistically, Guidry achieved as much or more than Sutton in significantly less time.

But, Guidry never received more than thirty-seven Hall of Fame votes during the five years that he and Sutton were both on the BBWAA ballot, while Sutton's smallest vote total in that period was 259. Clearly, both men's Cooperstown vote histories were impacted by the de facto pitching standard — Sutton's because he achieved 300 wins, Guidry's because his career ended 130 victories short of it. During the time that Sutton was on the writers' ballot, similar comparative circumstances also hindered the candidacies of Luis Tiant (229 victories) and Vida Blue (209). Like Guidry, both men were contemporaries of Sutton — with shorter careers and, perhaps, more impressive statistical achievements — but experienced similar fates in head-to-head competition with Sutton in the voting.

It's not that Sutton was undeserving of the honor he received. There are other pitchers in Cooperstown who are both subjectively and statistically less qualified than he is; and, if the Hall of Fame must have any de facto standard for hurlers, three hundred wins may be the best one available. It also may be true that neither Guidry, Tiant nor Blue have been unfairly excluded, as each of those men's credentials are debatable. But, by fixing the voters' attentions on one arbitrary level of career achievement, the existence of that — or any — de facto standard impacts the Cooperstown selection process in two ways, both of which are detrimental to the Hall of Fame. Achievement of the standard overshadows any and all negative aspects of a player's candidacy, and compels many electors to vote for him — based solely on the precedent that everyone else who achieved it is already in, so there's no reasonable justification to exclude him. At the same time, the failure to reach that standard comparatively demeans the candidacies of other players whose accomplishments may deserve far more consideration than they receive. Overall, in a process dominated by subjective evaluation, any standard based merely on cumulative numbers—

whether formal or de facto—must inevitably compromise the voters' ability to place a player's credentials in an appropriate relative context.

Given the 75 percent support required for election by either panel, the Hall of Fame's selection process obviously relies upon a belief in the collective judgment of its voters. But the wisdom of collective thinking can be undermined by the least thoughtful members of any group; and, in that context, the lack of formal performance criteria and the small number of de facto standards also make the process vulnerable to a wide variety of voter biases.

Some of those biases are based on individual achievement. At various times, they may include favoritism for hitters with high career batting averages (especially .300 or better) and or substantial totals of home runs, runs scored and batted in; pitchers with low career ERAs and or high strikeout or shutout totals; men who have won numerous yearly statistical titles in those and other categories; Most Valuable Player and Cy Young Award winners; players who were frequent all stars; and men who played for numerous pennant or World Series winners. These biases are relatively justifiable because they are based on some type of measurable performance.

But the absence of clear-cut standards also assures that the selection process is susceptible to other biases which have little or nothing to do with a player's true ability or achievement. These may include preferential treatment for candidates who were relatively more accommodating to the voting scribes (i.e., men who "gave good interview"), players who were popular with their teammates, men who were widely perceived as positive role models (on the field or in the broad social milieu), or—as some suspect—those who spent much of their careers in major media centers, especially New York. (The voters who represent New York, Los Angeles and—in an earlier era, Chicago—have never constituted a majority of the BBWAA electorate, but they have always represented a block of votes large enough to determine the HOF fate of a borderline candidate.) Conversely, these types of bias may injure the Hall of Fame prospects of candidates who were often surly or uncooperative with the media or other players, men whose careers were punctuated by personal problems (like alcoholism, drug use or legal difficulties), or those who played most or all of their careers in relatively small media markets like Cincinnati, Kansas City or Milwaukee.

Given the subjective nature of the process, it was inevitable from the beginning of Cooperstown voting in 1936 that bias among the BBWAA voters would lead to omissions of various worthy candidates. In fact, the scribes' failure to elect any nineteenth-century players during the first few years of voting was the impetus for creation of a second electorate, initially called a Centennial Commission (progenitor of the current Veterans Committee). Over the years, the VC and its predecessors have enshrined eight men — all of whom played (or at least began their careers) in the nineteenth century — who never received a single vote in any BBWAA election. Whether each of those men (discussed in Chapter Four) really belong in Cooperstown is arguable. But, their selections attest to considerable credentials in their candidacies, and their failure to gain even modest notice from the Hall's primary electorate testifies to the fallibility of the BBWAA voting.

Some forms of HOF voter bias manifest among both electorates, while others may be unique to just one. But their existence has left the selection process open to constant criticism, and the variety of biases in both election procedures makes it difficult to measure their various impacts on the selection process or to identify whether any specific or consistent pattern of preferences has been operative among the Hall of Fame electorate(s) over time. As a result, a consensus definition of a Hall of Famer may never have existed at any moment since the museum's first election.

Abetted by these biases, the voting outcome by both elective organs has also been vulnerable to charges of racism. Historically, African Americans and other men of "color" were barred from participating in the major leagues from the mid–1880s through 1947, when Jackie Robinson joined the Brooklyn Dodgers; and, in the absence of equal opportunity, various "Negro" major leagues operated during much of that period. Predictably, from the time the Cooperstown museum was opened in 1939 through Robinson's election as a Hall of Famer in 1962, the HOF roster was a "whites-only" country club. It was not until the early 1970s that the Hall opened its doors— albeit, begrudgingly — to those excluded players who never had the chance to perform at the major-league level; and, when it finally did, there were justifiable complaints that the initial effort to include Negro leaguers was mere tokenism. Inevitably, the number of blacks in Cooperstown has grown since 1962; by 2000 it included sixteen of the 185 players on the roster (about 9 percent of that total) plus the seventeen former Negro leaguers noted in the Introduction.

But, as the proportion of Afro-Americans in Cooperstown increased, their growing presence among the list of baseball's designated immortals also exposed the Shrine to similar charges regarding its treatment of players of Latin descent. Such claims were made during the late 1990s, when only three of the Hall's players (Roberto Clemente, Luis Aparicio and Juan Marichal) and one of its managers (Al Lopez) shared Hispanic ancestry and after the candidacies of first basemen Orlando Cepeda and Tony Perez were repeatedly rejected by the writers throughout the decade.

(Cepeda's BBWAA eligibility expired after the 1994 election; Perez was on the ballot as of 1992.) Those complaints had impact: Marichal was appointed to the Veterans Committee in 1998, the panel promptly enshrined Cepeda in 1999 and Perez was elected by the writers the following year.

Subjectively, Cepeda and Perez are more legitimate Hall of Famers than many other men in Cooperstown, including at least three men who played the same position (Jim Bottomley, Frank Chance and George Kelly). But their slow-coming recognition and the timing of their elections may be further evidence of bias-related flaws in the voting process, and they raise concern about hypersensitivity to criticism among those involved in the selection procedure. If both men are legitimate Hall of Famers, then they should've easily passed muster by the BBWAA (the writers rejected Cepeda fifteen times, and Perez was not elected until his ninth year on the ballot), and their failure to do so may be another example of the scribes' fallibility. But, in turn, their election at the height of criticism regarding potential anti–Latino bias may also evidence the same impulse for tokenism that haunted the early years of the Negro-league selections.

Exacerbating all of this is the fact that the Hall of Fame museum is a business. In turn, its success is dependent upon economic considerations—the primary one being that almost all of its customers visit during the summer (baseball season), and many of them come during the week of its annual induction ceremony (in late July or early August). Obviously, in order for the museum to succeed, there must be someone to induct each year. But, due to a lack of foresight to schedule voting every year and to the fact that an absence of standards (and an abundance of candidates) has occasionally precluded anyone from being elected, there were seven summers during the first twenty-five years of HOF balloting when — because no one was elected — no induction ceremony was held (1940–41, 1943–44, 1950, 1958 and 1960). This hurt the Hall of Fame, financially, and it is arguable that most of the "refinements" in its election procedures over the years were motivated as much or more by the need to guarantee an induction ceremony as by any effort to assure fairness or justice in the process.

The need to hold an induction ceremony has its strongest political impact on the Veterans Committee — because, in the years when the BBWAA fails to elect anyone, the panel feels added pressure to make a selection. As a result, it's no surprise that some of the most dubious VC choices ever — Elmer Flick (1963) and Dave Bancroft, Chick Hafey and Rube Marquard (all 1971), to name a few—came in years when there was no writers' balloting or when the scribes had failed to anoint someone. Since 1972, the only time there was no BBWAA inductee was 1996 (pitcher Phil Niekro topped the writers' ballot with insufficient 68.3 percent support), and two of the VC choices that year (hurler Jim Bunning and manager Ned Hanlon) were also debatable selections.

Regardless of the pressures that motivated their election, the relatively poor credentials of many VC selections have also exacerbated tensions between that panel and the BBWAA, which have persisted since the mid–1940s, despite the natural turnover in both organs' memberships. As a group, and for reasons which are delineated later, the writers have always regarded the committee with some disdain — as if the panel's mandate is somehow less valid than their own. The arrogance of that attitude is absurd, given that the voting rights of both electorates are a privilege granted by the Cooperstown trustees and by no means the scribes' birthright. But, although the writers' own failures are the reason for the existence of the VC and its predecessors, their criticism of the panel's selections has often been valid. The Hall of Fame's most glaring errors of selection over the years were made by the Veterans Committee, and the panel is blamed by most critics— especially the writers— for lowering the Hall's (undefined and nonexistent) standards of admission.

All of this demonstrates that both Cooperstown selection procedures are plagued by flaws and have been from their inceptions. As evidenced by SABR's consideration of establishing its own Hall of Fame, baseball's hallowed Shrine is rapidly losing credibility with its most ardent supporters, and it may not be too long before many among those who care most about the institution are calling it Blooperstown instead. While potentially blasphemous to some readers, any irreverence that follows is justified by those flaws in the Cooperstown selection process. But, before they can be identified clearly on a broad historical scale, it will be instructive to examine their impact in the microcosm of one small group of Hall of Fame candidates.

2

Seven Men Up

Through 2000, among the 185 men chosen for Cooperstown for their playing careers, ninety-three of them had been elected by the BBWAA. They included seven catchers, twenty-nine infielders, twenty-five outfielders and thirty-two pitchers. Except for some nineteenth-century players who were passed over by the writers in the early years of voting (notably Cap Anson), the group includes every man —five or six dozen in all—whose HOF legitimacy is undisputed.

As a result, the BBWAA selections are rarely faulted by anyone, even the most ardent Hall of Fame critics. Because first-year election has proved historically difficult, the thirty-four players who were chosen in their initial year of eligibility are virtually sacrosanct, as are the inductions of Lou Gehrig and Roberto Clemente in special elections resulting from personal tragedies. Among the other fifty-seven, only a few ever have been criticized for any reason. Generally, such criticism has focused on whether Rabbit Maranville and Luis Aparicio (good defensive shortstops, but neither man much of a hitter), Harmon Killebrew and Ralph Kiner (home-run savants with relatively poor batting averages and not great fielders), and Hoyt Wilhelm and Rollie Fingers (relief-pitching specialists) deserved recognition equal to that of players of more obvious all-around skill, or whether pitchers Ted Lyons, Phil Niekro and Don Sutton achieved their status as a result of longevity rather than superior ability. On the whole, however, such criticism also has been faint and fleeting.

But, the widespread respect for the BBWAA's selections as a whole is based on a bottom-line emphasis that ignores the manner in which the true flaw in the voting process—the lack of objective standards—often derails the front-door candidacies of players who, whether or not they merit Hall of Fame membership, deserve far more consideration than the scribes' subjective process affords them. It also overlooks the fact that ninety-two other HOF players were chosen by the Veterans Committee or one of its predecessors. Whether or not Tommy McCarthy, Chick Hafey or Jesse Haines deserve mention in the same discussion as Stan Musial or Lefty Grove, it's hard to fault the VC choices of Anson (elected in 1939), Ed Delahanty (1945), Kid Nichols (1949), Sam Crawford (1957), Tim Keefe (1964) and Amos Rusie (1977). The time spread involved in their selections indicates that deserving Hall of Famers have been overlooked by the BBWAA with some regularity. A full understanding of how that injustice occurs requires examination of the case histories of some men who may have been victimized by the procedure.

Because subjectivity in any form implies bias, it was inevitable from the beginning that the Hall of Fame trustees' and BBWAA's reliance upon it would lead to inconsistent treatment of analogous players. Typical of such inconsistency are the comparative Cooperstown voting histories of the seven players below, all of whom were immediate contemporaries who played the same key position — shortstop. Table 1 provides their career records in years played (YP), hits (H), home runs (HR), total bases (TB), runs scored (R), runs batted in (RBI), batting (BA), slugging (SA) and on-base averages (OBA), with the group leader for each category boldfaced.

TABLE 1
CAREER BATTING STATISTICS, KEY 1940s SHORTSTOPS

Player	YP	H	HR	TB	R	RBI	BA	SA	OBA
Luke Appling	20	2749	45	3528	1319	1116	**.310**	.398	**.399**
Lou Boudreau	15	1779	68	2500	861	789	.295	.415	.380
Pee Wee Reese	16	2170	126	3038	**1338**	885	.269	.377	.366
Phil Rizzuto	13	1588	38	2065	877	563	.273	.355	.351
Marty Marion	13	1448	36	1902	602	624	.263	.345	.323
Johnny Pesky	10	1455	17	1832	867	404	.307	.386	.394
Vern Stephens	15	1859	**247**	2991	1001	**1174**	.286	**.460**	.355

These stats demonstrate where each of the men usually hit in their team's batting order. Except for Stephens and Marion, all were fixtures near the top of their teams' lineups, evidenced by their preponderance of runs scored compared to runs batted in and justified by their on-base averages (anything above .380 is very good). Reese and Rizzuto were leadoff men or second-slot hitters for most of their careers, although both men hit lower in the order when they first came to the majors. Pesky usually batted second. Appling could bat in any of the first three slots, but his high RBI total is more reflective of career length than power, and he fits the one-two mold the best. Boudreau was usually a third-place hitter, but his lack of home-run power made him more analogous to the top-of-the-order guys than to Stephens, whose sock made him a bona fide clean-up man for the often inept St. Louis Browns and later with the mighty Boston Red Sox of Ted Williams and Bobby Doerr. Marion could've batted in the leadoff or second slot for a lot of teams, but the St. Louis Cardinals had enough offensive talent in the years he played for them that he often was number eight in their lineup (except when player shortages during World War II kicked him up a notch or two).

Stephens was the American League home-run leader in 1945 and led the AL in runs batted in three times (in 1944 outright, 1949–50 tied). Boudreau won a batting title in 1944 and was a three-time leader in doubles. Appling won two AL batting titles (1936 and 1943) and led the circuit in on-base percentage in 1943. Pesky topped the American League with more than two hundred hits in each of his first three seasons in the majors; but, due to World War II military service, the years were not sequential (1942, 1946–47). Rizzuto never led the AL in any major batting category. Reese led the National League in walks in 1947 and runs scored in '49. Marion led the NL in doubles in 1942. If you were looking for power, you'd pick Stephens. Otherwise, you'd probably prefer Appling, Boudreau or Reese (for his extra punch) near the top of your lineup; but, on a good team, you could install Pesky, Rizzuto or maybe even Marion and not lose much in terms of offensive production.

Defensively, Marion was regarded by a plurality of contemporary observers as the smoothest-fielding, widest-ranging shortstop of the era. But grace is not quantifiable, and the career defensive statistics of these men don't support that subjective consensus unequivocably. Table 2 gives the career fielding average (FA), assists-per-game (A/G), double plays-per-game (DP/G), and range factor (RF, i.e., chances-per-game, less errors-per-game) for the seven shortstops plus their combined total of league leaderships (Led) in putouts, assists, errors, total chances, chances-per-game, double plays and fielding average at their position (although usually perceived as a negative, errors are included because they also can indicate superior range, especially by a shortstop). The table also provides the average career stats for all shortstops from baseball's Postwar Era (1946–60) who meet the Hall of Fame's ten-year service minimum. Note, however, that — although they were primarily shortstops — Pesky (in the late forties) and Stephens (in the early fifties) both played several seasons as third basemen, and the smaller number of plays normal to that position negatively impacted their career figures. The career leaders among this group for each stat are boldfaced.

TABLE 2
CAREER DEFENSIVE STATISTICS, TOP FORTIES SHORTSTOPS

Player	FA	A/G	DP/G	RF	Led
Luke Appling	.948	**3.20**	.626	**5.18**	25
Lou Boudreau	**.973**	3.01	**.745**	5.03	21
Marty Marion	.969	3.10	.628	5.02	13
Johnny Pesky	.966	2.62	.500	4.29	12
Pee Wee Reese	.962	2.88	.589	4.82	15
Phil Rizzuto	.968	2.83	.738	4.78	12
Vern Stephens	.962	2.90	.554	4.55	8
SS Average	*.962*	*2.67*	*.552*	*4.33*	*8*

Defensive statistics are often misleading. A high fielding percentage may indicate a lack of range, and the number of double plays turned per game is also dependent upon the type of pitching staff a team has and the fielding skills of other players. But, the numbers indicate that Boudreau may have been the best of these guys defensively. His fielding average is the only one above .969, he turned double plays far more frequently than anyone else but Rizzuto and his overall range (assists-per-game and range factor) was comparable to Appling and Marion. But, note also that each of these men's stats are at least average, or above it, for the approximate era in which they played — so none of them was a slouch with a glove.

All of these men were starting shortstops in the majors during the years 1942–50. (Appling had only a partial season in 1945 and played third base for most of 1949, and Pesky played at the hot corner for the last three years of that period.) Among the seven, Appling was the only one not in his prime during the decade: he was born in 1907, his career began in 1930, he was a major-league regular for eight seasons before 1941, and he was thirty-four years old at the start of that season. But, except for one year, he remained a lineup fixture through 1949. Boudreau, Marion and Rizzuto all were born in 1917, but in 1938 Lou got to the majors first and had one at-bat his first season. Marion arrived in the bigs in 1940, Rizzuto in '41. Reese, Pesky and Stephens were born in 1918, 1919 and

1920, respectively. Reese reached the majors in 1940, Stephens the next year (for just two at-bats) and Pesky in 1942. Appling's cumulative statistics benefit from his longevity, Pesky's are hurt somewhat by the brevity of his career, and the rest of them are on a relatively equal footing, timewise.

World War II interrupted four of these men's careers. Pesky, Reese and Rizzuto each missed three seasons during their prime due to military service (1943–45), and Appling also served in 1944. Luck (whether bad or good depends on how you look at it) and or 4-F draft classifications resulting from injuries kept Boudreau, Marion and Stephens out of the military during the war (but Boudreau missed about a third of 1945 with a broken ankle). If you add their war-service years to their major-league careers, then Appling would've had twenty-one big-league seasons, Reese nineteen, Rizzuto sixteen, and Pesky thirteen, while the other three men's totals would not be changed.

Except for Appling, who had the misfortune to play his entire career for the Chicago White Sox when they were not very competitive, all of the men played for at least one pennant winner. Rizzuto's postseason career was the most extensive and successful. He played for nine of the New York Yankees' American League champs, seven of which won the World Series, and military service cost him participation in another series victory in 1943. But, four of those pennants and three world titles came after 1950, when Appling had retired and the seven were no longer playing at the same time. Reese played for seven Brooklyn pennant winners, but four of those — and his only World Series ring — also came after 1950. With the Cardinals, Marion played on four pennant winners, all in the 1940s, three of which won the series. As American Leaguers forced to play against the Yankee dynasty, rather than for it, Boudreau, Pesky and Stephens each performed for just one pennant winner, and only Lou's 1948 Cleveland Indians won the series. So, except for Appling, they all had postseason experience during the era in which they faced each other, although Rizzuto and Reese also benefited from the post–1950 good fortunes of their New York teams.

Each of these men was also an all-star. Reese was selected for the all-star squad ten times but missed one game due to an injury. Stephens was chosen eight times, also missing one game from injury. Appling was selected seven times, but three of those occasions were in the 1930s, before the others were in the majors. Boudreau was on eight squads, but injury cost him one game. Marion was chosen eight times, missing two from injury. Rizzuto was selected five times. Pesky made only one all-star team, in 1946. So, with few exceptions, one of these seven men was the all-star shortstop for his league throughout the 1940s. Table 3 lists their all-star appearances for the decade (due to wartime travel restrictions there was no game in 1945), indicating whether the man was a starter (S), played as a reserve (R), was selected but did not play (N), or was chosen but missed due to injury (I). Dashes (—) indicate the player was not selected at all, asterisks (**) show military service, and a blank ( ) indicates the player was not in the majors at the time of the all-star game that season. The totals on the right, in sequence, are the number of times each was the all-star starter (S), the number of times each was chosen to the squad (C), and the number of games each actually played in (P) during the decade.

TABLE 3
KEY SHORTSTOPS' ALL-STAR
APPEARANCES, 1941–50

Player (League)	'41	'42	'43	'44	'46	'47	'48	'49	'50	S	C	P
Appling (AL)	N	—	N	**	R	R	—	—	—	0	4	2
Boudreau (AL)	R	S	N	N	—	S	S	—	—	3	6	4
Pesky (AL)		—	**	**	S	—	—	—	—	1	1	1
Rizzuto (AL)	—	N	**	**	—	—	—	—	S	1	2	1
Stephens (AL)		—	S	S	R	—	R	R	N	2	6	5
Marion (NL)		—	—	S	S	S	S	I	N	S	5	7	5
Reese (NL)		—	R	**	**	I	R	S	S	R	2	6	5

Note: In 1941 Joe Cronin started for the AL, Arky Vaughan (starter) and Eddie Miller (reserve) played for the NL; in 1943 Miller was the NL reserve; in 1948 Buddy Kerr was the NL reserve; in 1949 Eddie Joost started for the AL.

Three of these men — Marion, Boudreau and Rizzuto — won Most Valuable Player awards. The rest of them all came relatively close once or twice in their careers. The writers who vote for the honor are basically the same ones who participate in Hall of Fame balloting, so examining the men's MVP histories may shed light on their separate Hall of Fame fortunes.

Marion's MVP came first, in 1944, at age twenty-six. He batted .267, with 135 hits, 6 homers, 50 runs scored and 63 RBI for St. Louis that year. Five other Cardinal regulars had higher batting averages than he did, six of them had more homers and runs batted in, four had more hits, and every lineup regular scored more runs. (Stan Musial, who was MVP in 1943, led the St. Louis offense in hits and batting average and was second on the team in RBI.) Marion topped the NL's shortstops in fielding that season with a .972 percentage, but it was the only major defensive category in which he led at his position. Nevertheless, Marty's defense and leadership were deemed by the voters to be so instrumental to St. Louis' third consecutive pennant that he won the MVP award by one point over the fourth-place Cubs' Bill Nicholson, who led the circuit in homers, runs scored and runs batted in. Marion never again placed among the top five in any MVP election.

Boudreau's trophy came in 1948 at age thirty-one. He batted .355, with 18 homers and 106 RBI (all career highs) and also led American League shortstops in double plays and fielding. Some other Cleveland players also had stellar seasons: second baseman Joe Gordon hit 32 homers and drove in 124 runs, third sacker Ken Keltner had 31 taters and 119 ribbies, pitchers Bob Lemon and Gene Bearden both won 20 games, and Bob Feller won 19. But, Boudreau also served as the Indians' manager that season and almost single-handedly beat the Red Sox in a one-game pennant playoff, hitting two homers, two singles and walking once in an 8-3 victory. Cleveland owner Bill Veeck, Jr., never revealed whether Boudreau also collected tickets at the turnstiles and sold beer between innings, but you couldn't ask for much more from a MVP shortstop with modest home-run power. Boudreau also finished third in the MVP voting for 1947, when he led the league in doubles and batted .307, and he placed fifth in 1940, the only other year he drove in more than one hundred runs in his career.

Rizzuto's award came in 1950 at age thirty-three, and it was one of the most curious MVP choices ever. After placing second in the 1949 voting, he had the only two-hundred-hit season of his career and batted a personal best of .324, which was the sixth-highest average in the league. (It was one of just two times he would bat above .284 in his career.) But, there were a lot of guys in the AL that year with far more impressive numbers in the power stats that usually equate with MVP success. One of them was Boston's Vern Stephens, who scored the same number of runs as "The Scooter" (125), had 185 hits, was fourth in the league in homers (30), second in total bases (321, compared to Rizzuto's 271), and tied teammate Walt Dropo for the league lead in RBI (144). Overall, eleven AL batters had more than one hundred ribbies that season. There would have been a twelfth, but Boston's Ted Williams, who had 97 for the year, broke his elbow in the July all-star game and missed most of the season's second half. Rizzuto's 66 RBI were only the fifth-best total on the Yankees in 1950, and more than two dozen other players had higher amounts in the league as a whole. But, Rizzuto led AL shortstops in putouts that season and also tied a (since broken) record for the highest single-season fielding average ever by a shortstop (.9817).

With too many sluggers to pick from in 1950 among the usual MVP-type statistical categories, the voters opted instead to notice the contributions of other people (Stephens, Dropo and Bobby Doerr of Boston, New York's Yogi Berra and Joe DiMaggio, Cleveland's Luke Easter and Al Rosen, Detroit's Vic Wertz and Chicago's Gus Zernial all surpassed 25 homers and 100 RBI). Rizzuto was the prime beneficiary with 240 MVP points. Boston's Billy Goodman, who led the league in batting at .354, but had only 6 homers and just 68 RBI, placed second with 180 points, in part for his positional versatility following Williams's injury, and Detroit's George Kell, who led the league in hits, batted .340, and had 101 RBI but hit only 8 home runs, was fourth. In contrast, New York's Berra was the only power hitter to finish among the MVP top five (third, with 146 points) and the only one with more than 75 points in the balloting. Despite his third consecutive stellar season (more on 1948–50 later), Vern Stephens got only 6 points in the voting.

Appling earned a second-place spot in MVP voting in 1936 and 1943, the years of his two batting titles. In the first of those seasons, when Chicago finished third and Luke was the only one of these shortstops in the majors, he batted a career-high .388. It was also the only time in his major-league tenure that Appling scored more than 100 runs (111), had more than 100 RBI (128), and had 200 hits or more (204). The winner that season was New York's Lou Gehrig, who topped the league in runs scored (167), home runs (49), and had one more hit than Appling, leading the Yankees to the pennant by nineteen and one-half games. The White Sox finished fourth in 1943, with Appling batting .328, leading the league with a .419 on-base average, and driving in 80 runs, the third-best RBI total of his career. The winner that year was the Yankees' Spud Chandler, who led AL pitchers with twenty wins, an .833 winning percentage (on just four losses), and five shutouts. Luke never finished among the top five in any other year.

In his rookie season of 1942, Pesky finished a distant third in the MVP race with 143 points, behind New York's Joe Gordon (270 points) and Red Sox teammate Ted Williams (249). As noted earlier, Pesky's 205 hits topped the AL that season, and his .331 batting average was second-best to Teddy Ballgame's .356. After Pesky's three years in the war, he placed fourth in the MVP voting of 1946, again topping the league in hits and ranking third-best among the league's batters (.335), helping Boston to its first pennant since 1918. Williams, who led the league in runs scored and was runner-up for the home run, RBI and batting titles, won the 1946 award, and teammate Bobby Doerr (with 18 homers and 116 RBI) was third, behind pitcher Hal Newhouser of Detroit (26-9, in his third consecutive season of 25 wins or more). Pesky's first two seasons in the majors marked the only occasions when he finished among the top five in MVP voting.

Reese finished fifth once (1949) and sixth twice (1946 and 1948), MVP-wise, but none of those seasons was statistically overwhelming, and there were other years when he was about as good but got less attention from the voters. In his fifth-place season he led the National League in runs scored (132), had a career high in home runs (16), collected 172 hits, had 73 RBI, and batted .279. He also led NL shortstops in putouts and fielding average. The performance earned him 118 points in the MVP voting (the only time he ever scored higher than 79); and the 1949 winner, Jackie Robinson, was his only teammate on the pennant-winning Dodgers ahead of him in the voting. In 1946 Reese scored 79 runs on 154 hits, with 5 homers, 60 runs batted in and a .284 average, but did not lead the league in any major fielding category. Two seasons later, he scored 96 runs on 155 hits, with 9 homers, 75 ribbies and a .274 average, leading the league in putouts, double plays and chances per game. Pee Wee had very similar years in 1951 and 1955 but didn't fare as well in the voting. In 1951, when the Dodgers lost the pennant on Bobby Thomson's playoff homer, Reese scored 94 runs on a career-high 176 hits, had 10 homers and a personal-best 84 RBI, and batted .286, but finished only fifteenth in the MVP vote with just fifteen points. In 1955, when Brooklyn finally won a World Series, Pee Wee scored 99 runs on 156 hits, had 10 homers, 61 ribbies and a career-high .309 average, while tying Hank Aaron for ninth place in the voting.

Stephens compiled one of the most confusing MVP-vote histories ever. He placed just third in the year of his only pennant winner — although he was clearly the dominant player on his team, and the second-place club had two MVP candidates of virtually equal merit — and he was fourth on two other occasions. But, statistically, none of these seasons was anything close to the best of his career, and in the years 1949-50, when he arguably had the most awesome back-to-back offensive seasons of any shortstop in history, he could muster no better than a seventh-place MVP finish.

In 1942, after his two at-bats with St. Louis the previous year, Stephens became the Browns' regular shortstop, helping them climb from fifth place to third, while scoring 84 runs on 169 hits, with 14 homers, 92 runs batted in, a .294 average, and (predictably, for a rookie) leading the AL with 42 errors. Although he was not among the top five in any major batting category, the performance earned him his first fourth-place finish in the MVP voting — with 140 points, behind Yankees second baseman Joe Gordon (270), Ted Williams (249), and fellow rookie Pesky (143 points and 37 errors).

Two years later, in the season of his only pennant win, Vern finished third in the voting while topping the junior circuit in RBI (109), being runner-up for the home-run title (20 taters, compared to Yankee Nick Etten's 22), and batting .293. "Junior" also led the club with 91 runs scored, 164 hits and 32 doubles. Only one other Brownie had more than 72 ribbies that year (third sacker Mark Christman with 83), and first baseman George McQuinn was second on the team in homers with a paltry 11. Pitcher Nels Potter went 19-7 with a 2.83 earned run average for St. Louis, but that performance was nowhere near those achieved by second-place Detroit's two aces Hal Newhouser (29-9 and a 2.22 ERA) and Dizzy Trout (27-14 and a league-leading 2.12), who placed one-two in the MVP vote ahead of Stephens (236 and 232 points, respectively, compared to Vern's 193). In the same year that the writers honored good-glove, no-hit Marty Marion, whose offensive contribution was—at best—negligible to his team's pennant, it seems amazing that Stephens, the only truly productive hitter on his flag-winning club, would place no better than third best in his league's voting, playing the same position in the very same city. The result seems to imply that the voters from each circuit applied very different sets of MVP standards, which is surprising when you recall that, in the 1940s, five of the eight teams in each league shared their city with at least one club from the other circuit (Boston, Chicago, New York, St. Louis and Philadelphia)—so a majority of the voting writers must've had some opportunity to witness play in each league.

Statistically, the American League's 1944 Most Valuable Player outcome is an absolute anomaly. It contradicted the predominant trend that MVP's come from pennant or division winners. Since the voting began in 1931, and through 1999, 95 of 139 Most Valuable Players (68.3 percent) have been members of first-place clubs. It was one of only thirteen times during the same period, and just the second time in history, that neither of the top two vote-getters came from a first-place team. And, although there have been twenty-two incidents when players on the same club finished one-two in the voting, 1944 was the only time they did not play for a pennant or division winner. Did the wartime talent shortage take a toll on the sportswriters too? Maybe the MVP voting that season was done by the journalistic equivalents of wartime baseball subs like Xavier Rescigno, Steve Gerkin and Pete Gray.

Stephens placed fourth again, behind Boudreau, in 1948, his first season with the Red Sox, who lost the pennant in that one-game playoff with Cleveland. He placed second in the league in runs batted in (137), fourth in homers (29) and total bases (299), and also scored 114 runs on 171 hits. But, second-place Joe DiMaggio had a bigger year for the Yanks—leading the AL in home runs (39) and RBI (155), plus scoring 110 runs on 190 hits, and batting .320—as did Ted Williams, who finished third in the MVP race while winning the league batting crown (.369) and scoring 124 runs on 188 hits, with 25 homers and 127 RBI. At age twenty-seven, inserted into the cleanup spot (behind Dom DiMaggio, Pesky and Williams, ahead of Bobby Doerr) in a Boston lineup whose offense posed far more pennant potential than any batting order Stephens had seen with the Browns, Junior appeared ready to combine his power and physical maturity into a burst of run production.

Stephens did not disappoint. In 1949-50 he put up offensive numbers that were comparable to the best back-to-back seasons produced by any major-league shortstop in history. In fact, at the time, Vern's combined total bases (650) were the highest consecutive-season total ever achieved by a shortstop, easily surpassing the old record (594) set by Joe Cronin in 1930-31. Since then, five other men have exceeded that total. Two of them, like Cronin, are also in Cooperstown (Ernie Banks and Robin Yount), and another is certain to be (Cal Ripken, Jr.). The other two (Alex Rodriguez and Nomar Garciaparra) are well on their way, but it should also be noted that their recent great seasons occurred at a time (1998–99) when major-league batting norms appear to have been greatly inflated by the effects of a rabbit baseball and or repeated expansion (1993 and '98). Table 4 compares the best consecutive-year performances by major-league shortstops based on combined total bases, with the group leader for each statistic boldfaced.

TABLE 4
Best Consecutive Seasons by Shortstops,
by Total Bases (1876–1999)

Rank	Player	Year	R	H	TB	HR	RBI	BA	SA	OBA
1	Ernie Banks	1958	119	193	379	47	129	.313	.614	.370
		1959	97	179	351	45	143	.304	.596	.379
		Total	216	372	**730**	92	272	.308	**.605**	.374
2	Alex Rodriguez	1998	123	213	384	42	124	.310	.560	.360
		1999	110	143	294	42	111	.285	.596	.357
		Total	233	356	678	84	235	.300	.571	.359
3	N. Garciaparra	1998	111	195	353	35	122	.323	.584	.362
		1999	103	190	321	27	104	.357	.603	.418
		Total	214	385	674	62	226	**.339**	.593	.389
4	Cal Ripken	1983	121	211	343	27	102	.318	.517	.373
		1984	103	195	327	27	86	.304	.510	.375
		Total	224	**406**	670	54	188	.311	.514	.374

Rank	Player	Year	R	H	TB	HR	RBI	BA	SA	OBA
5	Robin Yount	1982	129	210	367	29	114	.331	.578	.384
		1983	102	178	291	17	80	.308	.503	.387
		Total	231	388	658	46	194	.320	.542	.385
6	Vern Stephens	1949	113	177	329	39	159	.290	.539	.391
		1950	125	185	321	30	144	.295	.511	.361
		Total	238	362	650	69	303	.292	.525	.376
7	Joe Cronin	1930	127	203	301	13	126	.346	.513	.422
		1931	103	187	293	12	126	.306	.480	.391
		Total	230	390	594	25	252	.326	.496	.406

But, despite Vern's dazzling stats in 1949–50, he placed only seventh (with one hundred points) in the American League MVP voting for 1949 and (as noted earlier) earned a measly six points in 1950, tying him for twenty-fourth place in the balloting. The Red Sox finished second in 1949, once again losing the pennant by just one game, and were third in 1950, four games behind the champion Yankees. Recall that Rizzuto placed second in 1949 and won the award the next season, even though his totals for the two years combined (226 runs, 369 hits, 491 total bases, 12 home runs, 131 runs batted in, a .300 batting, .399 slugging and .386 on-base average) were nowhere near as impressive as Vern's overall. In fact, Stephens was so overlooked in the 1950 MVP voting that even Chicago shortstop Chico Carrasquel, whose White Sox finished in sixth place, 38 games out of first, actually garnered more MVP support than Vern (21 points, tied for sixteenth place), despite batting only .282, with 72 runs scored, 148 hits, only 4 home runs and 46 RBI, and leading the league's shortstops in absolutely zero defensive categories.

What the MVP voters ignored in 1949-50 were, simply, the two highest single-season RBI totals ever produced by a shortstop in the major leagues. They were also two of the four highest totals ever produced by a player who was not an outfielder, first baseman or catcher through 1999. Among shortstops, second and third basemen only Rogers Hornsby, who had 152 RBI in 1922, and Al Rosen, who drove in 145 runs in 1953, have had as many as Vern's 144 in 1950, and neither of them matched Junior's 159 from the previous year. The only other single-season RBI performances by shortstops to rank among the all-time top one hundred are the 143 ribbies by Ernie Banks in 1959 and (surprise!) Vern's 137 in 1948. Finally, note that three of the men above Stephens on the list above each won a MVP award in at least one of their two big back-to-back seasons. Banks won in both, even though his team did no better than tie for fifth place each year; Yount and Ripken won in 1982 and 1983, respectively, when their clubs won pennants.

There are no formal criteria for Most Valuable Player honors, not even for eligibility. So, the standards for election are entirely subjective — like weighing a player's credentials for the Hall of Fame. But, the MVP is also an award of the moment, contingent upon the temporal and sometimes fleeting mood shifts of the voters. Hence, in 1944, with wartime offense at a low, a pitcher (Newhouser) and a banjo-hitting, Gold Glove–type shortstop (Marion) earned their separate league's MVPs. Over the next five years, with offense on the upswing from the return of wartime players, the award was won mostly by sluggers or offensive catalysts (Stan Musial, Ted Williams, Joe DiMaggio, Jackie Robinson, Phil Cavarretta and Bob Elliott). Then, six years later, although offense was abounding and there were power hitters everywhere, the honor again went to a pitcher (NL reliever Jim Konstanty) and another banjo-hitting, Gold Glove–type shortstop who had a season above his head for a pennant winner (Rizzuto).

Presumably, there were justifiable reasons for these outcomes. If the subtle, intangible evidence supporting Marty Marion's and Phil Rizzuto's trophies (for example) is obscured from us now, a plurality of contemporary observers nonetheless saw something in their performance that was MVP-worthy despite the gaudier statistics of other players.

TABLE 5
KEY SHORTSTOPS' MVP-VOTE HISTORIES, 1942–50

	Ordinal Rank in MVP Voting										Top	Award	Car
Player	1	2	3	4	5	6	7	8	9	10	Ten	Pts	Pts
Stephens (AL)	0	0	1	2	0	1	1	0	1	0	6	33	710
Boudreau (AL)	1	0	1	0	0	1	0	1	0	2	6	32	896
Rizzuto (AL)	1	1	0	0	0	0	0	0	0	0	2	23	575
Marion (NL)	1	0	0	0	0	0	2	0	0	0	3	22	375
Reese (NL)	0	0	0	0	1	2	0	1	0	0	4	19	588
Pesky (AL)	0	0	1	1	0	0	0	0	0	0	2	15	300
Appling (AL)	0	1	0	0	0	0	0	0	0	1	2	10	427

But, whether they won an award or not, the overall records of each of these shortstops in the MVP voting for the period in which they were contemporaries show that all seven of them were held in high regard by the baseball writers of the era. In fact, in the period 1942-50 there was only one year (1945) that at least one of them was not among the top five in MVP balloting. Table 5 shows the number of times that each man finished in each of the top ten spots in MVP voting during that period and their total number of top-ten appearances for that era (Top Ten). Each is also awarded points for those finishes, based on the traditional MVP voting scheme (Award Pts, fourteen for first place, nine for second, eight for third, etc.), and the chart also gives the actual total of points they earned in all MVP balloting during their entire careers (Car Pts).

So, along with Hall of Famer Arky Vaughan (whose career as a regular was over by 1943) and Eddie Miller (who may have been better than any of them defensively, but couldn't carry Marion's bat, let alone one of the others'), these seven men were the best major-league shortstops of the 1940s. But, their combined batting, fielding, postseason, all-star and MVP voting histories do little to settle any argument about which was the best. Clearly, there were distinct differences in these men's skills; but, among the group as a whole, they tended to counterbalance in a way that reduced the overall distance between the best and least of them. Appling, Pesky and Boudreau were the best hitters for average, but Stephens had the most power by far. Marion had the best defensive reputation, but his career fielding stats are no more impressive than Boudreau's, and all of them were as good or better with a glove than the average shortstops of their era. Rizzuto and Reese had the most postseason appearances, but they also had the advantage of playing for teams that were loaded with talent, whereas Appling (for most of his career) and Stephens (for some of it) did not. Marion started the most all-star games, but Reese, Boudreau and Stephens were chosen for the game just as often. Boudreau, Marion and Rizzuto won MVP awards, but Stephens had a more consistent history of MVP support than either Marty or Phil.

With that in mind, and whether or not one, any, or all of these men belong in Cooperstown, you'd expect that their Hall of Fame voting histories would reflect the relative balance in their skills and career achievements; and, because the baseball-beat writers are the electors in both cases, you'd also think that the high regard shown to all of them in MVP voting would have manifested in relatively similar support for each man's enshrinement. But, it didn't happen that way.

3

Three Men Out

The seven shortstops discussed in Chapter 2 all became eligible for the Hall of Fame between 1952 and 1964. But, despite the relative similarities in their statistical, all-star and MVP credentials, they had very different fates in the voting. Table 6 shows the number of BBWAA elections in which each man was eligible for consideration in the balloting (Yrs El), the number of years in which they received votes (Yrs w/V), the highest number of votes (High Vote) and percentages of support (High Pct) that each received, and the overall total of votes they earned (Vote Total).

TABLE 6
KEY FORTIES SHORTSTOPS'
HOF-VOTING HISTORIES

Player	Years El	Years w/V	High Vote	High Pct	Vote Total
Appling	9	7	189	83.6	547
Boudreau	10	10	232	77.3	1146
Marion	12	12	127	40.0	1010
Pesky	12	1	1	0.4	1
Reese	14	14	186	47.9	1782
Rizzuto	14	14	149	38.4	1154
Stephens	13	0	0	0.0	0

Luke Appling, the first to retire, was elected by the BBWAA in 1964, receiving 83.6 percent support from the writers, fourteen years after his retirement, in his ninth year eligible. Lou Boudreau also was chosen by the writers, although just barely — getting 77.3 percent in 1970, eighteen years after his retirement, in the tenth year he received votes. Pee Wee Reese, who retired in 1958, and Phil Rizzuto, who was ushered out (i.e., released) at midseason by the Yankees in 1956, were both passed over by the writers in each of their fourteen years on the ballot (with Reese getting a high of 47.9 percent support and Rizzuto never receiving more than 38.4 percent), but both got into Cooperstown through the back door via the Veterans Committee (Reese in 1984, Rizzuto a decade later).

The other three men now appear unlikely ever to be enshrined. Marty Marion, who retired in 1953, got substantial support from the writers (as high as 40.0 percent in his ninth year on the ballot) but nonetheless missed in twelve chances with the BBWAA. Johnny Pesky got one vote in 1960, his first year on the ballot, but never received another even though he technically remained eligible through 1974. And Vern Stephens, whose home-run power made him the most distinctive of the group by not fitting the good-glove, no-sock stereotype for the position, never got a single vote from any Hall of Fame elector, even though he was eligible for consideration from 1962 through 1975. All three of them have been eligible for selection by the Veterans Committee since the early 1980s, but their Cooperstown prospects apparently have evaporated.

Appling ended his playing career after the 1950 season. At the time, there was a one-year waiting period between retirement and being placed on the HOF ballot, so Luke's first year of eligibility was 1952. Surprisingly, he got no votes at all that first year, but received two in 1953, none the next year, and three votes in 1955. In 1956 his vote total jumped to fourteen. The writers then took a semi-holiday, holding elections only in alternate, even-numbered years during the period 1956–65 — so Appling's next chance for election came in 1958, when his support jumped to seventy-seven votes, representing 28.9 percent support, the eighth-best total received that year. He dropped to seventy-two votes and 26.8 percent in 1960, but that was also good enough for eighth place. In 1962 the number of participating electors declined from 269 in the previous election to just 160. Commensurately, Luke's vote total fell to forty-eight, but it was actually his best showing to that point, as it represented 30 percent support and was the sixth-best total among the men who got votes that year, behind Bob Feller and Jackie Robinson (who were elected) and Sam Rice, Red Ruffing and Eppa Rixey (who were not).

By 1964, Rice and Rixey's eligibility had expired. That year the BBWAA also reprised a two-fold, preliminary- and runoff-vote procedure from the 1940s (discussed in later chapters). Appling responded like a good clutch hitter, jumping to first place ahead of Ruffing by one vote on the preliminary ballot (142–141), then increasing his margin in the runoff (189–184) to gain election.

Boudreau retired after 1952 and — under the old rules— would've been on the Cooperstown ballot as early as 1954. But, as of 1954, the waiting period for eligibility was extended to five years, so he should not have been on the ballot until 1958 (as there was no BBWAA vote in 1957). Nevertheless, he received two votes in 1956 (Marion and Rizzuto also got one vote apiece that year), apparently from writers who were ignorant of, or ignored, the new restriction. Boudreau received decent support (sixty-four votes for 24.1 percent) in 1958, his first official year on the ballot, but then fell to just thirty-five and twelve votes in the next two elections. Discounting the runoff elections of 1964 and 1967, his support climbed steadily from 1964 (33.8 percent) until he was elected in 1970. Note, however, that Boudreau actually received less support in 1964, his third official year on the ballot, than did Reese (36.3 percent)— even though Pee Wee was never elected by the writers.

Marion quit in 1953, and — after the "outlaw" vote he received in 1956 — his first official year of eligibility was 1960, when he garnered 37 votes for 13.8 percent support. He dropped to just 16 votes and 10 percent in 1962. But, beginning in 1964 (50 votes for 24.9 percent on the preliminary ballot), his vote totals increased steadily through 1970 (120 votes for 40 percent) then plateaued in the 120-vote range through the end of his eligibility in 1973. In Marion's last year on the ballot, he got 127 votes for 33.4 percent, and he averaged 23.2 percent support for the twelve elections in which he received votes (including runoffs). Marion's highest-ever ordinal finish was eighth in 1971 (123 votes for 34.2 percent). Although overlooked by the writers and the Veterans Committee, Marty received higher support levels than Rizzuto in nine of the ten years that they were both on the ballot and in five of the nine years that he competed with Reese.

Discounting his lone vote in 1956, Rizzuto's first official year on the ballot was 1962, when he got forty-four votes for 27.5 percent support. Except for the runoff elections of 1964 and 1967, his support fluctuated between 17.9 percent in 1966 and 29.2 percent in 1973. He topped the 30 percent barrier in 1974 and received his greatest support (149 votes for 38.4 percent) in 1976, the last year of his BBWAA eligibility. Overall, Phil averaged 22.5 percent support in the fourteen elections that he received votes. Ironically though, Rizzuto's highest ordinal finish came in 1962 — his first year on the ballot — when his vote total was the seventh best among all the players named. Rizzuto outpolled Boudreau only once in seven tries

(1962), bested Marion only once in ten years (also 1962), and trailed Reese in every year that they were simultaneously eligible.

Reese appeared on the ballot for the first time in 1964, which — because Appling was elected that year — was the only time that all seven shortstops were simultaneously eligible for consideration. Pee Wee received seventy-three votes that year for 36.3 percent support. Thereafter, excluding runoffs, his support levels fluctuated between 26.1 percent in 1969 and the 47.9 percent he earned in 1976, when he also received his highest vote total ever (186). In the fourteen elections in which he got votes, Reese averaged 33.1 percent support. Like Rizzuto, his highest ordinal finish came in his first year on the ballot — fifth place in 1964, although he finished sixth in 1976, his last year eligible. He outpolled Boudreau once (1964), topped Rizzuto in all twelve of their mutual elections, and bested Marion in four of the nine years that they were eligible together.

Appling had nearly a decade of accomplishments before any of the other men reached the majors, and therefore belongs as much or more to an earlier generation of players. Nonetheless, there were eight different ballots, including runoffs (1964–70), in which at least six of the shortstops were eligible for HOF consideration. Table 7 compares the HOF-support percentage levels that each man received in those elections, with the column for each player headed by their initials. Neither Pesky nor Stephens received a vote in any of them. That fact is difficult to defend given that both men's career accomplishments were competitive with, and in some cases superior to, the others, and recognizing that the fluctuations in support for Marion, Reese and Rizzuto (at least) are indicative that there was no firm consensus at the time about the relative hierarchy of their candidacies.

TABLE 7
FORTIES SHORTSTOPS' HOF-SUPPORT
PERCENTAGES, 1964–70

Year	LA	LB	MM	JP	PR	VS	PWR
1964	70.6	33.8	24.9	0.0	22.4	0.0	36.3
1964-RO	83.6	19.0	7.5	0.0	4.9	0.0	20.8
1966	—	38.1	28.5	0.0	17.9	0.0	31.5
1967	—	49.0	30.8	0.0	24.3	0.0	30.5
1967-RO	—	22.2	7.2	0.0	4.6	0.0	5.3
1968	—	51.8	31.6	0.0	26.2	0.0	28.7
1969	—	63.9	32.8	0.0	22.9	0.0	26.1
1970	—	77.3	40.0	0.0	26.3	0.0	32.3
Total	*154.2*	*355.1*	*203.3*	*0.0*	*149.5*	*0.0*	*211.5*
Average	*77.1*	*44.4*	*25.4*	*0.0*	*17.9*	*0.0*	*26.4*

In one sense, the numerical results of the BBWAA voting can be seen as a dialogue on each player's credentials for the Hall of Fame. If the dialogue is open, thoughtful and evenhanded, then each man deserving serious consideration should receive adequate "discussion" (i.e., votes) over a sufficient period of years to evidence an intelligent, defensible conclusion regarding the worthiness of their candidacies. Failure to gain election by the end of their eligibility should be ample proof, within the scope of the writers' presumed collective wisdom, that they don't belong there. Clearly, this dialogue took place regarding Appling, Boudreau, Reese, Rizzuto and even Marion.

But, if the HOF voting procedure constitutes a dialogue, then Johnny Pesky was mentioned only by a whisper in passing, Junior Stephens was never even discussed, and both men were denied anything close to appropriate consideration by the voters. Any explanation for this failure can only be speculative, because we cannot know with certainty what went on in the minds of the writers who voted during the years that Pesky and Stephens were eligible.

At the time they came on to the Cooperstown ballot, one problem Pesky and Stephens faced in their candidacies was that the BBWAA was mired armpit deep in a huge list of eligible players from earlier periods in major-league history. The length of this list made it difficult for anyone to get elected. In 1960, the first year that Pesky was eligible (with Appling, Boudreau and Marion also on the ballot), 131 different men received votes, a group that seems to include (but doesn't) every twentieth-century player who met the ten-year service requirement and had not been chosen for the Hall to that date. With the vote spread among so many men, the probability was greatly diminished that anyone would receive the 75 percent support required for election. As a result, although Edd Roush's 146 votes topped the ballot, they represented only 54.3 percent support, so there were no new Cooperstown members enshrined by the writers that year.

The overall quality of the candidates also made it tougher to get elected in 1960. Only four of the 131 men who received votes — Appling, Boudreau, Ruffing and Joe Medwick — were eventually elected by the BBWAA, which seems to imply that there weren't very many good choices available. But, the list also included thirty-three others who were chosen later by the Veterans Committee. So, although some of those players were dubious selections, there were many men deserving serious consideration from which each elector could choose to support only ten. Logically, whether the ballot is lengthy or not, it's much easier to get elected — or even get votes, for that matter — if there is only a handful of viable candidates than if there are three dozen or more.

Most of the men on the 1960 ballot also were players from the 1920s or thirties and some even had careers that began before World War I (Edd Roush first entered the majors with the White Sox in 1913). With this backlog, it also was predictable that many of the players from the more distant past would fare best in the voting, because many electors were bound to feel some obligation to decide the fates of the older players before the ballot became loaded with men from a more recent era. Predictably then, among the twenty-eight men who received 10 percent support or more that year, only ten of them had played as late as the 1940s, and only five of those — Appling, Boudreau, Marion, Johnny Mize and Johnny Vander Meer — also had been active into the early 1950s.

In 1962, when Stephens (and Rizzuto) became eligible, seventy-seven men received votes from the writers. They included seven players that were eventually enshrined by the BBWAA — Appling, Boudreau, Ruffing and Medwick (the four holdovers from 1960), plus first-time eligibles Ralph Kiner, Bob Feller and Jackie Robinson, the latter two of which were the only men elected in 1962. Roush's eligibility had expired (he and manager Bill McKechnie were selected by the Veterans Committee that year). But the list of men who received votes still included twenty-nine players that were chosen sometime later by the VC. In fact, despite the decline in the number of men receiving votes, it was just as difficult to get any votes at all in 1962 as it had been in the previous election. As noted earlier, the number of BBWAA voters dropped from 269 to 160 that year, so there was a maximum of only 1600 votes to spread around, instead of the 2690 in 1960. Commensurately, the 41 percent dip in the number of men who received votes (from 131 to 77) was virtually the same as the 40 percent decline in total electors.

But, none of these problems prevented Appling, Boudreau, Reese, Rizzuto or even Marion from getting votes in the elections of 1960–64, or later. So there were other reasons why Pesky and Stephens were almost totally ignored by the writers.

In 1947, hoping to assure that the voters had an appropriate historical perspective, the BBWAA restricted the franchise in Hall of Fame elections to active or retired members with at least ten years of service in the organization. As a result, the number of electors dropped from an average of 226 in the first eight BBWAA elections to a total of just 121 in 1948, the smallest number of voters ever to participate in that aspect of the Cooperstown balloting. The ten-year requirement should've helped to ensure that a substantial percentage of the people who voted in the HOF elections of the sixties and seventies had seen Johnny Pesky and Vern Stephens play at the peak of their careers. But it didn't work that way, because the map of major-league baseball changed dramatically in the fifties and sixties, radically altering the composition of the Hall of Fame electorate.

Five major-league franchises — the Braves, Browns, A's, Dodgers and Giants — had changed cities by the time that Pesky became eligible in 1960, and another one (the old Senators/Twins) moved before Stephens joined the ballot in 1962. Before their periods of eligibility had expired, there were two rounds of expansion (1961–62 and 1969) plus four more franchise relocations (the Braves and A's again plus expansion Seattle to Milwaukee and the new Senators to Dallas). When the moving vans finally stopped, the number of major-league cities with teams in both leagues had dropped from five as late as 1952 to just two by 1965 (Chicago and New York), and the number of cities with big-league teams had doubled from eleven in 1952 to twenty-two in 1973.

In turn, the number of BBWAA electors grew steadily during this period. By 1960, Pesky's first year of eligibility, the number of voters was up to 269; and, although it dropped to 160 when Stephens first appeared on the ballot in 1962, it rose all the way to 362 before his eligibility expired in 1975, a 199 percent increase over the 121 voters of 1948. On average, 308 electors participated in each of the thirteen HOF elections in the years 1960–75.

The growth accompanied a tremendous turnover in the composition of the BBWAA. The addition of each new city to major-league status meant that new writers from different newspapers joined the firsthand traveling coverage of their teams. The franchise shifts also meant that the ranks of baseball-beat writers in the abandoned cities were reduced, as papers were forced to cut their coverage from two teams (or three, in the case of New York) to just one. With retirements, deaths and the other normal causes of attrition, this meant that — even with the BBWAA's ten-year service requirement in force — the composition of the Hall of Fame electorate had changed considerably by the mid-sixties, with more change to come in the next decade.

Unless they were already middle-aged and had previously worked in one of the older major-league cities, the BBWAA's members from the new big-league locales could've had relatively little personal experience watching the seven shortstops from the forties play. So, by the mid-1960s, as they began to join the ranks of HOF voters, all many of them had to go by were the players' word-of-mouth reputations among veteran writers and baseball people plus the statistical records of the players' careers. In that atmosphere of change, Johnny Pesky and Vern Stephens lost their luster among the Hall of Fame's electorate.

Baseball writers rely on managers and coaches as a prime source of information about the teams they cover; and, in the process, they are strongly influenced by these men's opinions regarding the individual skills of current and former players. In that respect, the deck was stacked against Pesky and Stephens during the period that the two men were eligible for HOF consideration.

In the two decades from the end of World War II through the mid–1960s the Yankees and Dodgers were by far baseball's most successful franchises. Combined, the two clubs won almost 60 percent of the available pennants in the years 1946–66 (twenty-five out of forty-two), and — after the Dodgers moved to Los Angeles in 1958 — both clubs had comparatively enormous amounts of money to spend on player development and acquisitions. Because success encourages imitation, other clubs hoping to achieve similar results often sought to emulate one organization or the other. This manifested in a large number of men with backgrounds in the Yankee or Dodger organizations being hired as coaches and managers during the two decades from the late fifties through the mid-seventies. In addition to former Yankees pilot Casey Stengel (with the Mets through the mid-sixties) and Walt Alston (who managed the Dodgers during 1954–76), the skippers alone included Chuck Dressen, Gene Mauch, Joe Gordon, Cookie Lavagetto, Ralph Houk, Hank Bauer, Eddie Lopat, Gil Hodges, Yogi Berra, Herman Franks, Don Heffner, Eddie Stanky, Dick Williams, Clyde King, Preston Gomez, Billy Martin, Sparky Anderson, Don Zimmer, and Darrell Johnson, in roughly chronological order. All of these men spent portions of their careers in the New York or Brooklyn/Los Angeles organizations; many were either Yankees or Dodgers at heart at the time they became skippers; and several of them were former teammates of Reese and or Rizzuto.

In comparison, there were few ex-teammates of Stephens and Pesky managing or coaching in the majors during the same era. After all, absolutely no one wanted to emulate the St. Louis Browns, so Heffner, Don Gutteridge, Bob Swift, Joe Schultz, Less Moss and Floyd Baker were about the only former Brownies around who were managing or coaching. The list of Vern and Johnny's teammates with the Red Sox was about the same size — Ted Williams, Bobby Doerr, Birdie Tebbetts, Billy Hitchcock, Sam Mele and Cot Deal being the noteworthies. Pesky also managed and coached during this period. He piloted the Red Sox in 1963–64, he was a coach for the Pirates in 1965–67, then he returned to Boston for a decade as a coach beginning in 1975. But after Stephens retired in 1955 he never wore a big-league uniform again, unless it was to appear in an old-timers game.

As a result, there were a lot more people available who, if asked, were more likely to trumpet the skills of Reese and Rizzuto to the new generation of baseball writers than those of Stephens and Pesky. It also helped that Reese and Rizzuto were still visible too. Pee Wee broadcast the game-of-the-week with Dizzy Dean on network television through most of the sixties; the Scooter joined the New York announcers almost immediately after his release as a player in 1956 and made a second career that lasted more than four decades. Inevitably, this Yankees-Dodgers bias had a negative impact on Johnny and Vern's prospects for Cooperstown, as Pee Wee and the Scooter would've dominated any conversation among the relatively new sportswriters and veteran baseball men about the unelected shortstops of their era, and, because of competition from players at other positions, no HOF-voting writer was likely to support more than one or two shortstops in a given year.

Beyond that bias, Pesky and Stephens also were disadvantaged by subjective hindsight. As time passes, it's tempting to see the historical record as our safeguard against the misjudgment of legend and nostalgia — but reliance on the bare bones of data can lead us to conclusions just as false. One player's pinnacle of unrepeated success — a solitary MVP for example — might acquire an exaggerated importance that draws more Hall of Fame support than another man's record of consistently placing high in the MVP balloting without ever winning the award. One man may reap some Cooperstown benefit by being linked with teams that won multiple pennants, while another may be penalized because he played for clubs that regularly fared worse in the standings. Or, the image of a player's overall ability may become tainted in posterity by his association with a single, negative moment in time. With little else to distinguish them from the other shortstops of their era, Pesky and Stephens were victims of these kinds of subjective misreadings of history by the new generation of Hall of Fame electors, and both men were hurt by their misfortunes of having never played on a World Series winner and never won a MVP.

Appling had never won a World Series or MVP trophy either but was lucky enough to be elected to Cooperstown in 1964, before the big turnover in HOF voters. Among the others, Boudreau played for only one pennant winner — the same as Pesky and Stephens — but his 1948 Indians won their series, he had a MVP award to his credit, and the writers also enshrined him before the turnover in BBWAA membership was complete (1970). Marion won three of the four fall classics he played in and had the 1944 MVP in his pocket, which compensated somewhat for his own disadvantage from the Yankees-Dodgers bias — so he got a lot of votes, just never enough. Rizzuto had a trophy too; and, although Reese never won one, Pee Wee and the Scooter were in the World Series regularly throughout their careers — even late enough (the mid–1950s) so that most of the new generation of voters had actually seen them play in one, at least on television.

The Hall of Fame voters' favoritism for the MVP winners among the forties shortstops was not just myopic but also inconsistent with the treatment given other HOF candidates at that position. In the history of MVP voting, only thirteen shortstops have ever placed among the MVP top five more than once in their careers. One of them, Cal Ripken, Jr., is not yet eligible for Cooperstown. Among the others, Stephens and Pesky are the only ones who have been virtually ignored by the HOF electors. Table 8 lists these men in descending order, first according to the frequency that each one ranked among each of the top five ordinal spots in MVP voting (Top 5 Freq) and then by the total of Hall of Fame votes each later received (HOF Votes). Seven men on the list are enshrined at Cooperstown, and those who are not each received more support than Stephens or Pesky — including Alvin Dark, Arky Vaughan and Travis Jackson, none of whom ever won a MVP award.

TABLE 8
HOF-VOTE HISTORIES, SHORTSTOPS WITH
MULTIPLE, TOP-FIVE MVP FINISHES

Player	MVP Ordinal Rank					Top 5 Freq	HOF Votes	HOF Status
	1	2	3	4	5			
Ernie Banks	2	0	1	1	0	4	321	In
Lou Boudreau	1	0	1	0	1	3	1146	In
Vern Stephens	0	0	1	2	0	3	0	Out
Cal Ripken	2	0	1	0	0	3	—	NYE
Maury Wills	1	0	1	0	0	2	1680	Out
Rabbit Maranville	0	1	1	0	0	2	1282	In
Phil Rizzuto	1	1	0	0	0	2	1154	In
Alvin Dark	0	0	1	0	1	2	776	Out
Luke Appling	0	2	0	0	0	2	547	In
Arky Vaughan	0	0	2	0	0	2	244	In
Travis Jackson	0	0	0	1	1	2	67	In
Dick Groat	1	1	0	0	0	2	29	Out
Johnny Pesky	0	0	1	1	0	2	1	Out

Note: Robin Yount won two MVP awards, 1982 and 1989. But his second came as an outfielder, and he played no games at shortstop that season.

In addition, if anything, Pesky and Stephens's lone World Series appearances may have actually hurt both men's Cooperstown chances. Pesky was disadvantaged by his negative role in the deciding play of the 1946 series, when St. Louis right fielder Enos Slaughter scored the series-winning run from first base on Harry Walker's two-out double in the eighth inning of the decisive game. Many observers felt that Pesky hesitated on the throw to home after center fielder Leon Culberson's relay, allowing Slaughter to score; and, unfortunately for Johnny, the catch phrase "Pesky held the ball" became a haunting capsule description of his entire career. Pesky also led the 1946 series in errors, with four, and batted just .233 with no RBI against St. Louis. But Bobby Doerr and Wally Moses were the only Boston regulars to bat over .261 in the series (Ted Williams, who was injured in a pre-series exhibition game, hit just .200, with a lone RBI), and the Red Sox as a team batted only .240 against the Cardinals' pitchers. So Johnny wasn't the only one in the lineup who failed to deliver clutch hits. In the aftermath, the fact that Boston took St. Louis to the full seven games was largely forgotten, except to glorify Slaughter's dash to home, and Pesky became one of the most famous of World Series "goats."

In the 1944 World Series Stephens had an experience similar to Pesky's two years later. He and teammate Don Gutteridge tied for the series lead in errors, with three, and Vern batted only .227, with no homers or runs batted in against the crosstown Cardinals. One of his errors also led to the Browns' downfall. In the bottom of the fourth inning of game six, Junior's errant throw on a one-out attempted double play allowed Walker Cooper to score the tying run from third base and kept alive what proved to be the winning rally in the Cards' 3–1 victory in the series clincher. But, just like Pesky in 1946, Stephens was not the only wimpy hitter for the Browns in their lone fall classic. Only one of their regulars batted above .231 in the series, and the team as a whole hit a paltry .183 in the six games against the Cards. Vern's error never proved as famous or haunting as Pesky's supposed hesitation did, perhaps because no one ever took the 1944 Browns seriously. Their pennant that year is often dismissed as a fluke that resulted because the American League's usual contenders were decimated by wartime player shortages—a quirky anomaly in the otherwise dismal history of an inept franchise that was back in the AL cellar within three years of its only league title. So, even if Junior had batted .400 and gone errorless in the series, but the Browns had still lost, such a performance might also be forgotten or ignored.

No doubt, the two men's World Series miscues also contributed to the notion that neither was a good defensive shortstop, an idea that persists about both players long after their careers ended. But their reputations as inadequate glove men are entirely subjective, and the fielding records of both men contradict this third-generation (or older) hearsay. As shown in the previous chapter (Table 2), at worst both men were average defensively, if not above so, compared to the other HOF-eligible shortstops of their era. Beyond that, their fielding at the position was competitive with the other Hall of Fame candidates of the period. Table 9 compares the seasonal averages for games, putouts, assists, errors, total chances, successful chances (SC, total chances minus errors), range factor, double plays and fielding average compiled by the seven shortstops discussed in this chapter for only those specific years during the 1942–50 period that each man played the position (so, any years in which Appling or Pesky were primarily third basemen are excluded) and gives the group average for each stat. The leaders among the group are boldfaced in each category.

TABLE 9
SEASONAL FIELDING STATISTICS, KEY FORTIES SHORTSTOPS

Player	G	PO	A	E	TC	SC	RF	DP	FA
Appling	110	210	345	26	581	555	5.05	73	.955
Boudreau	132	277	401	**17**	695	678	**5.14**	101	**.976**
Marion	135	260	426	20	706	686	5.08	86	.972
Pesky	**152**	297	**458**	26	781	755	4.97	96	.967
Reese	148	**305**	451	27	**783**	**756**	5.11	97	.966
Rizzuto	143	303	419	23	745	722	5.05	**108**	.969
Stephens	143	258	445	29	732	703	4.92	91	.960
Totals	*963*	*1910*	*2945*	*168*	*5023*	*4855*	*35.32*	*652*	*6.765*
Averages	*138*	*273*	*421*	*24*	*718*	*694*	*5.05*	*93*	*.966*

Clearly, Hall of Famer Appling was the least of these shortstops defensively during this period, if only because his age must have limited his durability — as measured by games played — and his range. But, there is no definitive evidence here that either Pesky or Stephens was significantly worse than any of the others in the field. Pesky leads the group in games played per season and assists, so he was the most durable of the bunch for the three years he played the position, and Stephens also played five more games per season than the average man among the seven. That durability must've had a negative impact on their range factors and fielding averages. Boudreau and Marion played considerably fewer games per season but have two of the best range factors and the highest fielding averages in the bunch. This proves little more than that rested shortstops make more plays per game at a higher success rate, while tired ones get to fewer balls and make more errors. That's certainly no surprise, given the rigorous demands of the position. But, there's also no logic in arguing that either man was a liability because he was able, willing and or required to be in the lineup almost every day. If that was true, we would all think a lot less of Cal Ripken, Jr.

From the evidence in Table 9, except for Appling, Stephens appears to be the least of the other shortstops defensively. But, he was good enough at the position that, when traded to Boston in 1948, manager Joe McCarthy installed him at short for the next three seasons and shifted Pesky to third base. "Marse" Joe, who some consider to be the greatest major-league skipper of all time, must've seen something in Vern's defense that justified the move. McCarthy's intuition was rewarded, as the shift solidified Boston's infield: Pesky's thirty-five double plays in 1948 topped all major-league third basemen; over the 1948–50 period, with Junior at short, the Red Sox as a team turned sixty-nine more double plays than they had during the seasons that Pesky played the position; and, in 1950, when Phil Rizzuto tied the major-league record for shortstops with a fielding average of .9817, Stephens was right behind him at .9815. When Pesky and Stephens switched positions again in 1951, the move was dictated by a leg injury that limited Vern's range. So, maybe Pesky and Stephens would never have won a Gold Glove had the awards been given back then. But, neither man was anything like Dick Stuart (or even Jose Offerman) either, and their fielding statistics repudiate any notion that their gloves were colanders.

Stephens and Pesky also were hurt by what appears to be inconsistent treatment from the voters regarding World War II military service. Pesky may have been a victim of his military duty. As noted in Chapter 2, Johnny missed three seasons at the beginning of his career (1943–45) due to the war. In 1942 and 1946–47 he led the American League with more than two hundred hits each year, tying the all-time record for most times leading that category at the start of a career and batting .330 over the course of those three seasons. We'll never know what numbers Pesky would have produced in the three years he lost to military duty. But, before injuries began to slow him in 1952, he batted below .312 only once in his first seven seasons (1948, the year he had to adjust to a new position). Johnny had 1455 hits and scored 867 runs in his ten-year career. If he had played during 1943–45, any performance similar to the ones he gave in his first three seasons would've given him about 2000 career hits and easily pushed him over 1000 runs scored.

Of the twenty-seven shortstops in major-league history to reach both of those career totals through 1994, thirteen of them are in Cooperstown, three are not yet eligible, and seven of the other eleven received more Hall of Fame votes than Pesky did. As is, Johnny compiled the third-best career on-base average (.394) of all shortstops who have been eligible for

Cooperstown through 2000. Only Honus Wagner and Arky Vaughan did better, and they are both in the Hall. Similarly, Pesky owns the eighth-highest batting average among the same group of men (.307). Five of the seven shortstops above him are also enshrined (Wagner, Vaughan, Appling, Joe Sewell and Hughie Jennings), and a sixth (Ross Barnes, three votes from the 1936 Old-Timers Committee) got more HOF votes than Johnny did.

In contrast, Stephens seems to have suffered because he didn't have to serve his country during the war. A bad knee prevented Vern from being eligible for duty, and his career statistics benefited from that circumstance. In the same three years that Pesky, Reese and Rizzuto all fought in World War II, Stephens averaged 159 hits, 22 home runs and 96 runs batted in per season; in 1944 he became the first shortstop in AL history to lead the league in ribbies (109); and in 1945 his 24 homers made him the first at the position to ever lead either major circuit in four-baggers.

Despite all that, Junior's stats often have been discounted by many observers on the premise that he put up great numbers against inferior wartime pitching. But, the same is true of Lou Boudreau, and that didn't keep him from getting into Cooperstown, and the absence of wartime service didn't prevent Marty Marion from receiving over a thousand Hall of Fame votes as well, although his batting numbers weren't nearly as good as Vern's. Denigrating Junior's wartime achievements ignores the fact that his performance actually improved after the return of the missing wartime pitchers. In the five-year period 1946–50, Stephens averaged 166 hits, 25 homers and 117 RBI per season, each figure better than his numbers for the shorter period 1943–45. In 1949 Vern set an all-time record for home runs by a shortstop in a season (39, broken by Ernie Banks in 1955); and, as noted earlier, that same year he had more RBI than any middle infielder ever. So, Junior's batting feats were not just a mirage that resulted from facing Triple-A caliber or worse, wartime pitchers.

Stephens also may have suffered from moral high-handedness by some BBWAA voters. Vern had a reputation as a "player" on more than just the baseball field, and there are tales that he had more lady friends on road trips than sailors have ports. Reputedly, he also enjoyed a variety of beverages. One of his ex-roommates once guessed that Vern played hungover in about 80 percent of the Browns' games one season; and, during one road trip, he supposedly almost fell off of a train while intoxicated, nearly duplicating the premature demise of Hall of Fame outfielder Ed Delahanty in 1903. These stories about Stephens might be exaggerated, but his reputation as a good-time-loving swinger was well-known among the BBWAA long before he left baseball. So it's possible that some, perhaps many, writers ignored his credentials for that reason. But, even if so,

When Vern Stephens retired in 1955 he was the all-time leader in home runs by a shortstop, and only two men since then — Ernie Banks and Cal Ripken, Jr.— have surpassed his total at the position. Vern's all-star and MVP-vote histories also were as good or better than several of his contemporaries who've been elected to Cooperstown. But, he never received a single Hall of Fame vote, and his failure to do so exposes a major flaw in the subjective foundation of Cooperstown's selection process. (Photograph from *The Sporting News*)

Vern's lack of support from any BBWAA voter is grossly inconsistent with the plethora of other reputed boozers (e.g., Grover Alexander, Jimmie Foxx and Hack Wilson) and womanizers (e.g., Babe Ruth and Mickey Mantle) who the scribes have elected to baseball's Shrine.

When Stephens retired in 1955, he held the major-league record for most career home runs by a shortstop (Vern hit 213 of his 247 lifetime homers at the position). It took no less than Ernie Banks and Cal Ripken, Jr., to break that mark. (Ernie surpassed it in 1959 on his way to belting 292 taters as a shortstop, 512 in all. Ripken passed Vern in 1990, then supplanted Banks as the career leader three years later.) To date, the two men remain the only shortstops in big-league history with more homers than Junior. Banks is in the Hall. Ripken is sure to be. Among the top three men in career homers at each position (including first, second and third basemen, shortstops, outfielders and catchers, eighteen men in all) only three of them besides Stephens and Ripken are not yet enshrined at Cooperstown—first baseman Mark McGwire, second baseman Ryne Sandberg, and third sacker Graig Nettles—and none of them was eligible in 2000. McGwire is still active, and Sandberg will not be eligible until 2003. But, both men are almost certain to be elected by the scribes. Nettles was dropped from the ballot in 1997 when his 22 votes were less than the 5 percent required to be retained, but he did receive a total of 125 votes in his four years on the HOF ballot (1994–97). To date, Vern Stephens still has zero votes and is not about to get one.

Finally, Stephens and Pesky also may have been hurt by the relative dispersion of authoritative statistical sources available to Hall of Fame voters during the early years on the Cooperstown ballot. Until publication of Macmillan's first *Baseball Encyclopedia* in 1969, the most "official" sources available for individual player statistics from their era were the myriad of annual publications by *The Sporting News* (e.g., their *Baseball Guide, Dope Book* and *Player Register*). But, because no one of these books was ever as comprehensive as Macmillan's, any truly conscientious voter was required to sort through several publications for each of many different years to piece together a thorough statistical summation of any player's career and had to do the same for many other men in order to put them all in any thoughtful perspective. Such an effort was unlikely from most BBWAA electors, as reporters/editors in general are notorious for their preference for easily available facts.

Given their career achievements relative to their contemporaries, and regardless of whether either man belongs in the Hall of Fame, the failure of so many HOF voters over so many years to appropriately weigh the credentials of Vern Stephens and Johnny Pesky constitutes an injustice to both players and to the Hall of Fame as an institution. Merely explaining this failure by the various circumstances listed here makes it no more defensible.

If Stephens and Pesky were the only victims of that type of injustice, it might be dismissed as a fluke. But, they are not isolated cases, by any means. The list of players whose HOF candidacies never received an adequate "dialogue" from the BBWAA is a long one that includes men from every era of major-league history and Cooperstown voting. Even ignoring Stephens, Pesky and the eight men who've been elected to Cooperstown by the Veterans Committee but never got a vote from the BBWAA, a partial survey of such players includes Wally Berger, Rocky Colavito, Lave Cross, Bill Dahlen, Willie Kamm, Indian Bob Johnson and Ken

Williams, each of whom received no more than three votes in two BBWAA elections; plus Buddy Bell, Darrell Evans, Jack Glassock, Bobby Grich, Dave Kingman, Bill Madlock, Carl Mays, Al Oliver, Dan Quisenberry, Ted Simmons, Harry Stovey, Jim Sundberg and George Van Haltren, who got votes in only one election and earned no higher than 4.5 percent support; and Pete Browning, Charlie Buffinton, Bob Caruthers, Harlond Clift, Mike Cuellar, Hooks Dauss, Dave Foutz, Jeff Heath, Ed Konetchy, Jim McCormick, Tony Mullane, George Mullin, Jack Powell, Del Pratt, Ed Reulbach, Al Rosen, Bob Shawkey, Jack Stivetts and Hippo Vaughn, all of whom — like Stephens — never received a single vote from the BBWAA at any time.

That so many supposedly knowledgeable voters could virtually ignore all of these men, while noticing other players of roughly equal ability and (as the next chapter will show) throwing away votes on candidates who were far less qualified, explains why some kind of Veterans Committee has always been needed as part of the Cooperstown process. It also evidences the injustices inherent in the Hall of Fame and BBWAA's continued insistence upon using a subjective voting system.

4

Alphonse and Gaston

You see the play all the time. The batter hits a high pop fly to the infield or shallow outfield. Two or three fielders converge in the area where the ball is about to descend, but the wind, sun or lights combine with a failure to communicate that leaves each of them unsure who will, or should, make the catch. While they all look to each other for someone else to take charge, the ball drops untouched onto the grass between them.

In the not-so-distant past, that kind of team error was called the "Alphonse and Gaston Act." The term originated from a pair of cartoon characters created by someone named Frederick B. Opper, back before most of us were born. According to *The Dickson Baseball Dictionary*, the two characters always deferred to one another so much that they never got anything done — Gaston saying "After you, my dear Alphonse"; Alphonse responding, "No, after you, my dear Gaston." You don't hear the term very often any more — not in the last couple decades anyway — because most of the veteran baseball announcers who were familiar with the old cartoon from the time before World War II have died off, and their successors never really embraced the phrase with much enthusiasm.

Passé or not, the term is an appropriate descriptor for the Hall of Fame selection process. That's because from Cooperstown's very beginning, and throughout the sixty-five-year history of baseball's Shrine, the museum's trustees and its chief elective body — the BBWAA — have done almost everything imaginable to mimic Alphonse and Gaston. And, if they haven't failed as completely as their cartoon counterparts (after all, the writers have elected about half of the players enshrined at Cooperstown), they have certainly performed like the namesake fielders in every other respect, as their numerous efforts to refine the selection process have missed the catch by accomplishing virtually nothing to define or clarify any standards for admission.

When the Hall of Fame was created, the failure to establish any meaningful criteria for Cooperstown membership occurred because — as baseball historian and statistics guru Bill James has noted in *The Politics of Glory*—"The Hall of Fame selection process was an afterthought to an accident." James's work provides a far more detailed look at the Hall of Fame's institutional history than space permits here. But, in essence, the impetus for the museum was an amalgam of the Cooperstown city fathers' desire to boost the hamlet's depression-era economy by creating a tourist attraction based on the town's mistaken claim that baseball was invented there in 1839 by Civil War hero Abner Doubleday and of an unsuccessful effort by organized baseball to obtain federal funding during the 1920s for a monument in Washington, D.C., to honor the game's greatest players (one envisions a two-hundred-foot-tall monolith carved like a giant stone bat next to a fifty-foot-high granite fielder's glove with a giant marble baseball nestled in its pocket and the names of great players carved into the ball like autographs).

When those proposals were merged in the 1930s in anticipation of what was wrongly believed to be baseball's centennial in 1939 (year of the first Cooperstown induction ceremony), much attention was paid to how the museum would operate financially, but little coherent thought was given to who would be honored or precisely how the members should be chosen — except that successful candidates should receive 75 percent support in any vote taken. Deferring first, just like Gaston, the trustees left the incidental details to the whims of their chosen electors— an Old-Timers Committee (OTC) empowered to induct five players from the nineteenth century and a panel of 226 BBWAA members charged with selecting an equal number of "moderns" (players from 1901 or later).

So predictably, in reciprocating Alphonse fashion, the very first Hall of Fame election misfired when the seventy-eight electors on the OTC failed to award the required fifty-nine votes to any nineteenth-century player. In turn, the first group of inductees, announced 29 January 1936, was limited to the five men — Ty Cobb, Walter Johnson, Christy Mathewson, Babe Ruth and Honus Wagner — who, conveniently, were the only ones to receive 75 percent approval or better from the BBWAA. As a result, the HOF selection process was tainted by failure from its beginning, and the institution has never completely recovered from that first Alphonse-and-Gaston error.

Beyond the OTC's failure, the initial electoral system had other flaws. The original concept, to honor players only, excluded any consideration of managers, executives and key contributors to the game's early history and development. So, players like Hal Chase and Charlie Pabor received support in 1936, but Alexander Cartwright did not.

Chase was a one-time league leader in home runs and batting during the game's Dead-Ball Era. He also possessed a near-unanimous reputation as the premier-fielding first baseman of the period, perhaps of all time, despite the fact that his 402 errors at the position were (and remain) almost fifty percent more than any other first sacker who played exclusively since the start of the twentieth century. Apparently, many of those errors were not accidents. Chase was blacklisted from baseball after the 1919 season for alleged involvement in fixing games. Legend has it that his gambling shenanigans were so frequent and nefarious that, by comparison, he made the Chicago Black Sox who threw the 1919 World Series look merely gray. But, neither his own misdeeds nor his well-known, before-the-fact knowledge of the Black Sox fix prevented Chase from receiving eleven BBWAA votes in 1936 — more than future HOF first basemen Bill Terry or Frank Chance got that year — and eighteen more votes in the 1937 election.

Pabor, an outfielder and pitcher during the years of the National Association (1871–75), collected one whole pitching victory and 715 hits in five seasons, but never appeared in an official big-league game — because the NA (perhaps unfairly) is not recognized as a true major league. He did bat .360 playing for the association's sixth-place Brooklyn Atlantics in 1873, a feat which apparently prompted one member of the 1936 Old-Timers Committee to give him a lone vote for Cooperstown.

Cartwright, on the other hand, was nothing less than the Church of Baseball's Moses. In 1846 he descended from the heights of Manhattan to deliver unto his people the Law (i.e., baseball's first codified rules of play). His people, who called themselves the Knickerbockers and had gathered at the mythologically appropriate Elysian Fields in Hoboken, New Jersey, then became the first official converts to the Church of Baseball; and, although Cartwright's rules were not (so far as we know) dictated by a burning bush or inscribed in ancient Hebrew on stone tablets, they are credited with establishing nine-man teams, nine-inning games, ninety feet between the bases and fixed batting orders (apparently, nine was Alex's lucky number). So, more than any other person, Cartwright — and not Abner Doubleday — is rightly regarded as the true inventor of modern baseball, and his omission from consideration in the initial Hall of Fame voting evidenced the inadequate forethought invested in who should be considered for Cooperstown membership.

But, the biggest flaw in the initial voting process was the failure of the Hall of Fame's braintrust as a whole to establish any meaningful guidelines for an individual's election. Among other problems, this led to confusion regarding who was eligible for consideration by the two separate groups of electors: one Old-Timers Committee member actually voted for Jake Daubert, who was a very good first baseman but whose major-league career didn't begin until 1910 (so the only part of the nineteenth century that Jake ever saw was through the eyes of a child), and eight men whose playing careers overlapped the turn of the century — Jimmy Collins, Lou Criger, Ed Delahanty, Willie Keeler, Nap Lajoie, John McGraw, Honus Wagner and Cy Young — received votes on both 1936 ballots. The lack of clear standards also left the definition of what precisely constitutes a Hall of Famer dependent entirely upon the subjective opinions of each individual elector.

Initially, the BBWAA electors also could vote for any player, active or retired. So inevitably, Mickey Cochrane, Jimmie Foxx, Frankie Frisch, Lou Gehrig, Lefty Grove, Rogers Hornsby, Al Simmons, Bill Terry and Pie Traynor — each of them legitimate Hall of Famers but all of whose careers were ongoing and whose total accomplishments, therefore, were not yet fully known — were among the forty-seven men who received votes in the BBWAA's version of the 1936 balloting. If active players had been allowed to receive votes into the 1980s, Pete Rose clearly would've been elected to Cooperstown long before anyone had ever heard about his reputed betting on ball games.

In the beginning, and over the years, the absence of objective selection criteria might have been tolerable if every BBWAA elector voted thoughtfully and in good conscience. But, the history of Hall of Fame voting in each of its six decades is littered with evidence that some, often many, among the voting writers have failed to take their privileged mandate seriously. As a result, and beyond the mere effects of subjective bias about a player's skill, the voters' judgment often has been tainted by personal pique, cronyism, moral high-handedness and an impulse for the absurd.

Clearly, whim, prejudice, pique, senility and or outright stupidity was evidenced by some of the BBWAA voters in that first election when, somehow, Ty Cobb and Babe Ruth managed to avoid being chosen unamimously. Granted, Cobb was a paranoid, ill-tempered racist who succeeded in permanently offending almost everyone he met in life. So, perhaps it's more remarkable that only 4 of the 226 scribes left him off their ballots that year, giving him just 98.2 percent of the vote. Ruth had character flaws too, most of them involving the predictable self-indulgences of a man-child raised in an orphanage. Perhaps that's why eleven of the writers omitted his name in 1936, and he got only 95.1 percent support. But, by subjective reputation and statistical accomplishment, Cobb and Ruth were clearly the greatest all-around players of baseball's first sixty years, and it's hard to imagine how anything but pique or moral high-handedness prevented their unanimous election.

But, even if Cobb and Ruth lost votes because of their personality flaws, that still can't explain the failure of Honus Wagner, Christy Mathewson or Walter Johnson to achieve unanimity in 1936. Wagner and Mathewson were widely regarded as the best players of the twentieth century's first decade, and Johnson — statistically at least — was the greatest pitcher ever. Wagner could and did play almost every position with tremendous skill, and his reputation was bolstered by outperforming the much younger Cobb in their head-to-head competition during the 1909 World Series. Nearly a century after he played, Wagner is still regarded by most members of the Church of Baseball as the greatest shortstop ever. He also was so concerned about setting a bad example for youth that he insisted his baseball card be taken out of circulation because it was sold with tobacco— certainly with no idea that the action would eventually enhance the card's value to roughly twenty times his annual salary as a result (in October 1998 one of those cards sold at auction for $222,500). During the same era, Mathewson was regarded by many as the greatest pitcher ever, even better than his contemporary Cy Young, the all-time leader in games won. For most of his career and well beyond it, Christy also was perceived as the finest gentleman and role model for youth ever to don spikes and a woolen cap. Johnson ended his career after 1927 with 417 wins (second only to Young's 511, 44 more than Mathewson) and 3509 strikeouts (706 more than Young, his nearest competitor at the time). Walter threw the definitive fastball of the game's first fifty years, and legend has it that he was so concerned about maiming one of his era's helmetless batters with the pitch that he often was reluctant to throw as hard as he could, especially in twilight. So, none of these men should've lost any votes in 1936 because of doubtful moral fiber. Yet, Wagner did no better than tie Ruth with 215 votes and 95.1 percent support, Mathewson drew 205 for 90.7 percent, and Johnson somehow mustered just 189 for only 83.6 percent.

The 1936 failure of all five of these men to achieve unanimous election in a voting procedure in which guys like Hal Chase and Charlie Pabor also drew support exposed the flaw in the absence of formal standards for Cooperstown membership and a fickleness among the BBWAA electors. It also set a perverse precedent, as no man to date has ever been elected unanimously. Maybe, the voters since then have operated under the premise that if none of those first five inductees were good enough to be unanimous then no one else could possibly be. Or, they are merely saving that reward in the absurd expectation that someone will eventually bat 1.000, hitting a home run every time he comes to the plate, or pitch nothing but shutouts and never lose a game over a ten-year-plus career.

But, whatever the rationale and regardless of era, none of the game's true greats has ever achieved unanimous election. Through 2000, the highest percentage ever received in any BBWAA balloting was earned by pitcher Tom Seaver, who got 425 of a possible 430 votes in 1992 for 98.84 percent support. Seaver's support was nearly matched by fellow hurler Nolan Ryan, who got 491 out of 497 votes in 1999 for 98.79 percent, and the two men are the only ones ever to surpass Cobb's percentage of 1936. Everyone else has fared worse.

Also, for decades the HOF electorate completely ignored numerous players whose candidacies merited serious consideration. Through 2000, as noted in Chapter 1, eight men have been chosen for Cooperstown by the Veterans Committee or one of its predecessors who never got a single vote in any Hall of Fame election. Six of them were nineteenth-century players who should've gotten some support but didn't in the original OTC balloting of 1936: Jim O'Rourke (.310 career batting average, 2304 hits, elected in 1945); Pud Galvin (361 pitching victories, seventh-best, all-time, elected in 1965); Mickey Welch (307 wins as a hurler, chosen in 1973); Sam Thompson (.331 batting average, 1299 RBI, tabbed in 1974); Roger Connor (.317 average, 138 home runs and the career homer leader prior to Babe Ruth, elected in 1976); and Bid McPhee (no doubt the greatest defensive player of the nineteenth century, enshrined in 2000). The lack of attention those six received cannot be blamed entirely on the BBWAA (although, in the first two elections after 1936, the writers could've voted for any of them). But, the other two can. Vic Willis (249 victories, eight-time twenty-game winner, elected in 1995) pitched during the years 1898–1910, and George Davis (2660 hits, 1437 runs batted in, inducted in 1998) played almost half his career in the twentieth century. Whether some of these men really belong in Cooperstown is debatable. But, their eventual elections by the VC imply that they should've received at least some votes sometime during the early years of balloting; and, as detailed in Chapter 3, many other players worthy of serious consideration also have been completely overlooked (or nearly so) by the BBWAA electors.

At the opposite end of the spectrum, three Hall of Famers have actually received too many votes for Cooperstown. The first of these incidents apparently evidences a shameful inattention by a couple of BBWAA voters. The other two are indicative that whenever Cooperstown's Alphonse and Gaston have attempted to legislate fairness, they actually dispensed injustice instead.

Former Cubs, Yankees and Red Sox manager Joe McCarthy, whose .615 career winning percentage is the best ever among skippers, netted a total of just nine votes spread over five different BBWAA ballots beginning in 1939. Although insufficient to get him into the Hall through the front door, McCarthy was elected by the Veterans Committee in 1957. Amazingly, two BBWAA electors still felt compelled to vote for him in 1958 — several months after his induction! Maybe these two writers cast their ballots from life-support systems and are deserving of some sympathy. If not, their insistence upon voting for someone already chosen for the Hall evidenced a disinterest in the overall process that demeaned their credibility as electors.

In the early decades of Cooperstown voting, the large number of candidates on the ballot often made it difficult to elect someone. In an attempt to solve the problem, the BBWAA has used a two-tiered, preliminary- and runoff-vote system on four occasions—1946, 1949, 1964 and 1967 — with the the second ballot limited to the thirty men with the highest support on the first vote and a caveat each time that only one man could be elected in the runoff.

Three of those efforts misfired in predictable Alphonse-Gaston fashion. The 1946 runoff failed to produce any electee when first baseman Frank Chance led the ballot with just 57.3 percent support, far less than the 71.3 percent backing he earned in the preliminary vote. The 1949 procedure worked as intended, as Charlie Gehringer earned 85.5 percent support in the runoff, after leading the preliminary vote with 66.7. But the scribes screwed the pooch a bit again in 1964 and '67, when — although both runoffs produced an inductee — they left another man waiting unfairly. Luke Appling topped the 1964 preliminary ballot with 142 votes and 70.6 percent support, followed by pitcher Red Ruffing just one vote behind him at 70.1 percent. Appling was elected in the runoff, getting 83.6 percent support, but Ruffing's 81.4 percent also was enough to get him enshrined under the normal circumstances. That scenario was repeated in 1967 when Ruffing and Joe Medwick both tied on the preliminary ballot with 212 votes for 72.6 percent support apiece. Ruffing was elected in the runoff with 86.9 percent support; but, despite receiving 81 percent on the same ballot, Medwick had to wait another year before getting his Cooperstown ticket punched.

In every normal (one-ballot) year, there has been no restriction — beyond the practical math of the process — on the number of men who may be elected by the BBWAA, and you'd think the trustees would've been thrilled to have multiple inductees in either 1946, 1949, 1964 or 1967 (because a larger number of men honored was likely to draw more people to the induction ceremony). So, it's hard to fathom what prompted the Hall and or the voting scribes to impose the absurd, one-man-only requirement on the runoff system. Whatever their reasoning, the results were that Ruffing and Medwick became the only two Hall of Fame members who were (arguably) elected twice, and it was fortunate that neither man died in the interims between their false and actual elections.

During the same decades that Connor, Davis, Galvin, McPhee, O'Rourke, Thompson, Welch and Willis couldn't even buy a vote, some BBWAA electors were also subverting their credibility by supporting players who had no legitimate reason ever being considered for Cooperstown. Although the support was often minimal and fleeting, by the nature of the selection process— in which the writers are allowed to back no more than ten players per ballot — each of these spurious votes had meaning because they inevitably denied support to other more legitimate candidates. A few of the more inexplicable Hall of Fame votes are noted below.

- Eddie Grant, who had a .249 batting average and 844 hits over ten seasons as a Dead-Ball-Era third baseman, got a total of nine votes spread over five separate elections in the years 1938–46. In contrast, contemporary third sacker Heinie Groh, a much better hitter (.292 average, 1774 hits), got only fifteen votes in eight different elections. Grant was a favorite candidate of baseball's first Commissioner, Kenesaw Mountain Landis— not for his playing skills, but because he had been killed in action in France serving his country during World War I. Whether Eddie ever received votes for the Doughboys' Hall of Fame is unknown.

- Although he went 7–17 as a starter one season, Hub Pruett was primarily a relief pitcher during a seven-year career in the 1920s and 1930s. Pruett never played for a pennant winner; and, although they didn't have the statistic back then, retroactive research has shown he compiled a whopping total of thirteen saves in his career — only a little more than some present-day closers get in a month. Despite a 29–48 career won-lost record, he got one vote in each of five BBWAA elections (1949–53), perhaps from the same writer. There are only three possible reasons for his support. Either the writer(s) owed him money, thought for some reason that Hub was one of the game's first significant relief pitchers, or rewarded his ability to strike out Babe Ruth (Pruett sent the Bambino back to the bench without making contact ten of the first fourteen times he faced him in the Show). The latter justification sounds best — until you note that Ruth went down swinging 1316 other times in his career. Using that criteria might qualify more pitchers for the Hall than have ever visited Cooperstown, let alone received votes. In comparison, Firpo Marberry *was* the game's first significant relief pitcher during virtually the same era as Pruett, with a 148–88 won-lost record (including 53 wins in relief) and 101 saves in a career that included four pennant-winning teams. Despite that, Marberry fared little better than Pruett in the balloting, earning only eleven votes scattered over five elections.

- Moe Berg got three BBWAA votes in 1958 and five in 1960. They came despite his meager .243 batting average on 441 career hits in fifteen seasons (1923–39), a rate of about twenty-nine hits per year (a typical month for most .300 hitters). Berg served mostly as a backup and bullpen catcher and hit .287, with no homers and just 47 RBI in his only year as a regular, for the White Sox of 1929 — a time when almost everyone who was any good at all was batting .320 or better. Moe hung around so long because he became manager Joe Cronin's pet bench jockey with the Senators and Red Sox of the 1930s. Berg was also a Princeton alum who spoke several languages and his Irwin Corey–like gift of pseudo-intellectual gab mesmerized sportswriters well into the 1950s, when he hung around ballpark press boxes looking for freebies — so, it's a cinch the writers who voted for Moe didn't owe him any money. He also served as an American spy in Europe during World War II, reputedly assigned by the Office of Strategic Services (OSS, predecessor to the CIA) to assassinate Werner Heisenberg, the Nazis' leading nuclear physicist and potential father of an anticipated German A-bomb. Berg did no better at that assignment than he did facing American League pitching, as he reputedly saw Heisenberg, but decided not to kill him. His personality was a cross between that of an intelligent eccentric and a paranoid super patriot, and — except for pitcher Rube Waddell, whom opposing coaches often distracted with toy trains — Berg may have been the most unique person ever to play major-league baseball. But, his skills as a backup catcher were roughly comparable to Bob Uecker's, maybe worse. Nonetheless, he got more HOF votes than some contemporary backstops that were clearly more deserving of Cooperstown support like Spud Davis and Babe Phelps. Davis got only one vote in each of two years (1948–49) but batted .308 for his sixteen-year career and hit over .300 in eight of the ten seasons he was a regular. Phelps got no votes at all but hit .310 over an eleven-year stint in the majors and topped .300 in half of his six seasons as a starter.

- Grant, Pruett and Berg aside, Jewel Ens earns the award for the most inexplicable HOF support ever. Ens played in a grand total of sixty-seven major-league games and had all of 186 at-bats and 54 hits in a four-year career (1922–25). In Jewel's rookie season he batted .296 on 42 hits as a part-time second baseman for Pittsburgh. He did smack one home run in his career, his only safety in five at-bats during his final big-league campaign. He also managed the Pirates for two seasons and part of a third, leading them to an overall record just nine games better than .500 and two fifth-place finishes. Despite that modest record, some of his contemporaries regarded him as a great manager, and he was a coach for the Bucs and three other clubs for twelve seasons through 1941. But, even if Ens was the Marcel Marceau of bunt signs, why he should've received a lone Hall of Fame vote in 1950, or any other year, is anyone's guess.

The votes received by Grant, Pruett, Berg, Ens and other guys unqualified for Cooperstown represent an absurd impulse among some BBWAA electors over the years to support men because they were cronies or merely provided good copy. One can easily understand the motives of a writer who wants to cast what he knows will be a lone vote for someone who has been a good friend or drinking buddy just to make the guy feel good (and, given his reputation as a late-night carouser, it's a wonder Vern Stephens didn't receive a truckload of those votes). But, that type of sentiment inevitably deprives votes to other players more deserving of support; it raises doubt about the expertise of the elector(s) who cast them; and it wouldn't take too many votes like that in a given year to deny a man his rightful place in baseball's Valhalla.

In fact, that actually may have happened. In 1985, when Nellie Fox missed election by just two votes in his last year of BBWAA eligibility, Jesus Alou and Dock Ellis both got one vote each.

Alou was a decent player who batted .306 one year, but his lifetime stats—as evidenced by a .280 average, 1216 hits and just 377 runs batted in—were nowhere near the performance you'd require from a Hall of Famer, unless your encephalogram was flatlining. No doubt, some writer voted for him knowing that he was the least accomplished of the three Alou brothers who played during the 1960s, just so Jesus—like Felipe and Matty—could say at family picnics that he also got some HOF support. To reprise a joke that was prevalent during their time, it's a wonder that same writer never voted for their other (fictional) brother, Boog Alou, as well.

Ellis won 138 games in twelve seasons including a career-high nineteen victories for the World Champion Pirates of 1971. He had a colorful personality and was certainly good copy. But, his big achievement, he has claimed, was being the only pitcher to throw a major-league no-hitter while tripping on LSD. If true, it's a wonder he didn't lose his concentration on the mound while staring at those wispy, paisley skies the drug produces. It also makes you wonder how many of Dock's 119 career losses were psychedelic too. Regardless, he apparently met that writer's personal de facto standard for psychotropic career wins.

In fairness, both men were competent players, but neither's qualifications compare favorably to Nellie Fox, the American League's premier second baseman of the 1950s. Because we don't know whether or not the writers who voted for Alou and Ellis in 1985 also supported Fox that year, we can't be certain that these two votes were the ones that forced Nellie to enter Cooperstown much later, through the Veterans Committee's back door. But, they might have been.

The voters' penchant for supporting unqualified candidates has not gone unnoticed by the Hall of Fame's braintrust. As early as 1945 the trustees attempted to clarify the electors' identification of worthy Cooperstown prospects by decreeing that "Candidates shall be chosen on the basis of playing ability, integrity, sportsmanship, character and their contribution to the team on which they played and to baseball in general." Unfortunately, this rule lacked any specificity and established no objective standards for membership, so it did nothing to prevent guys like Pruett, Berg and Ens from receiving votes in later years.

For practical purposes, the rule was nothing more than a morality clause inserted into the criteria for Cooperstown eligibility to prevent men like Hal Chase and "Shoeless" Joe Jackson from getting any more votes. As noted earlier, Chase got a total of twenty-nine votes in the BBWAA's first two elections. Jackson, the most famous member of the 1919 Black Sox, possessor of the third-best career batting average in the game's history (.356, behind only Cobb and Hornsby), and a much better player than Chase, received two votes from the writers in 1936.

The votes for Chase and Jackson were aberrations. In the wake of the Black Sox scandal, Judge Kenesaw Mountain Landis had been hired as commissioner in 1920 specifically to clean up baseball's soiled image; and, although the eight Chicago players allegedly involved in the World Series fix were acquitted in a Chicago courtroom, Landis had publicly banned them from the game anyway (and blacklisted several other supposedly shady players). At the time of the first Hall of Fame elections, with Landis just past midway through his twenty-four-year tenure as commissioner, there was no way that Shoeless Joe, or any other blackballed player, was going to be elected to Cooperstown on the judge's watch, regardless of his on-field qualifications.

Also, Jackson was the only one of the eight Black Sox to receive any Hall of Fame votes in 1936 or later. Eddie Cicotte never got any, although his career pitching record (a 208–149 won-lost mark, for a .583 winning percentage and a 2.38 career ERA) merited more than a handful. Buck Weaver, who some observers during the World War I era thought might be the next Honus Wagner, also never got any — despite his insistence that he had played the 1919 series on the level and his repeated, unsuccessful petitions to Landis for reinstatement to the game. Even Fred McMullin, the utility infielder who went one-for-two in his only at-bats in the tainted series and whose main role in the fix apparently was to sit on the Chicago bench and root for Cicotte and Lefty Williams to mishandle grounders and nail batters with intentional wild pitches, never got any either — although he compiled forty-eight more career hits than Jewel Ens's total of big-league at-bats.

But Landis died in November 1944, and it must be more than mere coincidence that the Hall of Fame trustees — who also comprised the version of the Veterans Committee extant at that time — imposed the morality clause so soon after his death. They probably feared the old coot as much as everyone else and didn't want the irate spirit of the autocratic judge haunting them at night from beyond the grave. Ironically, after ten years of non-support from the BBWAA electors, Joe Jackson got two more votes in 1946, the last ones he ever received. No doubt, they were a pyrrhic protest against the recently imposed morality clause by two disgruntled writers who didn't like being told how they could fill out their ballots — a BBWAA mindset that would resurface in the early 1990s with devastating results for the future of the Cooperstown roster.

In the big picture, the morality clause accomplished nothing. Until very recently, when none less than Hall of Famer and VC member Ted Williams initiated a campaign to get Jackson into Cooperstown, Shoeless Joe and the other banned players had about as much chance of getting elected to the Shrine as the Pope does of being a married Buddhist. In practical terms, all the rule did was to subtly dictate to the scribes that blackballed players were off limits for any future consideration. So, it defined only what a Hall of Famer is not — but only in vague, indirect terms — and did zilch to help identify what one actually is. It also muddled the issue even more, because it failed to provide any specific definitions of "integrity," "character" and "sportsmanship," let alone "playing ability," thereby reinforcing the absolute subjectivity of the selection process.

The morals clause of 1945 also failed to address the timeliness of player eligibility. By the mid–1940s, with many players in the military and some older men coming out of retirement to fill the void, the electors again were casting votes for guys whose careers were not finished. Pepper Martin, who retired after the 1940 season, got two votes in 1942 but then came back to play in 1944 (at age forty), the height of the wartime player shortage — perhaps an unforeseeable circumstance. But servicemen Bill Dickey (seventeen votes), Ted Lyons (four votes), Hank Greenberg (three), Joe DiMaggio and Joe Gordon (one apiece) all drew support in the 1945 election when — provided they didn't become wartime casualties like Eddie Grant — their careers were obviously not over. Dickey and Lyons both played one more season after the end of World War II, Greenberg played for two more years, Gordon played through 1950, and DiMaggio didn't retire until 1951.

In response, and with their usual timely efficiency, the Hall of Fame trustees and BBWAA fiddled until 1954 before they instituted a provision that each player had to wait until five years after his retirement to be eligible for the writers' ballot. In theory, this rule prevented any further voting for men who were still active, or might be; and, ostensibly, assured that the electors had ample time to place the players' career achievements in their appropriate historical perspective. But, like the morals clause, the five-year-wait rule contributed nothing substantive to the definition of a Hall of Famer. If anything, it only forced the biggest doofusses among the BBWAA voters to wait a little longer before exposing their ignorance about any specific candidate's credentials.

In the first two decades of Hall of Fame voting, one obvious example of that ignorance was the writers' penchant for supporting candidates whose major-league careers were of relatively brief duration. Between 1936 and 1960 various BBWAA electors cast votes for about forty men who played less than ten seasons in the Show. A few of them had playing credentials that were worthy of some consideration, like pitchers Addie Joss (160–97 won-lost record), Noodles Hahn (130–94) and George Earnshaw (127–93), and shortstop Ray Chapman (a four-time .300 hitter over nine seasons for Cleveland whose possible Hall of Fame career was cut short because he had the misfortune of leaning in too far on a high hard one thrown by New York's Carl Mays during the heat of the 1920 American League pennant race — long before the advent of batting helmets — and became baseball's first on-field casualty when he died from the beaning).

A couple other short-timers apparently got votes for their non-playing achievements: Jack Dunn, who had a seven-year career as a 64–59 pitcher around the turn of the century, later distinguished himself as owner of the International League's Baltimore Orioles, where he created one of the minor leagues' great dynasties and developed stars like Babe Ruth and Lefty Grove before their matriculation to the majors; and Al Schacht, a 14–10 pitcher in his three seasons with the Washington Senators (1919–21), later became famous for his lifelong, physical-comedy routine as "the Clown Prince of Baseball," an act later taken over by the late Max Patkin. But, although the careers of the other short-timers who received votes were more substantial than that of Jewel Ens, it's difficult to explain what prompted any support at all for most of them, and at least one of them could have been voted for only by the baseball writers from tabloids like *The Globe*, *The Star*, or *The National Enquirer*, had there been any among the electors. A few of them included:

- Joe Boley, Bill Cissell and Charley Gelbert, three Live-Ball-Era short-stops whose major-league careers totaled just twenty-four years combined, about the equivalent of either Bobby Wallace (twenty-five years) or Rabbit Maranville (twenty-three), who are both Hall of Famers at the same position. The trio also combined for 2234 big-league hits, just fifteen short of the career total by Bert Campaneris—another shortstop who isn't in Cooperstown and will never get there but has a far more legitimate claim than any of them. Careerwise, Boley batted .269, and Cissell and Gelbert hit .267, in an era when there were trainloads of guys hitting fifty points higher. Gelbert received five BBWAA votes, the other two got one each, apparently because their careers were statistically superior to all but about the top 150 shortstops who ever played in the bigs.

- Dickie Kerr won fifty-three games in the majors, including twenty-one for the 1920 White Sox, and compiled a .609 career winning percentage. But, his big-league career lasted just four seasons, nowhere near the span you expect from a Hall of Famer. All the same, he received the amazing total of seventy-five BBWAA votes spread among eleven different elections (1937–55), presumably because he was remembered as the "honest" pitcher among the 1919 World Series starters for the Black Sox. Nemo Leibold was the team's honest right fielder that year, too, but he never received any HOF votes, despite the fact his playing career was far more substantial than Kerr's. And, fortunately, the Chisox's honest peanut vendors of 1919 never received support either.

- Gabby Street was a Dead-Ball-Era catcher whose big-league career included an eighth season only because he once inserted himself as a forty-eight-year-old pinch hitter while managing the Cardinals in 1931. He made an out that time up, which hurt his Cooperstown chances, because it left him only ninety-two points shy of being a career .300 hitter. He did pilot St. Louis to two pennants (1930–31) and was the Senators' regular backstop at the start of Walter Johnson's career (1908–11). But, perhaps his biggest claim to fame was trying to catch a ball dropped from the Washington Monument. For all that effort, he got one vote in 1937, 1938 and 1953.

- The tabloid support went to Marty Bergen (four votes overall, two in 1937, one each in 1938–39). A catcher, Bergen played only four seasons in the majors (1896–99) and just one as a regular. He batted .265, with career totals of 10 homers and 339 hits. His tabloid fame came in January 1900 when he murdered his wife and two children then killed himself. It's sardonic that Bergen's vote total was equal to the body count related to his tragedy.

There should probably be room somewhere in the Hall of Fame selection process to consider the credentials of unique candidates like Jack Dunn and Al Schacht, whose contributions to the game were substantial but had nothing to do with their on-field performance as major leaguers. But the rest of these men drew support, one of them (Kerr) frequently, only because the Hall of Fame failed to give its electors any meaningful guidelines to judge an individual's credentials, and because — left to their own subjective whims— some BBWAA electors over the years have been incapable of making credible decisions about who deserved votes.

By 1960 it became apparent to someone in authority that short-term players didn't belong on the ballot. So, a rule was enacted requiring all future candidates to have at least ten years service in the majors. The ten-year rule eliminated the possibility of any more two-cup-and-sweet-roll guys like Jewel Ens receiving support for Cooperstown. It also greatly reduced the number of eligible players, mainly so the BBWAA voters wouldn't have to labor over a ballot of biblical length. As noted in Chapter 1, there were almost twenty-three hundred ten-year men among the fourteen thousand major leaguers through 1994, so — over time — the ten-year rule has reduced the number of HOF-eligible players by a factor of about six. But, in that light, any thoughtful person must also suspect that the rule's true intent was merely to trim the number of players eligible for the ballot enough to facilitate the annual election of someone — anyone — and, thereby, insure that an induction ceremony would be held each year.

Also, although it remains the only objective standard for Cooperstown membership in force to date, the ten-year rule did very little to clarify the definition of what a Hall of Famer is or should be. After all, there's no way that each of the guys who are technically eligible is really deserving of consideration. A lot of men like Hawk Taylor, Luis Aguayo and Jamie Easterly hang on in the majors for ten years or more because they possess some lone, specialized skill that managers find situationally useful (e.g., as a pinch hitter, late-inning defensive replacement, or left-handed middle reliever), but they are not about to crack the everyday lineup unless someone gets hurt and are never going to be confused with the greats of the game — except, maybe, by HOF electors flaunting their subjective devices. So, despite the ten-year rule, guys like Hal Lanier and Gates Brown continued to receive support from BBWAA voters as late as the 1970s and 1980s.

Lanier, whose father Max was a member of the Cardinals' pitching rotation in the mid–1940s, was the regular shortstop for the Giants during most of his ten-year career (1964–73). He batted all of .228, with 843 hits, eight home runs and 273 career RBI (fewer than Vern Stephens had in 1949–50). Hal was a good fielder but never was selected for an all-star game. He also was an epileptic. So was Grover Cleveland Alexander, who compounded his problem with booze. One of them is in Cooperstown, and belongs there — but it isn't Lanier. Regardless, one writer gave Hal a vote in 1979, apparently crediting him for risking injury and personal embarrassment every time he took the field — obviously a noble gesture by that voter. But, in comparison, Gene Alley and Ed Brinkman, two contemporary shortstops with marginally better offensive stats, comparable or superior defensive skills, and one all-star appearance apiece, never got a single vote. So, what made Lanier more worthy?

During Brown's thirteen-year career with the Tigers (1963–75), he was primarily a pinch-hitting specialist. Gates twice led the American League in pinch hits for a season and batted one point higher as a substitute swinger (.258) than he did for his career overall — an uncommon occurrence. Brown's bat might've made him a regular for another team, but the Tigers of his era were loaded with outfielders (Al Kaline, Rocky Colavito, Billy Bruton, Don Demeter, Jim Northrup and Mickey Stanley) who could hit as well or better than Gates did (except for Stanley) and also could run. The encyclopedias list Brown at five-foot-eleven and 220 pounds, but he always looked much heavier, moved in no manner resembling a gazelle, and it was obvious that he was fond of the training table — or any dining surface for that matter. One writer, probably from Detroit, felt compelled to vote for Gates in 1981 as a likely payback for his pinch-hit heroics, especially during the Tigers' championship season of 1968. But, there were several better outfielders from his era — Tommie Agee, Bob Allison, Alex Johnson, Cesar Tovar, Leon Wagner and Vic Davalillo (who was also a better pinch hitter), for example — who never got a vote.

Over time, the ten-year service requirement also has led to some absurd injustices regarding who has been eligible for Cooperstown, technically, and who has not. Comparatively, two of the more extreme examples include:

- Technically, John Vukovich has been eligible, but Tony Conigliaro has not. Vukovich was a third baseman who played in ten different seasons between 1970 and 1981. He was never a regular for any team and never had more than 217 at-bats in a season. In his five best years (1971, 1973–75 and 1980) he batted a composite .162 (about a hundred points below his league's norm for those seasons) and averaged 105 at-bats, one home run and eight RBI per year. His career numbers included six home runs and a .161 batting average — so his very best was not much different from his norm, and both were decidedly sub-standard for his time. Conigliaro was a right fielder who matched Vukovich's career homer output in his first few weeks in the majors with the Red Sox of 1964. Tony led the American League in homers the next season at age twenty, becoming the youngest man to do that in the history of the circuit. On 18 August 1967 he was struck by a fastball that broke his cheekbone and impaired his vision so badly that he missed all of 1968. He came back to hit a combined 56 homers in 1969–70, but his vision was still so poor that he was out of baseball by the end of 1975, after just eight seasons. He hit 166 home runs in his career (almost thirty times more than Vukovich) and finished with a .264 average (more than a hundred points above John's).

- Bobby Tiefenhauer met the ten-year requirement, but Don Gullett did not. Tiefenhauer played in ten big-league seasons during 1952–68, bouncing back and forth between the majors and minors. In his best season, with the Braves of 1964, Tiefenhauer won all of four games and lost six. He finished his big-league stint, at age thirty-nine, with a 9–25 career won-lost record, for a winning percentage of .265. Gullet played in only nine seasons, most of them with the great Cincinnati teams of the mid–1970s. He twice led the NL in winning percentage, and his overall record was 109–50, for a .686 career mark that is surpassed by only four other hurlers in the history of the bigs. A rotator-cuff injury forced him to retire after 1979, at age twenty-eight.

One possible injustice caused by the ten-year service requirement was "corrected" in 1978. After some heavy lobbying by then–Commissioner Bowie Kuhn, the Veterans Committee waived the ten-year rule to induct pitcher Addie Joss. Joss had received a total of 128 BBWAA votes spread over seven different elections in the years 1937–60 but never got more than the thirty-three votes and 14.2 percent support he received in 1942. As noted earlier, he posted a 160–97 won-lost record. That equates to a .623 winning percentage, and his 1.89 career earned run average is second-best, all-time. Joss also threw two no-hitters, including a perfect game in 1908, before his nine-year tenure with Cleveland was cut short by his death at age thirty-one from tubercular meningitis.

Since Addie's election, his induction has drawn considerable flack. Some critics believe Joss was chosen primarily because of his near-record ERA, the value of which — they argue — is a mirage caused by the combined effects of a relatively short career and the advantage of pitching in the Dead-Ball-Era (during the period Joss played, 1902–10, the typical yearly earned run average for the American League as a whole was approximately 2.70; so he was almost one earned run better than the rest of his league throughout his career, at a time when runs were hard to come by). Others complain that the Veterans Committee's decision to waive the ten-year rule set a bad precedent which, eventually, might be used to justify enshrinement of some truly flash-in-the-pan phenom.

Whether Joss deserves to be in Cooperstown or not, his selection emphasizes the real problem with the ten-year-service rule: although it provides the only objective criteria for Hall of Fame election currently extant, it is nonetheless entirely arbitrary and — as a result — almost as subjective as the rest of the selection process. Like the morals clause, albeit a tad more specifically, it also defines mainly what a Hall of Famer is not — that is, someone who didn't play in the majors in at least ten seasons. So, it excludes some very good players like Conigliaro and Gullett but allows guys like Vukovich and Tiefenhauer to qualify for (at least initial) consideration.

To prevent less-qualified players from stealing votes from truly deserving candidates, the BBWAA formed a Screening Committee in 1968, whose function was to reject any new eligibles who were not viable candidates and to limit the ballot to a maximum of forty players — another move that can also be interpreted as an effort to assure annual inductions. Neither Vukovich nor Tiefenhauer ever passed this screening. But the plan went awry in 1979, when the committee somehow left pitcher Milt Pappas, a 209-game winner (110 victories in the American League, 99 in the National) off the list. Milt then complained loudly, and with justification, that he was being shafted and was placed on the ballot. Pappas received five votes that year. But the writers apparently didn't appreciate the ruckus Milt had raised, as they were the last votes he ever got. Since then, any player who receives at least two votes from the six-man Screening Committee has been placed on the ballot.

To date, the morals clause, the five-year wait provision and the ten-year service requirement are the only standards in place to determine initial Hall of Fame eligibility. But, none of those rules facilitates any substantive definition of a Hall of Famer, and the slow timing of their implementations exposes the Alphonse-Gaston relationship between the HOF trustees and their primary electorate.

5

Subjective Follies

The Hall of Fame's ten-year service requirement and the persistent application of the de facto standards for cumulative achievement in games won, hits and homers strongly imply that Cooperstown election is intended to reward achievement over the length of a man's career, and it's clear that, over time, most BBWAA electors have voted consistent with that view. But, it was never determined at the beginning of voting — and has not been to date — whether the honor should also be given to players who accomplish feats which are momentary, or incidentally unique, and failure to resolve that issue has led to the Bill Wambsganss Syndrome.

Wambsganss was a starting second baseman for eleven of his thirteen major-league seasons (1914–26), spent mostly with Cleveland. In the fifth inning of game five of the 1920 World Series between the Indians and Dodgers, Bill was playing near the bag with no outs and men on first and second. With both baserunners moving on the play, he caught a line drive off the bat of Brooklyn pitcher Clarence Mitchell, stepped on second to double up Dodgers second sacker Pete Kilduff, and turned to tag catcher Otto Miller, who was moving to second base.

The only unassisted triple play in World Series history would've headlined all the Plays-of-the-Day features on local television, if there had been any back then. It was also the high point of Wamby's career. Anyone who's a big-league regular for eleven seasons has to be a decent ballplayer. But, if Bill had played in the 1990s, he would've been the rough equivalent of Joey Cora or Mickey Morandini — a heady second sacker with decent foot speed, who hits about .285 every third year or so and has no power to speak of — hardly Cooperstown material. In 1919, perhaps his best season,

71

Wambsganss had career highs of 146 hits and 60 runs batted in, while batting .278. He hit .295 in 1918, the highest average of his career, once scored 93 runs (1924), and never hit more than 2 homers in a season. Overall, he had just 1359 hits, 7 home runs, 520 ribbies and a .259 average as a major leaguer.

In 1942 Wambsganss received the first of what would prove to be thirteen Cooperstown votes spread over six different elections through 1956. Because there is nothing else especially notable about his career, there's no doubt that he got those votes solely because of his World Series fielding gem. The result was the Bill Wambsganss Syndrome, whereby BBWAA voters are seized by a compulsion to vote for players because they achieved or participated in a single remarkable event. This malaise is a syndrome of the voting process, rather than a full-blown effect, simply because no one has actually been elected to Cooperstown yet as a result (unless you count Hack Wilson, but more on him later). Nonetheless, in chronological order of their Hall of Fame support, Table 10 lists some of the men who have benefited from the Wambsganss Syndrome, notes the incident that made them famous, gives the range of years when they received HOF votes and the total of votes they earned. Perhaps there are others who could also be listed, but these are the most obvious.

TABLE 10
WAMBSGANSS SYNDROME BENEFICIARIES

Player	Achievement	Years	Votes
Bill Wambsganss	World Series triple play	1942–56	13
Johnny Vander Meer	back-to-back no-hitters	1945–71	700
Leon Cadore	longest game in history	1948	1
Joe Oeschger	longest game in history	1948	1
Fred Toney	double no-hitter	1949	1
Bobby Thomson	Coogan's Bluff homer	1966–79	114
Harvey Haddix	12-inning perfect game	1971–85	81
Don Larsen	World Series perfecto	1974–88	492
Roger Maris	61 homers in 1961	1974–88	1632
Bucky Dent	playoff-winning homer	1990	3

The second person to benefit from the Wambsganss Syndrome, beginning in 1945, was pitcher Johnny Vander Meer, who threw consecutive no hitters for Cincinnati against Boston and Brooklyn on 11 and 15 June 1938. Subjectively, given the Hall's lack of formal selection criteria and the

Bill Wambsganss, with arm outstretched at upper left, is shown at the end of his unassisted triple play in the 1920 World Series. Wamby received thirteen BBWAA votes spread over six different Hall of Fame elections, beginning in 1942. Although a decent player, there was nothing else Cooperstown-worthy about his career, and there is no doubt his support from the writers rewarded the uniqueness of his post-season moment of glory. The votes set a precedent which encouraged later, often substantial support for other unqualified men. (Photograph from *The Sporting News*)

achievement's definite uniqueness this might have been worth a dozen votes in a process that seems to be based on career accomplishment. But Johnny got seven hundred spread over fourteen different ballots, which is an awful lot of support for a guy whose career won-lost record was just 119–121—so, for whatever reasons, a lot of Cooperstown voters held his feat in very high regard.

Next in line came Leon Cadore and Joe Oeschger in 1948. They were the dueling pitchers who, on 1 May 1920, hooked up to go the distance in a twenty-six-inning, 1–1 tie game that was baseball's longest. Cadore's career won-lost record was 68–72, Oeschger's 82–116 — so neither merited any support for Cooperstown, despite their moment of unresolved glory.

There is some irony in Fred Toney's Wambsganss Syndrome support. Like Cadore and Oeschger, he was involved in one of baseball's greatest pitching feats. On the mound for Cincinnati on 2 May 1917 he threw a ten-inning, no-hit shutout to beat the Cubs' James "Hippo" Vaughn, who gave up no hits or runs himself for the game's first nine innings. The "double no-hitter," as it usually is called, was probably the greatest pitching duel in big-league history. One irony is that, although Vaughn — six-foot-four and 215 pounds — was nicknamed "Hippo," Toney was possibly even bigger. Macmillan's *Baseball Encyclopedia* lists him at six-foot-six and 245, but its rival, *Total Baseball* (the current "official" record), indicates he was only six-foot-one and 195. It makes you wonder whether there were two Fred Toneys, just some bad vital-statistics research somewhere, or if there is some *X-Files* aspect to this that Muldur and Scully should investigate (call it "The Case of the Inflatable Pitcher").

The other irony, more relevant to Cooperstown, is that — although Toney got his lone vote in 1949 for being the victor in the double no-hitter — Vaughn never got a Hall of Fame vote, ever, even though his career was considerably more impressive. Toney was 139–102, with a 2.69 ERA and 718 strikeouts over a twelve-year career. He won twenty-four games in the year of the dual no-hitter, and twenty-one contests in 1920. But, his only statistical blip was topping the National League with three saves in 1918 — and, since they didn't have that stat back then, his "leadership" had no meaning in Toney's era, or in 1949 for that matter (saves were invented by sportswriter Jerome Holtzman in the late 1950s, weren't adopted as an official statistic until 1969, and weren't measured retroactively until some-time later). In comparison, Vaughn pitched for thirteen seasons, finishing with a record of 178–137 (for a .565 winning percentage), a 2.49 career ERA, and almost twice as many strikeouts (1416). He won twenty games or more on five different occasions and twice led the league in strikeouts and innings pitched. In 1918 he might've won a Cy Young Award, had there been one back then, as he led the senior circuit in wins, shutouts, innings, strikeouts and earned run average.

The other men on the Wambsganss list are more recent and familiar. Bobby Thomson was a good player in his own right, and it might seem unfair to include him. A three-time all-star, Thomson hit 264 homers, had 1705 hits, 1026 RBI, and batted .270 for his career. Among the players who had been eligible for Cooperstown through 2000 and who never got a single HOF vote, only five of them had more career taters than Bobby, and just ten had more ribbies— so some of his credentials aren't shabby. But, there also were thirty men with more career hits and about three hundred with higher batting averages who'd also been completely overlooked in the voting. In that light, and given that he smacked the most famous four-bagger in baseball history, it's clear that a significant portion of his 114 votes were motivated by the Miracle of Coogan's Bluff.

Harvey Haddix also may have deserved some Hall of Fame support. Haddix got nowhere near the votes that Vander Meer did. But his career record (136–113) was better; and, for his comparable size (five-foot-nine and 170 pounds after a really big meal), Harvey got nearly as much out of guts and guile as did Hall of Famer Whitey Ford. All the same, Haddix is best remembered for his heartbreak of 26 May 1959: after twelve innings of no-baserunner perfection against the Braves, his pitching gem was spoiled when Felix Mantilla reached base on an error to lead off the thirteenth inning; and, one out later, the scoreless game quickly became a loss for the Pittsburgh hurler when Joe Adcock followed an intentional walk to Hank Aaron with a homer.

Don Larsen was luckier. Except for Vander Meer and maybe Roger Maris, Larsen clearly got the most Wambsganss Syndrome benefit from his sole moment in the sun, and if he had preceded Wamby chronologically, the malaise could (and should) be named for him — because his World Series perfect game for the Yankees is the quintessential once-in-a-lifetime feat. Larsen had a 10–4 won-lost record in 1956, the year of his perfecto, was 11–5 the previous season, and went 45–24 in his five-year stint with New York. But Don's other nine seasons were nothing to get excited about: he never won more than eight games in any other year; he was 3–21 for the 1954 Orioles; and, away from the talent-laden Yankees, he was just 36–67, producing an 81–91 career ledger.

Among the Wambsganss group, Bucky Dent's Hall of Fame support rewarded the least-impressive achievement, by far — his 1978 playoff-winning homer over the Green Monster in Boston (Felix Mantilla was better at lobbing balls over that wall, so maybe he should be enshrined). Dent was a competent defensive shortstop for a dozen seasons and provided the White Sox and Yankees with some positive emotional leadership. But his career stats (forty homers, 423 RBI and a .247 average) inspire no visions of Cooperstown among anyone who truly cares about the institution.

Like Bobby Thomson, and as evidenced by the large number of votes he received, Roger Maris deserved some Hall of Fame support even without the singular achievement that made him famous. Even before Maris broke Babe Ruth's single-season home-run record, Roger was recognized as one of the best defensive right fielders in the game, and he was the American League's Most Valuable Player in 1960–61. But Maris batted just .260 in twelve seasons, and his career stats (1325 hits, 275 homers, 851 RBI and 826 runs scored) are nothing special without his first three seasons in New York (451 hits, 133 taters, 354 ribbies and 322 runs). So his 61-homer season is the hallmark of his credentials, and his candidacy is an AC/DC proposition — you can go either way about it.

In many ways, Roger's Hall of Fame credentials mirror those of Hack Wilson, who set the major-league record with 190 RBI for the Cubs in 1930 and who — as noted above — could've been included on the Wambsganss list. Both men had twelve-year careers in which their peak performances were relatively meteoric: Maris had seven good-to-great seasons, all of them consecutive (1958–64); Wilson had six (1926–30 and 1932). They both set all-time records in stats that are the definitive measures of a slugger — home runs and RBI (Wilson's 56 taters in 1930 also stood as the National League's all-time standard until Mark McGwire and Sammy Sosa broke it and Roger's mark, in 1998). Both men's records are also tainted for some observers because of abnormal playing conditions in the seasons they were set. Wilson's big year marked the height of a period when the baseballs in use had been intentionally juiced by owners in order to stimulate offense in general, home runs in particular, and — most important — attendance. So the NL (including pitchers) batted .303 as a circuit that season. Maris set his mark in 1961, the first-ever campaign that featured diluted expansion pitching, when the number of home runs per game in the American League rose by 8 percent over 1960 and was 22 percent higher than the circuit's seasonal average for the previous decade. Unlike Maris in 1961, Wilson didn't win his league's MVP in 1930, in part because the BBWAA award didn't begin until the following season (but *The Sporting News*'s version of the honor went to the Giants' Bill Terry, who batted .401 and tied the NL mark for hits in a season).

But Maris and Wilson did share the same fate in the writers' version of Cooperstown voting. Wilson got 550 votes spread over sixteen ballots (including one runoff) in the years 1937–62 but never got more than the ninety-four votes he received in 1958, or the 38.3 percent support he earned two years earlier. Maris was on the ballot during 1974–88, topping out with 184 votes and 43.2 percent support in his last year eligible. Both men also experienced personal problems which — given the biases operative among some electors — may have limited their support in the voting. Wilson was a drinker whose premier seasons came under the guidance of manager Joe McCarthy (who also imbibed on occasion), and his career went south after Marse Joe jumped to the Yankees and was replaced by the less-tolerant Rogers Hornsby. Maris was a small-town boy who was never comfortable in the Big Apple limelight, and his inclination to withdraw from the media onslaught during his pursuit of Ruth's homer record prompted many writers to conclude that he was surly and uncooperative. Both men also died young: Wilson's abuse of alcohol hastened his death at age forty-seven in 1948; Maris died of cancer in 1985 at age fifty-one.

Wilson was elected to Cooperstown by the Veterans Committee in 1979, but his candidacy was adamantly opposed for several years by at least one VC member (see Chapter 7), and his election is still criticized by many observers. A lot of people thought that Maris would follow in 1999, because the home-run chase by McGwire and Sosa had returned him to the spotlight the year before. But Roger failed to make the panel's final ballot in 1999; and, although that doesn't preclude his future election, it dimmed his prospects considerably. Given all of the similarities between them, the two men's Hall of Fame candidacies are like two sides of the same coin: if you think Wilson belongs in Cooperstown, you probably believe that Maris does too; and if you don't like one's credentials, you probably won't buy the other man's either.

It's amazing that the Wambsganss Syndrome never prompted Hall of Fame support for Jimmy Sebring (who—discounting the nineteenth century—hit the first-ever World Series home run for Pittsburgh in 1903) or even E. Clise Dudley (an obscure hurler who is in the record books as the first man ever to hit a home run on the very first pitch he faced in the majors, for the Dodgers in 1929). And, if the ten-year service requirement had not been in effect by the late 1950s, it's a cinch that some deranged writer(s) would've voted for Bobo Holloman—as Bobo's no-hitter in his first major-league pitching start for the 1953 Browns earned him an inordinant amount of fame for a guy whose career won-lost record was 3–7 and was out of the majors for good by the end of that season.

Nonetheless, absent any objective standards for HOF membership, the support for the players listed in Table 10 was inevitable, and it's a sure bet that, occasionally, some BBWAA voters will be afflicted by the syndrome again. When they are, it's also certain that—in most instances—their whimsy will mean that some other, more-deserving candidate(s) will be deprived of votes.

But, because none of the men in Table 10 has ever been elected by the writers to date, the mindset that compelled votes for guys like Wambsganss, Cadore, Oeschger, Larsen and Dent has—thankfully—had no visible impact on the Cooperstown roster. In contrast, another of the scribes' more prevalent attitudes, which persisted for several decades, kept some of the best-qualified players waiting for inordinate periods before receiving their deserved recognition.

As noted at the start of Chapter 2, through the 2000 voting thirty-four players had been elected in their first year of eligibility. Sequentially, they included: Ty Cobb, Walter Johnson, Christy Mathewson, Babe Ruth and Honus Wagner (1936); Bob Feller and Jackie Robinson (1962); Ted Williams (1966); Stan Musial (1969); Sandy Koufax (1972); Warren Spahn (1973); Mickey Mantle (1974); Ernie Banks (1977); Willie Mays (1979); Al Kaline (1980); Bob Gibson (1981); Hank Aaron and Frank Robinson (1982); Brooks Robinson (1983); Lou Brock (1985); Willie McCovey (1986); Willie Stargell (1988); Johnny Bench and Carl Yastrzemski (1989); Joe Morgan and Jim Palmer (1990); Rod Carew (1991); Tom Seaver (1992); Reggie Jackson (1993); Steve Carlton (1994); Mike Schmidt (1995); plus George Brett, Nolan Ryan and Robin Yount (1999). In fairness, Roberto Clemente should also be added to this list, because his 1973 election on a special ballot three months after his death in a 31 December 1972 plane crash also came on the first time he was considered by the BBWAA (but, although it occurred for analogous reasons, the 1939 election of Lou Gehrig cannot be included, as — due to some writers' insistence upon voting for active players in 1936 — it was not the first time that Lou received votes from the scribes).

For much of Cooperstown's voting history, many of the game's all-time best could not get elected in their first year of eligibility. When the first five players were chosen in 1936, it marked the only time before Bob Feller and Jackie Robinson's enshrinements in 1962 that any man was elected in his first year on the ballot. For decades the BBWAA electors operated with a mindset that election in the initial year of a player's candidacy was reserved only for men deemed as baseball's true immortals.

There's nothing especially wrong with that approach, provided that there is a viable consensus definition of a baseball "immortal" in use. But, in predictable Alphonse-Gaston fashion, neither the Hall of Fame trustees nor the BBWAA ever established such a definition; and, because of their insistence upon willy-nilly, subjective criteria instead, some of the game's very best players experienced considerable frustration in the process. Sans Lou Gehrig, Table 11 lists the men elected by the BBWAA during the years 1937–61. It includes the year of each man's election, the number of ballots it took to enshrine each candidate (Num Bal; including runoff elections, but excluding the 1936 Old-Timers Committee voting), the support percentage each man received in his first year on the writers' ballot (Yr1 Pct), the percentage earned in the year he was elected (Elec Pct), and the average support percentage earned on all BBWAA ballots (Avg Pct). Men whose first-year support came while they were still active are noted by an asterisk.

TABLE 11
BBWAA Electees, 1937–61

Player	Year	Num Bal	Yrl Pct	Elec Pct	Avg Pct
Nap Lajoie	1937	2	60.2	83.6	71.9
Tris Speaker	1937	2	58.8	82.1	70.5
Cy Young	1937	2	49.1	76.1	62.6
Grover Alexander	1938	3	24.3	80.9	55.8
Eddie Collins	1939	4	26.5	77.5	57.0
Willie Keeler	1939	4	17.7	75.3	54.5
George Sisler	1939	4	34.1	85.5	60.2
*Rogers Hornsby	1942	5	46.5	78.1	46.5
*Mickey Cochrane	1947	7	35.4	79.5	39.7
*Frankie Frisch	1947	7	6.2	84.5	36.3
*****Lefty Grove**	1947	5	5.3	76.4	30.3
Carl Hubbell	1947	4	9.7	87.0	43.8
Herb Pennock	1948	9	7.5	77.7	27.0
*Pie Traynor	1948	9	7.1	76.9	29.7
Charlie Gehringer	1949	7	4.0	85.5	42.1
*****Jimmie Foxx**	1951	8	9.3	79.2	39.3
Mel Ott	1951	4	61.4	87.2	71.7
Harry Heilmann	1952	13	5.0	86.8	28.9
Paul Waner	1952	7	2.0	83.3	48.3
Dizzy Dean	1953	11	6.9	79.2	44.8
*Al Simmons	1953	10	1.8	75.4	39.6
*Bill Dickey	1954	11	6.9	80.2	40.1
*Bill Terry	1954	15	4.0	77.4	36.8
Rabbit Maranville	1954	16	12.4	82.9	37.4
*Joe DiMaggio	1955	4	0.4	88.8	50.7
Gabby Hartnett	1955	12	0.8	77.7	27.5
*Ted Lyons	1955	11	1.6	81.7	31.3
Dazzy Vance	1955	17	0.4	86.5	26.5
Joe Cronin	1956	11	3.7	78.8	28.3
*Hank Greenberg	1956	10	1.2	85.0	38.5

Not everyone listed in Table 11 is a true baseball "immortal," whatever that may be. Few people would argue that Willie Keeler, Herb Pennock, Rabbit Maranville or Ted Lyons (at least) belong on any short list of the very greatest players in history (certainly not the top fifty). But several men on that list would seem to qualify as immortals by almost any subjective standard imaginable — at minimum Cy Young (the all-time leader in pitching wins), and Joe DiMaggio (by force of legend and public image alone).

Table 11 also includes nine men (Young, Lajoie, Speaker, Alexander, Collins, Grove, Ott, Foxx and Waner, all boldfaced) whose career stats surpassed at least one of the current de facto standards for election and who therefore — if only by default — meet the BBWAA's *operative* definition of an immortal. Given the de facto standards, why were Foxx, Grove or Young (for example) any less deserving of first-year election than Willie McCovey, Tom Seaver or Nolan Ryan?

At minimum, the perverse habit of delaying the election of obvious Hall of Famers persisted into the 1970s, when five men (Koufax, Spahn, Mantle, Banks and Mays) became first-year inductees. And, it was really not until the next decade — when ten men were anointed with first-ballot election — that a different generation of BBWAA voters completely discarded the ill-begotten insistence upon making obvious Hall of Famers wait unnecessarily to be honored.

That mindset had other repercussions. Four of the Hall's initial inductees (Cobb, Ruth, Wagner and Mathewson) earned 90 percent support or better in 1936. But it was not until 1962 — when pitcher Bob Feller earned 150 of a possible 160 BBWAA votes for 93.8 percent support — that anyone again received at least 90 percent approval from the writers. Through the 2000 voting, only sixteen other men among the Hall's 185 players ever achieved that much support in the writers' voting, and all of them were first-year inductees. Chronologically, they include: Ted Williams (93.4 percent); Stan Musial (93.0); Sandy Koufax (96.9); Willie Mays (94.7); Hank Aaron (98.1); Brooks Robinson (92.0); Johnny Bench (96.2); Carl Yastrzemski (94.4); Jim Palmer (92.6); Rod Carew (90.3); Tom Seaver (98.8); Reggie Jackson (93.6); Steve Carlton (95.8); Mike Schmidt (96.5); Nolan Ryan (98.8) and George Brett (98.2).

At the same time, with no objective definition of an immortal in place and nothing but their disparate, subjective opinions to guide them, the writers applied their irrational caveat against first-year election so rigorously that it was just as difficult to be elected in one's second year on the ballot. When Nap Lajoie, Tris Speaker and Cy Young were chosen in 1937 — except for first-year winners Feller, Jackie Robinson, Williams, Musial and Koufax, and special-ballot selection Lou Gehrig — they became the last men before Yogi Berra was tabbed in 1972 to gain election as early as their second year of eligibility, and only three others — Whitey Ford in 1974, Rollie Fingers in 1992, and Carlton Fisk in 2000 — have done so since. Meanwhile, great players like Grover Alexander (three ballots), Rogers Hornsby and Lefty Grove (five), Jimmie Foxx (eight), and even the revered Joe DiMaggio (four) were forced to wait absurd lengths of time before their inevitable, rightful enshrinements.

The comparative landslide of first-ballot electees since the start of the 1980s may indicate that recent BBWAA voters have had an easier time than their predecessors identifying Cooperstown-worthy players. In one sense that's appropriate, because there is now a much larger slice of history available as a context for comparison of individual achievements than existed in the Hall's first few decades. But, the rarity of first-year electees and of 90 percent support levels during the early years of Cooperstown balloting apparently evidences considerable doubt among voters about the credentials of players like Alexander, Foxx, Grove, Hornsby and DiMaggio. In hindsight, that much uncertainty about their candidacies is hard to justify, and one is amazed that 10 percent or more of the voters in a given year could believe that any of those five was not a Hall of Famer.

The writers have been restricted to voting only on players for several decades (the last Hall of Fame manager to receive any BBWAA votes was Al Lopez in 1967). Currently, to be eligible for the scribes' ballot, a player must have been active at some point during a period not more than twenty years nor less than five years prior to the date of a given election. So, an eligible player can remain on the ballot for no more than fifteen years. If he is not elected in that period, he goes into limbo and has to wait three more years before he can be considered by the Veterans Committee (in the past, the length of this waiting period has varied from zero to five years). But if, at any time, a player receives less than 5 percent support in any BBWAA election, he is dropped from all subsequent ballots, even if his fifteen-year eligibility period has not expired.

The 5-percent support rule has been in force for just a decade or so, and the only apparent reason for its existence is to limit the number of players on the ballot. On the surface, that seems like a good idea. Since the major leagues' first expansion in 1961, the number of men who meet the ten-year service requirement has grown substantially, commensurate with the increased number of roster spots created by repeated expansions that raised the number of big-league teams from sixteen (and 400 yearly roster spots) in 1960 to thirty ball clubs (and 750 spots) in 1998. In turn, of the almost 2,300 players who had ten years or more of major-league experience during the period 1876–1994, almost half of them were active during some part of the years 1961–94. So, without the rule, the size of the BBWAA ballot would inflate annually, reducing the probability that someone might be elected (and that an induction ceremony could be held) every year.

But, despite that benefit (if it is one), the rule's most significant effect has been to derail further consideration of players whose career achievements merited far more scrutiny by the electors than they received as a result of it. The list of 5 percent victims includes third baseman Darrell Evans (414 home runs, 1354 RBI), outfielders Dwight Evans (382 homers, 1384 ribbies) and Al Oliver (2743 hits, .303 career batting average), second baseman Bobby Grich (224 home runs) and catcher Ted Simmons (2472 hits, more than any other man who played mostly as a backstop, and 1389 RBI, second only to Yogi Berra among the same group). Each of them has better credentials, subjectively and statistically, than several men enshrined at Cooperstown from their respective positions.

If those were the only men shortchanged by the 5 percent rule, the case against it might be marginal. But there have been others, of somewhat lesser light, including Dave Kingman (442 home runs), Fred Lynn (only man to win MVP and Rookie of the Year honors in the same season), Kent Tekulve (one of only six pitchers ever to appear in at least one-thousand games), Bill Madlock (four-time batting champion), Graig Nettles (390 four-baggers, 1314 RBI), plus Ron Cey, Sparky Lyle, Jim Sundberg and several more.

All of these men were dropped from the writers' ballot in the 1990s for failure to earn at least 5 percent support, most of them after just one year of eligibility. Some of them are not legitimate Hall of Famers. Possibly, none of them are. But each deserved far more consideration than the 5 percent rule afforded them.

As noted above, few men get elected to the Hall on their first try. Including Roberto Clemente, the thirty-five first-year inductees represent 37.6 percent of the ninety-three players enshrined by the BBWAA through 2000. That leaves fifty-eight others, almost two-thirds of the writers' selections, who needed two or more ballots to earn their spot in Cooperstown. Excluding Lou Gehrig (whose election percentage is unknown), the latter group averaged just over 25 percent support in their first year on the ballot and typically required more than seven elections (including runoffs) to earn the 75 percent support needed for induction. So, a lot of guys' candidacies start very slowly, some with no obvious momentum, and build over a period of years—as the passage of time (in theory anyway) enhances the voters' perspective on their credentials.

But, if the 5-percent support rule had been in force since the beginning of the BBWAA voting in 1936, many worthy Hall of Famers never would've made it into Cooperstown by the front-door route. A glance back at Table 11 reveals that ten of the men elected by the scribes in the years 1937–61—(in sequence) Gehringer, Waner, Simmons, Terry, DiMaggio, Hartnett, Lyons, Vance, Cronin and Greenberg—also could've been first-year victims of the rule, along with Luke Appling (no votes in 1952, 0.8 percent support in 1953), Lou Boudreau (1.0 percent in 1956), Ralph Kiner

(3.1 percent, 1962), Joe Medwick (0.8 percent, 1948) and Red Ruffing (3.3 percent, 1948). In addition, Pie Traynor got just 1.1 percent support in the second year he received votes, Harry Heilmann dropped to 2.9 percent in his third year, and Bob Lemon got just 1.3 percent on the second (runoff) ballot of 1964, his first year eligible. These eighteen BBWAA selections averaged just 2.9 percent support the first time they received votes; among them, only Lemon (11.9 percent) and Traynor (7.1 percent) would've escaped elimination by the 5 percent rule on their first BBWAA try, and the group as a whole averaged more than eleven ballots each to gain election by the scribes. Imagine "the Yankee Clipper" having to enter Cooperstown through the back door!

Granted, several of these men's first-ballot support came when they were still active or serving in the military and they shouldn't have received votes at all. But that's not true of all of them. Regardless, as a unit they posted a mean score of 81.7 percent support in the years of their inductions—ample evidence that a man's performance in his early years on the ballot is not indicative of how the writers may ultimately judge the merits of his candidacy.

Overall, including men chosen by the Veterans Committee, more than seventy Hall of Famers—about one-third of all current members who were not umpires or players in the Negro leagues—received less than 5 percent support in their first year on the ballot. So, if the rule were applied retroactively and these men were tossed out, Cooperstown would now have only about 145 members, a number that might satisfy those who perceive the Shrine is tainted by mediocrity. But, it's certain most of those narrow constructionists would not agree that Cronin, Gehringer, Greenberg, Simmons, Waner and DiMaggio, of all people, should be the ones expelled on that technicality.

It may state the obvious, but it's important to keep in mind that—except for the first-year electees—there is no meaningful correlation between the support percentage received in a man's first appearance on the ballot and the percentage he later earns upon election by the scribes. That's because 75 percent approval is required to earn induction, regardless of how he has fared in the past, and electees who begin their BBWAA vote histories with very poor support eventually meet the same minimum standard as men chosen on their first try. Table 12 clarifies this fact. It displays the first- and last-ballot (i.e., year of election) support percentages received by all BBWAA electees through 2000 (excluding Lou Gehrig and Roberto Clemente) and groups them by whether they were chosen on their first or various subsequent ballots of their eligibility. The data includes the number of electees in each ballot-range group (Tot Els), the highest (1st High) and lowest (1st Low) first-ballot support percentages earned by individuals within that group, and average first-ballot support percentage (1st Avg) among the group as a whole. It then gives the same information (Last High, Last Low and Last Avg) for the members of each group on the ballots on which they were elected (note that the first- and last-ballot data for first-year inductees is necessarily identical). At the bottom, it also gives the same extremes and averages for all ninety-one electees, as a whole, and for only those men chosen after their first try.

TABLE 12
FIRST- AND LAST-BALLOT SUPPORT
FOR BBWAA ELECTEES

Ballot of Election	Tot Els	1st High	1st Low	1st Avg	Last High	Last Low	Last Avg
Elected on First Ballot	34	98.8	77.5	90.5	98.8	77.5	**90.5**
Elected on Ballots 2–3	12	67.9	24.3	57.5	85.6	75.2	**79.9**
Elected on Ballots 4–5	14	65.7	0.4	35.7	88.8	75.3	**81.7**
Elected on Ballots 6–7	7	57.2	2.0	22.2	85.7	79.2	**83.2**
Elected on Ballots 8–9	6	50.0	0.8	19.4	83.6	76.9	**79.7**
Elected on Ballots 10–11	9	21.0	0.8	6.8	86.5	75.4	**81.2**
Elected on Ballot 12 or Later	9	12.2	0.4	3.2	86.9	75.4	**81.0**
All BBWAA Electees	*91*	*98.8*	*0.4*	*51.0*	*98.8*	*75.2*	*84.6*
After Ballot One, Only	*57*	*67.9*	*0.4*	*27.5*	*88.8*	*75.2*	*81.1*

Although there is a descending correlation among the first-ballot-high and average-support percentages received by each group in Table 12, there is no corresponding relationship to any of the group scores on the (last) ballot of election. Absence of any correlation indicates that — except for first-year electees—first-ballot performance is no valid predictor of how the writers will eventually perceive the merits of a successful candidate's credentials. Granted, the relationships might be much different if the table also included every man who has been rejected by the scribes. But their data is not relevant to whether the 5-percent support rule precludes viable candidates from further consideration. Beyond that, it's also clear that, since most of the 5 percent victims have been dropped after their first year on the ballot, their eliminations are not justifiable from this data.

So, who's to say that — given a number of chances equal to those of Bill Terry (fifteen), Harry Heilmann (thirteen), Bill Dickey (eleven), or even Mickey Cochrane (seven)—Darrell or Dwight Evans, Al Oliver,

Bobby Grich, Ted Simmons or any of the other 5 percent victims could not, or would not, have climbed from their poor initial support from the writers to eventually earn election to the Hall? And where is the justice in drawing an arbitrary time line for a player's retirement (around the middle of the 1980s) which gives favored treatment to everyone who came before that date, but shortchanges their relative equals who came later?

In one respect, there seems no justifiable reason why the 5 percent rule and the BBWAA's Screening Committee need be utilized simultaneously (as they presently are), because their purposes are redundant. If the committee is doing its job appropriately, you shouldn't need the rule at all, and anyone who merits a spot on the ballot should stay there until his fifteen-year eligibility expires and he has received the scribes' full consideration. Conversely, if the rule has to be there, then the Screening Committee seems unnecessary.

Without doubt, elimination of the 5 percent rule would lead to gradual inflation in the number of players annually listed on the writers' ballot and eventually make it more difficult than it is now to achieve election. But, that would impose no greater hindrance to the Cooperstown prospects of recent players than was shared by all the men from previous eras who are listed in Table 11, along with almost everyone else who appeared on a BBWAA ballot before the early 1990s. Clearly, any ballot-limiting benefits of the rule, as currently applied, are negated by the injustice imposed (relative to men of previous eras) upon any recent player who fares poorly in his early years of eligibility, and that absence of fairness is an excessive price to pay for the rule's expedience.

A partial solution to those problems would be to retain the 5 percent rule, but apply it only after a man has used up eight years (or just over half) of his fifteen-year eligibility. In that way, anyone likely to gain momentum over time probably will have achieved a support level indicative of his viability, and those dropped after eight years will at least have had ample opportunity to gain notice from the scribes. Within eight years of its application, it would also eliminate the same number of men annually as the current rule, only later in the process. But, even with that change, the 5 percent rule still would not provide a substantive definition of what a Hall of Famer actually is or should be.

Finally, one might also argue that the exclusions of Oliver, Grich, Simmons, the Evanses and the other men listed as 5 percent victims can be corrected by the Veterans Committee when those men become eligible for the panel's consideration. But, as a later chapter will show, that won't happen — because the VC's current eligibility rules include a Catch-22 that precludes their future consideration by the panel.

With all of that in mind, the subjective follies noted in this chapter provide added evidence that the BBWAA selection process was inadequately conceived from its beginning and has remained seriously flawed throughout the six decades of voting. Although some of the changes instituted by the Hall of Fame trustees and or BBWAA have attempted (in relatively good faith) to rectify the faults in that process, others (a majority it seems) have been the products of expedience and nothing more — flagrant attempts to enhance the prospect that an induction ceremony can be held each year, with inadequate consideration given to any injustices they impose.

6

Not-So-Wile E. Coyote

The BBWAA may have performed like Alphonse or Gaston over the years, but the writers' organ is only one of Cooperstown's two elective bodies, and much of the blame for mistakes among the Hall of Fame roster must also be directed at the scribes' counterpart, the Veterans Committee (VC). As noted earlier, the VC has received most of the criticism for the Hall's perceived errors of selection and is almost universally regarded among the Church of Baseball as the culprit in the gradual slide toward mediocrity that many perceive as having lowered Cooperstown's appropriate — if never defined — standard of excellence. In that regard, the panel has been analogous to the hapless cartoon character Wile E. Coyote, for many of its attempts to catch the Roadrunner (i.e., correct injustices in the BBWAA voting) have blown up in its face, like all that dynamite from Acme.

On the surface, much of the criticism levied against the Veterans Committee appears justified by the Hall of Fame's elective demography. Through 2000, the BBWAA had elected just 93 of Cooperstown's 249 members, of which only a half-dozen or so are ever singled out by critics as possible errors of selection. That leaves 156 men who were selected by some other means. Nine of the other members were chosen in the 1970s by a special committee formed to honor men from the defunct Negro leagues whose careers preceded major-league integration in 1947. The remaining 147 members, about 59 percent of the Cooperstown roster, were selected by the VC or one of its two predecessors — a Centennial Commission that operated in 1937–38 and a second Old-Timers Committee that existed during the 1940s (at times, for simplicity, all three will be treated in the text as a unit, under the label "veterans committees").

4ed.

Among those 147 inductees, and depending upon just how stringently one defines a Hall of Famer, less than half of those men have an unassailable claim to be in Cooperstown, and the rest of their selections have all stirred some controversy. Table 13 is a chronological list of the Hall of Fame's various elective organs over the years, including the periods in which they operated, the number of inductees elected by each and their respective percentage of the overall Cooperstown membership (the discrepancy from 100 percent resulted from rounding).

TABLE 13
Inductees Chosen by Cooperstown Voting Organs Through 2000

Organ	Years	Inductees	Pct
Old-Timers Committee 1	1936	0	0.0
BBWAA	1936–00	93	37.3
Centennial Commission	1937–38	7	2.8
Old-Timers Committee 2	1939–49	30	12.0
Veterans Committee	1953–00	110	44.2
Negro-league Committee	1971–77	9	3.6
Total		249	99.9

Where the BBWAA votes only on players, the veterans committees have also assumed the role of electing members in other capacities; 55 of their 147 inductees—about 22 percent of the Hall's total membership—have been men whose elections resulted from service as big-league managers, executives, umpires, and pioneer contributors to the game (plus eight Negro leaguers chosen by the panel after the special Negro League Committee of the 1970s disbanded). That leaves ninety-two men who've been chosen by the veterans panel and its progenitors for their careers as major-league players. Among those, at least fifty of the selections—and probably more—have been identified in print at some time or another as errors of selection.

On the other hand, whether or not one endorses most of the committees' selections, the fact that virtually half of the 185 men elected to Cooperstown solely for their playing skills have been added to the Hall of Fame roster to atone for real or imagined oversights by the writers is also ample evidence of flaws in the BBWAA's voting performance. So, the preponderance of criticism aimed at the veterans committees' choices over the years has also misplaced significant responsibility for the errors among

Cooperstown's membership, and these committees might never have existed at all if the original HOF electors of 1936 had fulfilled their intended roles.

The 1936 failure by the original Old-Timers Committee (OTC1) to elect anyone at all meant that, from its start, the Hall of Fame roster was inadequately representative of the nineteenth century — which, as of that year, comprised almost half of organized baseball's history dating to the formation of the National Association in 1871. The absence of any nineteenth-century players prompted creation of two different panels during the Hall of Fame's first decade — the current Veterans Committee's predecessors — that were intended to redress the oversight. The two groups accomplished very little in that regard during the years 1937–44; and then, in 1945–46, the second one went overboard in compensation for the previous failures.

It's also hard to believe that the 1936 Old-Timers Committee included many electors who had firsthand knowledge about the players they considered, because the greatest authorities on the skills of nineteenth-century players were already dead. Henry Chadwick, who had covered baseball for the Brooklyn *Eagle*, New York *Clipper* and other publications in the years 1856–94, invented the box score, and was the game's first true statistician, had died in 1908; Albert Spalding and Alfred James Reach, whose baseball guides are the most authoritative source of historical information and statistics for the 1800s, died in 1915 and 1928, respectively. Besides, in order to have witnessed the majority of any legitimate nineteenth-century player's career, the seventy-eight voters on the OTC1 would have had to have been born around 1860–65 at the very latest and have begun covering big-league baseball by about age twenty (or, by 1880–85). Even if they had, those men would've been in their seventies (or older) by 1936, and it's doubtful there were seventy-eight of them still living by then, let alone that number whose memories remained sharp enough to give their assigned task its appropriate consideration. At present, no one knows precisely who comprised the original Old-Timers Committee. But, even if we did, odds are that most of them voted either by tenuous, perhaps feeble, memory or (more likely) by second-generation, hearsay reputation.

Surprisingly then, if you ignore its failure to elect anyone at all, the OTC1 didn't do a bad job of separating HOF contenders from pretenders. The top five vote-getters — Cap Anson, Buck Ewing (both tied with forty votes and 51.3 percent support), Willie Keeler, Cy Young and Ed Delahanty — were all legitimate Hall of Famers who were enshrined by 1945; everyone who received eight votes or more was worthy of at least some consideration; and only three or four of the fifty-seven men who got any votes at all were of dubious merit, like Charlie Pabor. But, because of the increasing length of time between the nineteenth century and all subsequent elections, the panel's failure to fulfill its mandate gave short shrift to the players of that era and assured that all future consideration of those candidates would be made by electors with even less, or absolutely no, firsthand knowledge of the players' subjective credentials.

Soon after the original Old-Timers Committee failed to elect anyone, it was replaced by a six-man Centennial Commission (CC) mandated to redress the OTC1's oversight. The group included Kenesaw Mountain Landis, the baseball commissioner; Ford Frick and Will Harridge, presidents of the National and American Leagues at the time; John Heydler, a former NL president; William Branham, president of the National Association (umbrella administration of the minor leagues and a different organization than the NA of the 1870s); and George Trautman, the president of the minor-league American Association. All of these men were born in the nineteenth century. Landis, the oldest, was born in 1866; Frick, the youngest, in 1894. But, only two of them — Landis and Heydler — were really old enough to have any personal, observational knowledge of the players of that era; and, because most of Landis's career before 1920 was spent as a jurist, it's debatable whether he really knew George Wright (star shortstop for the 1869 Cincinnati Red Stockings, the first team comprised entirely of professionals) from George Armstrong Custer (who unwittingly became a "shortstop" playing against Native Americans at "Little Bighorn Park" in 1876, the year of the National League's formation).

In 1937–38, while the BBWAA was electing Nap Lajoie, Tris Speaker, Cy Young and Grover Alexander as Cooperstown's next inductees, the Centennial Commission chose seven nineteenth-century men to compensate for the OTC1's failure. Unfortunately, only three of the seven ever appeared in a major-league baseball game, and none of them were chosen specifically for their skills as a player. The three former players on the list were George Wright, Connie Mack and John McGraw. Wright had played in the National League during 1876–82, batting .256 on 383 hits; but his most significant accomplishments occurred before the league was formed; and upon his election he was cited as a "pioneer contributor" to the game. Mack and McGraw also had been nineteenth-century players of some skill. Mack was a first-string catcher for three different teams in the period 1886–96. McGraw, a third baseman, became famous with the National League's Baltimore Orioles of the 1890s. He continued to play through 1906 while serving as manager for the same city's American League team of 1901-2 and, later, the NL's New York Giants. To date, McGraw still owns the third-best on-base percentage in major-league history, behind only Ted Williams and Babe Ruth. But both men were far more renowned and elected to Cooperstown for their lengthy careers as managers. By 1937 McGraw's thirty-three-year managerial career was over, and Mack was in his fortieth of fifty-three seasons as a skipper. As pilots, McGraw won a record ten pennants (later tied by Casey Stengel), and Mack won nine.

The Centennial Commission's other four selections were strictly non-players: Alexander "Moses" Cartwright and Henry "Box Score" Chadwick also were cited as pioneer contributors; and Morgan Bulkeley and Ban Johnson, the first presidents of the National and American Leagues, were chosen as executives. (Although the AL didn't become a "major" league until 1901, Johnson had founded the circuit from the minor Western League in the 1890s and could be rationalized as a nineteenth-century selection, if one wished.) So, technically, the CC's first group of inductions redressed the 1936 omission of nineteenth-century players by failing to elect any of them — at least for their achievements in the lineup.

There was little complaint that the CC had taken it upon itself to cite the seven new HOF members for non-playing capacities. Perhaps no one wanted to buck Landis, who was given carte-blanche power over all aspects of baseball when he was chosen as commissioner and did not respond kindly to challenges of his authority. In one sense, it made perfect sense to enshrine the game's best managers, executives and other significant contributors to baseball's history. But, the move also went against the grain of the original intent of both the failed monument in Washington, D.C., and the Cooperstown museum to honor only players, and it gave members of the Church of Baseball a whole new set of Hall of Fame selections to criticize — notably, the managers. It also set a precedent that eventually was used to justify the induction of umpires, for whom there are absolutely no statistics to measure their abilities and whose selections are therefore the most purely subjective of all HOF members (managers and club executives at least have team records by which they may be judged). Perhaps the only evidence relevant to umpire inductions was cited by Bill Klem, one of the first two men in blue chosen for Cooperstown in 1953, who always asserted that he had never missed a call in a career that spanned 1905–41 — no doubt the self-assessment of every confident arbiter who is not Don Denkinger. Ironically though, Klem had once characterized Landis' job as commissioner as nothing more than "window dressing"— so the old judge might've had second thoughts about the precedent had he lived long enough to see Klem inducted.

In 1939 — when the BBWAA elected Eddie Collins, Willie Keeler, George Sisler and Lou Gehrig (the latter on a special ballot) — Landis, Frick and Harridge appointed themselves as the second Old-Timers Committee

(OTC2) and finally succeeded in choosing some actual players from the nineteenth century. They included the OTC1's vote leaders, Cap Anson and Buck Ewing, plus pitcher Charles "Old Hoss" Radbourn. Until very recently, when revisionist research pared the number to 2995, Anson was recognized as the first major-leaguer to achieve the 3000-career-hit plateau which has become one of Cooperstown's de facto standards for batters (and some sources still credit him with as many as 3041). Cap played in the remarkable total of twenty-seven seasons (1871–97), including all five years of the old NA's existence and twenty-two in the National League, where he was a four-time batting champion, an eight-time leader in runs batted in, and compiled a .329 career batting average. Ewing, a catcher-third baseman-outfielder during 1880–97, batted .303 with 1625 hits and — due largely to his versatility — was regarded by many contemporary observers to be the best all-around player of his era. Radbourn was a star in the 1880s for the NL's Providence Grays. He won 309 games, and his 60 victories in 1884 represent the all-time, single-season record (although, as with Anson, revisionists have since cut the total to a less aesthetically pleasing 59). On the down side, Anson was also a key figure in the ban of African-Americans from organized baseball in the 1880s, a disgraceful decision that stood up for more than half a century. But, racial politics aside, there is little reason to fault the selection of any of these men for their on-field skills.

Predictably though, Charles Comiskey, Albert Spalding and Candy Cummings, the other three selections made by Landis, Frick and Harridge in 1939, were not chosen as players. Comiskey had been a first baseman and player-manager for the St. Louis dynasty in the defunct American Association (AA, 1882–91, the NL's first rival "major" league and not the same circuit for which George Trautman later was president), a founder of the Players League (another nineteenth-century "major," which operated for one season only in 1890), and also played three years for the NL's Cincinnati franchise after the senior circuit absorbed the disbanded AA's remnants in 1892. But by 1939, Comiskey was far more famous for being the founding owner of the American League's Chicago White Sox (he was the tightwad whose penury prompted the Black Sox scandal), so Cooperstown labels "the Old Roman" as an executive rather than a player or manager.

Spalding was the best pitcher in the original National Association, compiling a 204–53 won-lost record for a .794 winning percentage in the years 1871–75. He then went 47–12 as a teammate of Anson, leading Chicago to the first National League pennant in 1876, and finished his playing career with a 1–0 record the next season. But, he gained even more fame for his sporting goods company (which for years supplied the National League with its baseballs) and for the seasonal guides he published with

Alfred Reach — so, he was also inducted as a pioneer contributor to the game. Reach has thus far been ignored by Cooperstown.

In the perfection of hindsight, the OTC2's final inductee of 1939 was the Hall of Fame's first true error of selection. Like Spalding, Candy Cummings had been a star pitcher in the old National Association, where he compiled a 124–72 won-lost mark and .633 winning percentage in the years 1872–75. But, as noted earlier, the NA is not yet regarded as a true major league; and, although Cummings also pitched in the first two NL seasons of 1876–77, his skills had diminished to a point that his career big-league record was just 21–22 and in no way comparable to Spalding's. Cummings also was elected as a pioneer contributor because of the unverified — and probably unprovable — legend that he personally invented the curveball while playing for amateur teams in Brooklyn sometime between 1866 and 1871. There is much dispute among baseball historians regarding Candy's invention of the pitch. Also, just how dazzling this "curveball" could've been is debatable, as hurlers of the era were required to release the ball below their waists, and batters were allowed to request pitches that were high or low in the strike zone. So odds are good that whatever Cummings tossed up to the batters of his day was nothing like the demon offerings of Sandy Koufax or Bert Blyleven.

Cummings would not be the only Cooperstown member to benefit from the "Candy Cummings Effect" (i.e., to be inducted because of an unprovable legend of responsibility for some baseball innovation). Folklore has it that Roger Bresnahan's induction in 1945 was rationalized — in part, at least — on the belief that he was the first catcher ever to wear shin guards, hardly a prerequisite for greatness as a backstop (although it evidenced undoubted good sense). It's a wonder that Landis, Frick and Harridge didn't embarrass the Shrine for all of posterity by choosing baseball's false inventor Abner Doubleday as a pioneer contributor as well, and it's probably a good thing there were no legends back then regarding which player was the first to wear a protective cup.

So, after three separate attempts in a four-year span to honor nineteenth-century players, by the end of 1939 the Hall of Fame roster included thirteen "modern" players chosen by the BBWAA (Cobb, Ruth, Wagner, Mathewson, Johnson, Lajoie, Speaker, Young, Alexander, Collins, Keeler, Sisler and Gehrig) and fourteen nineteenth-century personalities, of which only three (Anson, Ewing and Radbourn) were actually enshrined for their on-field performance in the major leagues. This meant that nineteenth-century players were still grossly under-represented, even though — among the BBWAA inductees— Young and Keeler also played during most of the 1890s.

Meanwhile, the BBWAA had petitioned Commissioner Landis in the summer of 1938 for the right to have all future authority over selection of candidates who played any time after 1900 (including men whose careers began earlier). Landis approved the request, ostensibly giving the (then) Centennial Commission jurisdiction over the nineteenth century and the writers power over the twentieth. Then, after making the second incarnation of the Old-Timers Committee's initial set of selections in 1939, Landis, Frick and Harridge passed their membership on the committee to four others who comprised the OTC2 through 1944: Ed Barrow and Bob Quinn, who were presidents of the Yankees and Braves, respectively; plus Connie Mack and veteran baseball writer Sid Mercer.

During 1940–44, the rejuvenated OTC2 elected absolutely no one. But, the writers weren't doing much better, as the BBWAA held no votes in 1940–41 or 1943–44, and Rogers Hornsby (1942) proved to be the only man elected by the scribes between 1939 and 1947. The lack of new inductees infuriated everyone with a financial interest in the Cooperstown museum, because — with no reason to hold an induction ceremony — it was difficult to sell the Shrine as a tourist attraction, especially at a time when leisure mobility was limited by wartime travel and gasoline restrictions.

In response to those concerns, in August 1944 the seventy-seven-year-old Landis suffered a brain burp of major consequence when he expanded the OTC2, adding Stephen Clark, director of the foundation that controlled the Cooperstown museum, and Boston sportswriter Mel Webb. With only one BBWAA selection made in the five years prior to Clark's appointment, his main agenda was — doubtless — to assure there were ample inductions to keep the museum solvent. But, whether it represented true belief or mere expedience, his support for the legend that Abner Doubleday invented baseball at Cooperstown was probably the best indication of his relative expertise as a horsehide historian. In hindsight, Webb's ability to judge ballplayers is also suspect, because he was the writer who later omitted Ted Williams from his Most Valuable Player ballot in 1947, depriving Williams of the award by one point in the year of his second American League Triple Crown. To make things even worse, Landis also dictated that the OTC2's members would function thereafter as the Hall of Fame's trustees, giving them ultimate authority over the entire selection process.

When Landis died three months after these appointments, the committee — meeting at his funeral — promptly voted to enshrine him. At the same time, they tinkered with the delineation of powers that Landis had approved in 1938, extending the OTC2's jurisdiction to include players whose careers began in the nineteenth century but extended to 1910, and formally limiting the BBWAA to voting only on men whose careers began after 1900. Since the writers were allowed to retain jurisdiction over all men who played exclusively in the twentieth century, the apparent intent of this was to liberalize the definition of nineteenth-century players, in order to facilitate better representation for that era (of course, it extended the OTC2's powers as well).

But, the six-man OTC2's real legacy was delivered in 1945–46, when — while the BBWAA failed again to elect anyone — the committee inducted a total of twenty-one men in a massive reprisal for the writers' hiatus and elective failures of the early to mid–1940s. Table 14 lists the men enshrined by the OTC2 in 1945–46, the year of their election, their HOF positional citation, and the inclusive dates of their careers as major-league players.

TABLE 14
OTC2 SELECTIONS, 1945–46

Player	Year	Position	Career
Roger Bresnahan	1945	catcher	1897–15
Dan Brouthers	1945	first base	1879–04
Fred Clarke	1945	outfield	1894–15
Jimmy Collins	1945	third base	1895–08
Ed Delahanty	1945	outfield	1888–03
Hugh Duffy	1945	outfield	1888–06
Hughie Jennings	1945	shortstop	1891–18
Mike "King" Kelly	1945	outfield	1878–93
Jim O'Rourke	1945	outfield	1876–04
Wilbert Robinson	1945	manager	1886–02
Jesse Burkett	1946	outfield	1890–05
Frank Chance	1946	first base	1898–14
Jack Chesbro	1946	pitcher	1899–09
Johnny Evers	1946	second base	1902–29
Clark Griffith	1946	executive	1891–14
Tommy McCarthy	1946	outfield	1884–96
Joe McGinnity	1946	pitcher	1899–08
Eddie Plank	1946	pitcher	1901–17
Joe Tinker	1946	shortstop	1902–16
Rube Waddell	1946	pitcher	1897–10
Ed Walsh	1946	pitcher	1904–17

As a whole, these selections were a disaster. Among the group, Delahanty and Plank are about the only ones whose Hall of Fame status has not been criticized at some point. Tinker, Evers and Chance were enshrined, perhaps as much as anything else, because of the fame they received as subjects of Franklin Pierce Adams's 1908 poem in the New York *Globe*, "Baseball's Sad Lexicon," which extolled their skills as the game's supposedly peerless double-play combination of their era — although, in the years they played as a unit (1903–10), they never once led their league in twin killings. And, without doubt, Chance, Evers, McCarthy and "Shinguard" Bresnahan all rank — statistically, at least — among the worst Cooperstown selections ever.

Most of the 1945–46 selections were also ill-advised politically, as they did little to equalize the representation of nineteenth-century players, and many of the choices violated the new jurisdictional rules that the OTC2 itself had imposed. Among the twenty-one inductees, eleven of them — Brouthers, Burkett, Collins, Delahanty, Duffy, Griffith, Jennings, Kelly, McCarthy, O'Rourke and Robinson — had enjoyed their most significant seasons as players during the 1800s; but two of those (Griffith as an executive, and Robinson as a manager) were cited only for accomplishments that occurred strictly during the twentieth century. Also, although six of the other ten choices had begun their careers in the 1890s (Bresnahan, Chance, Clarke, Chesbro, McGinnity and Waddell), only the latter three had stopped playing by 1910. The remaining four (Evers, Plank, Tinker and Walsh) all had begun their careers after 1900 and should, therefore, have been in the sole domain of the BBWAA. Overall, and even worse, the playing careers of nine of these twenty-one men extended beyond the 1910 limit that the OTC2 had imposed upon itself; and, roughly half the selections were, in truth, Dead-Ball-Era players from the first two decades of this century.

Apparently, the OTC2 got away with this because its members also comprised the HOF board of trustees at the time. No doubt, many among the BBWAA grumbled about it, but with Landis dead, there was no one around with the *chutzpah* to chastise them. Albert "Happy" Chandler had succeeded Landis as commissioner in 1945, but — consistent with the "What, me worry?" tenor of his nickname — showed no special interest in the problem and avoided any intervention in the issue.

So, by the mid–1940s, with the Hall of Fame less than a decade old, the failures of the original Old-Timers Committee, the Centennial Commission, and the second OTC had coupled with the Hall of Fame's overall lack of standards for election and the BBWAA's separate, temporary difficulty in choosing anyone at all to prompt several truly dubious selections for Cooperstown and to create an increasingly adversarial relationship between the Hall's two sets of electors. The OTC2 chose what proved to be its final pair of inductees in 1949, pitchers Kid Nichols and Morde-cai "Three-Finger" Brown. But, because Brown had played only during the twentieth century and his career did not end until 1916, his selection also violated the committee's self-imposed time boundaries and perpetuated the unnecessary confusion over the jurisdiction of the Hall's two elective bodies.

By 1952, after sixteen years of Hall of Fame balloting, and with the BBWAA (as of 1947) once again electing people on a relatively annual basis, the number of players in Cooperstown had reached forty-nine, with an almost equal total having been chosen by each the Hall's two methods (twenty-five by the BBWAA, two-dozen by the early veterans committees). But, although twenty-three of them had played some portion of their careers during the nineteenth century, only fourteen — Anson, Brouthers, Burkett, Delahanty, Duffy, Ewing, Jennings, Kelly, McCarthy, Nichols, O'Rourke, and Radbourn (all chosen by the CC or OTC2), plus BBWAA selections Keeler and Young — were truly, or even arguably, representative of the pre–1901 era. To some observers, this meant that the nineteenth century was still under-represented, with less than one-fourth of the Hall's player population even though it still comprised a third of major-league history.

What's more, of the eleven men inducted by the BBWAA in the period 1947–52, all had played the most significant portions of their careers in the 1920s or later, and only three — second baseman Frankie Frisch (one year), outfielder Harry Heilmann (five years) and pitcher Herb Pennock (seven) — had played during any part of the game's Dead-Ball Era (1901–19). With most of the stars from baseball's Live-Ball Era (1920–45) having retired within a couple seasons after the end of World War II, if not sooner, by 1952 it also appeared that these players — from what was generally considered the game's golden age — would dominate the HOF selections for years to come and that the prospects of election for anyone from the game's first half century were getting slim. In fact, Rabbit Maranville and Dazzy Vance — chosen in 1954 and 1955, respectively — would be the last players ever elected by the BBWAA whose careers began before 1920; and, of those two, only Maranville can be said to have enjoyed a significant part of his prime during the Dead-Ball years.

Beyond all that, by 1952 the members of the second Old-Timers Com-mittee had reached an age where it was obvious that — at the very least — some changes had to be made in the composition of the committee (e.g., Ed Barrow was eighty-five in 1952 and died the next year; Connie Mack was ninety and died in 1956). So, in 1953 the OTC2 — which, by then, had made no new selections for four years — was replaced by the Veterans Com-mittee as the Hall of Fame's second-line electorate.

Like the second Old-Timers Committee, the membership of the Veterans Committee comprised primarily former league and team executives, sportswriters and one representative of the Hall of Fame's braintrust (league presidents Warren Giles and Will Harridge, and J. G. Taylor Spink, publisher of *The Sporting News*, were the best-known members of the original panel from the first two groups; Paul Kerr was the museum's representative). But, the size of the committee was expanded over that of the OTC2 (from six members to eleven); and, this time, the committee as a whole did not simultaneously comprise the museum's trustees, as only Kerr and the two league presidents were allowed to serve that double duty.

But, none of those changes did anything to enhance the immediate prospects of nineteenth-century players being added to the Cooperstown roster. During its first decade of operation, the new panel enshrined nine men for their careers as major-league players—pitcher Charley Bender and shortstop Bobby Wallace (1953), third baseman Frank Baker and catcher Ray Schalk (1955) and outfielders Sam Crawford (1957), Zach Wheat (1959), Billy Hamilton and Max Carey (1961) plus Edd Roush (1962). Hamilton, the first significant player in big-league history to score more runs than the number of games he appeared in (1691 tallies in 1591 contests), played in the majors during 1888–1901, and he is the only real nineteenth-century player in the group. Among the others, only Wallace (who reached the Show in 1894 but played in twenty-five seasons through 1918) and Crawford (who entered the majors in 1899) had any portion of their careers occur before 1903.

In subsequent years the VC has done more to redress the shortage of nineteenth-century representation. During 1963–2000, among the fifty-nine other men elected as players by the panel, a dozen of them played all or most of their careers before the twentieth century, including first basemen Jake Beckley and Roger Connor, second sacker Bid McPhee, shortstops George Davis and Monte Ward, outfielders Joe Kelley and Sam Thompson, and pitchers John Clarkson, Pud Galvin, Tim Keefe, Amos Rusie and Mickey Welch. But several of these additions were slow-coming, as only four of those men were enshrined before 1971, and two of the others (Davis and McPhee) were not inducted until 1998 and 2000, respectively.

Recall also that six of those men — Connor, Davis, Galvin, McPhee, Thompson and Welch — never got a single vote in any Hall of Fame election. Similarly, the other seven as a unit (including Hamilton) earned a total of only forty-six votes on sixteen different Cooperstown ballots (most of them coming in the OTC1 voting of 1936). That equates to an average of just 2.9 Hall of Fame votes per man and a mean support of only 2.0

percent per ballot. Given that history, it's probable that the elections of these nineteenth-century players reinforced the BBWAA's ongoing perception that the Veterans Committee has tended to anoint the scribes' most unqualified rejects.

That particular criticism is obviously unfair, because nineteenth-century players were out of the BBWAA's purview by 1939, at the latest. But several of these selections have also been criticized for another reason that has no connection to the BBWAA-VC rivalry.

Predictable for the infancy of any sport, the rules of baseball changed radically and often from the formation of the National League in 1876 through the mid–1890s, as almost everything except the roundness of the ball was tinkered with on a nearly annual basis. Initially, pitchers were required to deliver the ball from below the waist; in 1883 the rule was changed to anything beneath the shoulder; and, for the following season, even that restriction was eliminated — so hurlers didn't throw overhand until 1884. Prior to 1887, the batter could request pitches that were high or low, above or below the waist. Stolen bases were deemed gauche at first and disallowed until 1886. Throughout the 1880s, rulemakers also changed the number of balls pitched out of the strike zone required for the batter to earn a walk, dropping the total one at a time from nine in 1879 to the since-used four in 1889.

Despite all that, the most influential changes probably involved the distance from which the pitcher threw the ball. At the National League's inception, hurlers had to toss from within a line-enclosed area whose front was at a distance of forty-five feet from home plate. That box was moved back to fifty feet in 1881, and it wasn't until 1893 that the precursor of today's pitching rubber was placed at the current sixty-feet, six inches. Predictably, this had a liberating effect on offense (after all, if Nolan Ryan was hard to hit at sixty feet, he might've tossed two hundred no-hitters from just fifty). Commensurately, the NL batted a paltry .245 as a league in 1892; the circuit's average jumped to .280 the year the distance was changed; it went as high as .309 in 1894; and then it stayed in the .280s throughout most of the Gay Nineties thereafter.

These rule changes cause many among the Church of Baseball to argue, with some merit, that the real, modern game did not exist prior to 1893; that, for comparative purposes the performance of batters and (especially the three hundred-victory) pitchers before that year is suspect; and that all major-league records from prior to that time should be denoted by a Maristerisk, or some such symbol. In turn, all of that prompts criticism of some — if not all — of the nineteenth-century pitchers selected for Cooperstown; and, unless you count Cy Young as one of those hurlers (his career spanned 1890–1911, and 286 of his 511 wins came before 1901), each of them (John Clarkson, Pud Galvin, Tim Keefe, Kid Nichols, Amos Rusie and Mickey Welch) was enshrined by the VC or one of its predecessors.

So, for some observers, the Cooperstown memberships of Radbourn (elected by the OTC2 in 1939), Clarkson, Keefe, Galvin and Welch (all tabbed by the VC in an eleven-year span that began in 1963) are especially dubious — because each of those five played all or most of their careers before the mound was moved in 1893. Galvin (361–308, .540), Radbourn (309–195, .613) and Welch (307–210, .594) all were gone from the majors by the end of 1892; Keefe (342–225, .603) pitched through 1893, going 10–7 in his last campaign; and Clarkson (328–178, .648) quit after 1894, with a combined record of 24–27 in his last two seasons. But, in fairness to the latter two, most players' performances decline in their last couple seasons. What's more, all of these men also spent the first part of their careers tossing underhand to locations requested by the hitters, which — for all we know — may have (at least partially) counterbalanced any advantage inherent in the shorter pitching distance they enjoyed.

Complicating things even more is the fact that Clarkson, Galvin, Keefe, Radbourn and Welch also were the first five hurlers in major-league history to meet or surpass the Hall's three-hundred-win, de facto standard for pitchers. Galvin got to three hundred victories first in 1888; Keefe and Welch followed in 1890; Radbourn joined the club in 1891; and Clarkson reached that mark the following season. Welch was the last of these men elected by the VC (in 1973), and there are some reasonable arguments that his selection lowered Cooperstown's nonexistent minimum standards for pitchers, despite his de facto achievement.

In that light, and with regard to the other de facto standards, the Hall of Fame and its electors are fortunate that Cap Anson's official career-hits total has been downgraded to 2995 — because the first 1357 occurred when he was allowed to request a pitch location, and all but the last 670 came before the mound was moved to its present distance. Even if you credit Cap with 3041 safeties, he is the only member of the 3000-hit club whose career began before 1893 (the next two were Nap Lajoie and Honus Wagner, whose major-league tenures began in 1896 and '97, respectively).

It's also good that almost no one hit home runs in any quantity before Babe Ruth came along. Cooperstown member Roger Connor, elected by the VC in 1976, was the pre–Ruth career leader with 138, and only six other players — Hall of Famers Sam Thompson (127), Dan Brouthers (106) and Hugh Duffy (104) along with Harry Stovey (122), Mike Tiernan (106) and Jimmy Ryan (105) — surpassed one hundred career taters prior to

1901. All but thirty-nine of Connor's homers occurred before 1893. And —
like Anson (1876–97) and Connor (1880–97)— Brouthers (1879–96),
Thompson (1885–98) and Duffy (1888–906) all played some part of their
careers before that date. Predictably, all three of them were also enshrined
by the VC (Thompson in 1974) or its predecessor, the OTC2 (Brouthers
and Duffy in 1945).

So, although the Veterans Committee eventually increased the representation of nineteenth-century players on the Hall of Fame roster, those
choices also prompted inevitable criticism and abetted the establishment
of at least one de facto standard which may have widely different meaning when applied to baseball's various historical eras. In that sense — like
the election of Candy Cummings, the selections of 1945–46 and the OTC2's
failure to abide by its own jurisdictional rules— they were one more stick
of dynamite exploding in the face of Cooperstown's not-so-Wile E. Coyote. Unfortunately, all of these foibles pale in comparison to the biggest
errors in the Veterans Committee's conduct.

7

The Good Ol' Boys Club

Like the BBWAA, Veterans Committee inductees are required to receive 75 percent support for election, but the complete numerical results of the panel's elections have never been released to the public (at least not formally). Also, where the BBWAA has been allowed to elect whatever number of candidates receive the required support level, the VC — through most of its history — has been limited to choosing a maximum of two inductees per year. Exceptions to this rule occurred in 1953 (when six men were chosen), 1963–64 (a total of ten inductees combined), and 1970–77 (three per year, except for 1971 when there were seven). The panel was also allowed to choose as many as four men per year in the period 1995–2000, but the two extra inductees were limited to one each from among men who played prior to 1920 and from those who played in the Negro leagues. Initially, the committee also was allowed to consider any former major-league manager, umpire or executive who had been retired for at least five years, but that was amended in 1966 to accommodate men who had been retired for at least six months and had already reached the age of sixty-five (allowing the hastened election of manager Casey Stengel).

Also, for the first time (unless you count Connie Mack), a Hall of Fame player was added to the panel upon its formation in 1953 — former Detroit Tigers second baseman Charlie Gehringer, who had been elected by the writers in 1949. The number of Hall of Fame players on the committee has increased gradually over the years and by the 1990s was in approximate parity with that of the executives or sportswriters. Branch Rickey, a catcher with four years of major-league service during the Dead-Ball Era, also was on the original VC and served on the panel through 1965.

But, he was not yet a Hall of Famer when appointed; and, when he was inducted in 1967, he was cited only for his career as an executive.

On the surface, the inclusion of HOF players made perfect sense. It gave the Hall's living members (a few of them, anyway) a more direct involvement with the institution. Presumably, their sense of pride in their own accomplishment would also encourage them to maintain a high standard of admission. Plus, it also meant that future VC candidates would be judged, in part, by their peers from the playing field — who, in theory, would have a keener sense of the subtle differences in each man's abilities than that possessed by baseball executives or sportswriters. Apparently, no one in 1953 was especially concerned whether the clubhouse allegiances or on-field animosities of these former players might also encourage favoritism or spitefulness among the committee's selections, although that result was inevitable in a process that lacked any objective standards.

As noted in Chapter 3, sportswriters are inevitably influenced by the views of ballplayers about the relative skills of other players, especially their contemporaries. Sure, the writers have opinions of their own, especially if they've seen the man in question play. But, in terms of HOF qualification, if their own view is not set in cement, some scribes might defer to a player's expertise the same way that most of us who aren't auto mechanics accept the advice of a skilled wrenchman when our car isn't working properly. So, the opinions of former players who are on the Veterans Committee at any time are likely to be influential among the writers who share that duty and probably among the baseball executives as well.

Gehringer and Rickey were the only ex-players on the VC for most of the panel's first decade until Joe Cronin was added in 1961. One of the panel's selections in its first year can be viewed as an example of possible favoritism on Rickey's part. Shortstop Bobby Wallace had been Branch's teammate on the St. Louis Browns of 1905–6 and briefly in 1914 during Rickey's term as player-manager. Wallace batted .300 or better just twice (1897 and 1901) and averaged only .268 over the course of his career. But, at the time of his election, his 2309 career hits were the sixth-best total ever among men who played primarily at shortstop, and his twenty-five-year stint as a player was (and still is) the longest by any man from that position in history. So, although the wisdom of his selection is doubtful now, it must've seemed far more justifiable in 1953. Also, because Rickey was chosen for the VC in the role of executive rather than player, the validity of citing Wallace's election as an example of favoritism by Hall of Fame players on the panel is arguable.

Whatever weight Gehringer's opinions had among the rest of the VC doesn't seem to have manifested in any favoritism during the first few years, when the committee was busy judging the credentials of nineteenth-century and Dead-Ball-Era guys who were not Charlie's contemporaries. Gehringer's major-league career began in 1924; of the six men inducted by the VC as players in the years 1953–60, four of them had retired before Charlie ever reached the majors; only one (Ray Schalk) was his American League contemporary for any meaningful period; and none of them was an ex-teammate. Among those six, Sam Crawford, inducted in 1957, also had played for Detroit through most of his career, and Gehringer's opinion of him may have been influenced by teammates whose tenures with the Tigers overlapped both. But, Crawford was also the most deserving HOF selection among the group; and, although Wallace was a marginal candidate, only one of the other players chosen during 1953–60 (Schalk) was of truly doubtful merit.

When Joe Cronin joined the Veterans Committee in 1961 his opinions probably overshadowed Gehringer's among the rest of the committee — assuming they ever disagreed strongly — because Cronin was as good a politician as he was a shortstop, maybe better. He had been a player-manager by age twenty-six and served as Red Sox vice president, treasurer and general manager from 1948 until 1959, when he was chosen for what would become a fourteen-year term as president of the American League — the first ex-player ever tabbed for that role. He also became one of the Hall's directors in 1959, two years before he joined the VC.

One of the committee's selections in 1964, three years after Cronin joined the panel, was outfielder Heinie Manush. Manush had been a very good hitter. He'd led AL batters with a .378 average in 1926; he had twice topped the circuit in hits and doubles; and ended his career with a .330 average, 2524 hits, 110 home runs and 1183 RBI. Despite all that, his best showing ever in MVP voting was 1933, when he placed third behind Philadelphia's Jimmie Foxx and the Senators' Cronin, and he finished among the top ten in balloting for the award only one other time during his career. His BBWAA voting history for Cooperstown was also unimpressive — a high of only twenty-two votes in 1958 and a best of 9.4 percent support in 1962. But, Manush had been a teammate of Cronin's at Washington (1930–34) and Boston (1936) and had also worn a Tigers uniform with Gehringer in the period 1924–27.

Manush's statistical credentials for Cooperstown are debatable, especially relative to the offensive excesses common in his time. And, ignoring the earlier selection of Wallace, his election by a committee that included two former teammates set a precedent for that panel and opened a door that could never be closed.

In 1968 the VC inducted outfielder Goose Goslin, another former teammate of both Cronin (in 1930 and 1933) and Gehringer (1934–37), who had career stats that were marginally better than Manush's (a .316 average, 2735 hits, 248 homers, 1609 RBI). Goslin's history in the MVP and HOF balloting was similar to Heinie's: a personal best of sixth-place MVP finishes in 1927–28, a high of thirty Cooperstown votes in 1960 and 13.5 percent support in 1956. Goslin wasn't a bad choice overall, but by 1968 the VC's apparent trend toward cronyism was irreversible because the year before the panel had added Frankie Frisch as its third player-member.

Frisch's brief but pivotal role on the committee is analyzed in far more depth than space permits here by Bill James in *The Politics of Glory*. Frisch had only five years on the panel before he died following an auto accident in 1972. But, in that time, the VC chose four of his former teammates for Cooperstown — shortstop Dave Bancroft (elected in 1971) and outfielder Ross Youngs (1972) from the Giants of the early 1920s and pitcher Jesse Haines (1970) and outfielder Chick Hafey (1971) of the Cardinals from later in that decade.

Except for the selection of Haines, Frisch had some help electing his buddies. Bill Terry, Frankie's teammate on the Giants during 1923–26, joined the VC in 1971 and served through 1976. Terry was on the panel when Bancroft, Youngs and Hafey were elected, and two more of both men's former teammates from the Giants—first baseman George Kelly (1973) and third sacker Fred Lindstrom (1976)— also were chosen during Terry's tenure, after Frisch had died.

Former Yankees pitcher Waite Hoyt was also on the committee during the same years as Terry. Hoyt had briefly been a teammate of both Kelly (with the 1932 Dodgers) and Lindstrom (the Pirates of 1933–34) and had played in New York during most of the years that the ex-Giants were stars in that city. During Hoyt's VC tenure, the panel also enshrined two other men he had played with — outfielder Harry Hooper (elected in 1971) was Waite's teammate with the Red Sox in 1919–20, and pitcher Lefty Gomez (1972) played with Hoyt on the Yankees for about a month in 1930.

All of the principals are dead now, allowing only for speculation. But, to make things worse, the elections of Hafey and Lindstrom also may have been motivated — at least in part — by perceived debts owed to each man by Frisch and Terry, respectively.

Throughout his big-league career, Hafey was plagued by a chronic sinus condition that required several surgeries and diminished his vision in an inconsistent fashion, which forced him to switch among three sets of eyeglasses with varying prescriptions. As a result, he was one of baseball's first "stars" to wear visual aids. He also was hampered by a nearly as chronic overestimation of his importance to the Cardinals, which prompted him to hold out after both of the 1930–31 seasons, and prompted Chick's trade to the Reds during the second holdout.

A left fielder, Hafey led St. Louis to a pennant in 1931, a season in which he scored 94 runs, had 157 hits, 16 homers and 95 RBI, while leading the National League in batting and on-base averages (with figures of .349 and .404, respectively, although the latter statistic wasn't kept back then). But, in the BBWAA's first-ever version of MVP voting, Chick placed only fifth. The senior-circuit honor went instead to his teammate, Frisch, who scored 96 runs, had 161 hits, only 4 homers and 82 ribbies and batted .311 with an OBA of .368. So Hafey's stats were better that season, and — given his self-perceptions — it's possible Chick felt slighted by his failure to cop the award. Hafey was still alive in 1971, and it's possible that his election to Cooperstown that year was, in part, Frisch's payback for "stealing" that first MVP trophy.

When John McGraw retired as the Giants' skipper in 1932, Bill Terry was named to replace him. At the time, Fred Lindstrom believed he had been promised the job. Irate, Lindstrom demanded a trade, and Terry obliged, shipping him to Pittsburgh. So, it's also possible that Fred's election in 1976, the last year that Terry was a VC member, was Bill's ultimate apology for taking that plum.

The elections of Manush, Goslin and (arguably) Wallace, with help from ex-teammates Cronin, Gehringer and Rickey, may have been justifiable, well-intended and relatively innocent. But the enshrinement of Frankie Frisch's cronies clearly was not the latter, nor was Frisch's adamant opposition to the election of other players like outfielder Hack Wilson. Regardless of intent, the election of Manush and the momentum of the Haines-Bancroft-Hafey-Youngs selections of 1970–72 created a snowball effect that was unstoppable. Table 15 lists former players who have served on the Veterans Committee, their ex-teammates who've been chosen for Cooperstown by the panel during each man's tenure and the year of their "crony" elections. Through 2000, there have been only four former players who served as members of the Veterans Committee without having any of their one-time major-league teammates elected to Cooperstown — past members Monte Irvin, Billy Herman and Pee Wee Reese, plus newcomer Hank Aaron (that doesn't mean they didn't try; a couple may have, but just never succeeded).

Note that two of the men listed, Birdie Tebbetts and Bill White, are not Hall of Famers. Tebbetts had a fourteen-year career as a major-league catcher, was a manager for eleven seasons, and was added to the VC as a "former executive" for the latter capacity. White was a first baseman (1956–69) but earned his VC position as a former National League president. As noted earlier, Rickey also was a former player, whose committee membership stemmed from his lengthy front-office experience. Lopez (a Hall of Fame manager) and Irvin (one of the nine original Negro-league selections) also played in the majors. All of them are included on this list because they had big-league playing careers, although they were either not enshrined at all, or not for those roles.

TABLE 15
POSSIBLE "CRONY" SELECTIONS BY
THE VETERANS COMMITTEE, 1953–2000

Committee Member	VC Tenure	Former Teammates Elected
Branch Rickey	1953–65	Bobby Wallace (1953)
Charlie Gehringer	1953–90	Heinie Manush (1964), Goose Goslin (1968)
Joe Cronin	1961–84	Manush (1964), Goslin (1968)
Ted Williams	1966–	Earl Averill (1976), George Kell (1983), Bobby Doerr (1986)
Frankie Frisch	1967–72	Jesse Haines (1970), Dave Bancroft (1971), Chick Hafey (1971), Ross Youngs (1972)
Waite Hoyt	1971–76	Harry Hooper (1971), Lefty Gomez (1972), George Kelly (1973), Fred Lindstrom (1976)
Bill Terry	1971–76	Bancroft (1971), Youngs (1972), Kelly (1973), Lindstrom (1976)
Stan Musial	1973–	Johnny Mize (1981), Enos Slaughter (1985), Red Schoendienst (1989)
Burleigh Grimes	1977–85	Travis Jackson (1982), Arky Vaughan (1985)
Roy Campanella	1978–93	Pee Wee Reese (1984), Vaughan (1985)
Al Lopez	1978–94	Hack Wilson (1979), Vaughan (1985), Ernie Lombardi (1986)
Birdie Tebbetts	1979–94	George Kell (1983), Doerr (1986), Hal Newhouser (1992)
Monte Irvin	1983–98	none
Billy Herman	1991–92	none
Pee Wee Reese	1993–99	none
Yogi Berra	1994–	Phil Rizzuto (1994)
Bill White	1994–	Jim Bunning (1996)
Juan Marichal	1998–	Orlando Cepeda (1999)
Hank Aaron	2000–	none

Nine of these committee members—Rickey, Cronin, Frisch, Terry, Grimes, Lopez, Tebbetts, Williams and Berra—also served as managers, and you might expect that their apparent favoritism would've extended to men who had played for them at some time or another. But, discounting periods when some of them were player-managers, only two of their former players have been elected by the committee during any of their tenures. Outfielder Lloyd Waner was inducted in 1967 during Frisch's term on the committee, after playing for "the Fordham Flash" in Pittsburgh during 1940–41. Ironically, Frisch had traded Waner to the Braves early in 1941, Frankie's second season as the Pirates' skipper. Pitcher Hal Newhouser was elected in 1992 during Al Lopez's tenure on the panel and had played for "El Senor" at Cleveland during 1954–55, the last two seasons of Newhouser's career. But, similar to Waner's circumstance, Lopez had released Newhouser after just two pitching appearances in the 1955 campaign. So, when it comes to HOF voting, the bond between former teammates seems much stronger than that between manager and pupil.

Beyond exposing the Veterans Committee process to ongoing charges of favoritism, the inductions of Haines, Bancroft, Hafey, Youngs, Kelly and Lindstrom were among the panel's worst choices ever. Along with the election of Ray Schalk in 1955, their Hall of Fame memberships encouraged a spate of arguments implying that if one of them was good enough for Cooperstown, so were any number of other men who played the same positions or during the same era. So, their inductions energized the Marching-and-Chowder Societies of (among many others) players like pitchers Carl Mays, Paul Derringer and Mel Harder, first sackers Johnny Mize and Charlie Grimm, third baseman Stan Hack, outfielders Hack Wilson, Chuck Klein, Lefty O'Doul and Babe Herman, plus catchers Rick Ferrell and Ernie Lombardi to press for the election of their favorite candidate — as all of these advocates could claim, many with justification, that their choice had better Cooperstown credentials than Schalk or any of the Frisch-Terry-Hoyt "Crony Six." Inevitably, some of those advocacies also succeeded: Wilson was elected by the VC in 1979 (with Frisch no longer around to scuttle his candidacy); Klein was chosen the following year; Mize was tabbed in 1981; Ferrell in 1984; and Lombardi in 1986.

In turn, the same type of "if, then" argument was later applied to men from other eras and likely influenced the VC elections of guys like Post-war-Era infielders George Kell and Pee Wee Reese in 1983–84, and Dead-Ball-Era pitcher Vic Willis in 1995. No doubt, committee members themselves are reduced to using such "if, then" arguments in their debates on the merits of various candidates.

Clearly, that very situation occurred with the 1994 election of shortstop Phil Rizzuto, whose induction also merits scrutiny as evidence of the absurd level of politicking that often influences VC selections. Without repeating all the data from chapters 2 and 3, recall that Rizzuto was an integral part of many pennant and World Series winners with New York, that he won one AL MVP, was released by the Yankees at midseason in 1956, almost immediately joined their broadcast team, and — although he got one technically illegitimate vote in that same year — first became eligible for the BBWAA ballot in 1962, receiving 27.5 percent support.

While serving as a Yankee announcer, Rizzuto watched his HOF vote totals grow from forty-four in 1962 to 103 a decade later. Although Phil was once quoted as saying, "I never thought I deserved to be in the Hall of Fame," whether or not he meant it, it's safe to say that — like any of us who are human beings with feelings — the increased votes must have raised his private hopes for eventual election. In 1973 his vote total went up to 111, raising those hopes a little more, but stalled at the same number the following year, no doubt lowering them a bit. In 1975, his next-to-last year of BBWAA eligibility, Rizzuto's total climbed again (barely) to 117, representing 32.3 percent support. At that point, if he's a realist, Phil probably realized that it was far more likely the Arctic ice caps would melt all at once than that he would somehow double his support level and be elected in his final year on the ballot. In 1976, typical of many candidates in their last year of BBWAA eligibility, his vote total climbed to 149 — but that was equal to only 38.4 percent support, barely half the amount required for induction.

By the time Rizzuto's BBWAA eligibility expired, he'd been a Yankee broadcaster for two decades. He was an affable and visible personality in the nation's biggest city and (at the time) — much like his Hall of Famer teammates, Joe DiMaggio, Yogi Berra and Mickey Mantle — a living symbol of the glory days of its greatest sports franchise, the most successful in baseball history. Beyond Phil's achievements as a player, he had re-legitimized the once trite "Holy Cow!" among the East Coast vernacular (although Harry Caray deserves more credit for revitalizing the phrase among America as a whole), and a lot of people liked him. As a result, by 1979 (perhaps earlier) it was rare to watch or hear a Yankees broadcast in which Rizzuto's fellow announcers, one of whom was Bill White, failed to lament how it was a shame that "the Scooter" had been overlooked for the Hall of Fame and how they hoped that — when Phil became eligible for the VC process — the committee would enshrine their much-deserving buddy. Apparently, it didn't matter to them back then that there were lots of other players better qualified for Cooperstown than Rizzuto. It didn't matter that, at the time, there were other shortstops in baseball history — George Davis, Bill Dahlen, Arky Vaughan, Pee Wee Reese, Herman Long and Vern Stephens among them — whose credentials for the Shrine were as good or better than Phil's. It didn't even matter that other Yankees from the Scooter's era — second baseman Joe Gordon, plus pitchers Spud Chandler and Allie Reynolds, for instance — had as much or more claim to be in the Hall as Rizzuto did.

Rizzuto became eligible for VC consideration in 1983. His fellow announcers continued to blow Phil's cornet for him, and his candidacy also picked up support from some influential New York sportswriters. But, the campaign for the Scooter really got going in 1984, when the committee voted to enshrine Reese, his crosstown contemporary at the same position for the Dodgers. At that point, among the New York media, Rizzuto's absence from Cooperstown evolved from being a mere oversight to an absurd injustice — in part, no doubt, because the carpetbagging Dodgers had left town almost three decades earlier (and, therefore, no longer deserved any loyalty from New Yorkers), and because the committee that elected Pee Wee had included his former Brooklyn teammate Roy Campanella, plus Reese's longtime National League playing rival Stan Musial, both of whom were his most likely advocates in the pre-voting discussion. It also didn't matter to the New York writers that they had been part of the BBWAA electorate which, over the years of the two men's front-door eligibility, had given far more votes to Reese than to Rizzuto (1782 to 1154, a 54 percent difference).

By 1993, almost a decade after Reese's induction, Rizzuto still had to buy a ticket to get into Cooperstown. But, the campaign for Phil had grown so loud that, in that year, Bill James devoted much of *The Politics of Glory* to analysis of the Scooter's credentials—concluding that, in the event of Rizzuto's election, the Hall already had several members who were less qualified (a position that was hardly an endorsement and revealed a sense of resignation about the inevitability of Phil's election). Sure enough, after Campanella's death that year, there were a couple openings on the committee that were filled by Yogi Berra (Rizzuto's former teammate) and Bill White (his ex–broadcast partner), and Rizzuto was promptly enshrined by the panel in 1994. Clearly, the coincident timing of Berra and White's appointments, plus the crescendo of media politicking on Rizzuto's behalf, tipped the scales in favor of the Scooter's election; and, it's probable that, as Phil's most likely advocates on the panel, Berra and White both must've argued that if Reese was in Cooperstown, Rizzuto belonged there too.

The lingering effects of cronyism and its attendant politicking are threefold. First, they encourage individual VC members to become — perhaps with good intentions—spokesmen for their former playing buddies rather than staunch advocates for a high standard for HOF membership. In turn, odds are that over the long run — whenever they succeed — most crony selections will lower the subjective standards for Cooperstown rather than raise them (and one can argue, with much merit, that most of the inductees listed in Table 15 lowered Cooperstown's undefined minimum standard at their respective positions). Finally, all of this extends the apparent legitimacy of "if, then" rationales to a whole new set of players whose candidacies would not, otherwise, deserve serious consideration. So, as a result, rather than correct the oversights and injustices among the Hall of Fame roster, the panel's behavior actually multiplies and exacerbates them.

Another problem with the Veterans Committee has been that there is no enforced term of office. Currently, committee members are supposed to serve no more than two three-year terms, but that limit has only been on the books for a decade (or less), and through 2000 no one had ever been required to leave the panel after six years of service. So, in reality, membership has been open ended, like appointment to the U.S. Supreme Court. Once on the committee, a man could stay until he chose to leave or died in office, whichever came first. The longest term ever on the VC to date was that of Charles Segar, a member of the original panel of 1953, who remained on the committee for four decades, through the early 1990s. Some of the former players and executives who've been VC members stepped down before their deaths: ex-commissioner Ford Frick, who served during 1966–69, died in 1978; Bill Terry was on the committee during 1971–76, but lived until 1989; and Waite Hoyt, who served during the same years as Terry, passed away in 1984. But many others have stayed until they knew that death was at their door or the Reaper actually came and took them: Warren Giles (on the committee during 1953–78) died within a year after stepping down; Frisch lived for only a short time after his auto accident; and Branch Rickey, Joe Cronin, Burleigh Grimes, Billy Herman, Roy Campanella and Pee Wee Reese all died in office, as have others.

The trouble with open-ended membership isn't the disruption caused by people dying on the job, because that happens in every line of work. But, it guarantees that — regardless of a man's age at the time of his appointment — the committee will always, inevitably, comprise very old men. The nineteen former major-league players who have served on the VC at some time since 1953 had an average age of sixty-six at the time of their appointments. The oldest at the time he joined (1977) was Burleigh Grimes, who was a mere eighty-three; and the next-oldest, Billy Herman, was a spry eighty-one when he came on in 1991. In comparison, the youngest ex-player ever named to the committee was Charlie Gehringer, who was just forty-nine when he joined the original VC in 1953, and only a couple others have been as young as their early fifties. Among the

former big-league executives who've served on the panel (excluding Branch
Rickey, who was counted among the ex-players for this purpose), Ford
Frick was seventy-one at the time of his appointment, Will Harridge was
sixty-nine, Gabe Paul sixty-seven and Warren Giles a relative toddler at
fifty-six — so, an average in the mid–sixties probably applies to all the non-
player members too.

On one hand, the advanced age of these men seems appropriate,
because the members are required to weigh the credentials of candidates
from the distant past, and older men are — or should be — more likely to
have some firsthand knowledge about such players' skills. That argument
even made some sense in 1953, because a man who was seventy or older
at the time (like Branch Rickey) could have seen most of this century's
best players in action. But, the logic falters today when you realize there
is no way that even very old men of the millennium can have any firsthand, observational knowledge about many of the candidates who fall
under the VC's current purview.

For example, the oldest former big-league players on the panel for
the 1998 voting were Ted Williams and Pee Wee Reese, both born in 1918.
One of the committee's selections in 1998 was a former Negro-league
teammate of panel member Buck O'Neil, "Bullet" Joe Rogan, whose pitching career ended with the Kansas City Monarchs of 1938, one year before
Williams, and two seasons before Reese entered the majors. Another 1998
selection was shortstop George Davis, whose major-league playing career
ended in 1909, almost a decade before Williams and Reese were born. It's
probable that the panel's two former Negro leaguers, O'Neil (who was
born in 1911, played just two seasons with Rogan on the Monarchs, and
was eighty-six years old at the time of Bullet Joe's election) and Monte
Irvin (who was born in 1919 and also witnessed only the last two seasons
of Rogan's playing career), were the only committee members with more
than hearsay knowledge about Bullet Joe's skills, and it's certain that no
one on the 1998 committee who wasn't at least 110 years old could con-
tribute an iota of observational expertise to any discussion of Davis' credentials.

Granted, many of the VC's selections in the 1990s were men whose
careers came after World War II, and the former players on the committee who voted in 1998 — Stan Musial, Williams, Reese, Berra, White and
Irvin (who resigned and was replaced by Juan Marichal after the 1998 election) were all familiar with their skills. But, during the decade, in addition to Davis and Rogan, the panel also enshrined Vic Willis (whose career
spanned 1898–1910), William Hulbert (one of the founders of the National
League, who became its president in 1877), Bill Foster (a Negro leaguer

who last pitched for the Chicago American Giants in 1938 and — like Rogan — stopped playing before anyone on the committee reached the majors), and Ned Hanlon (a National League outfielder of the 1880s, cited for a managerial career of 1889–1907). Most of the VC members of the 1990s could've had no more firsthand knowledge about any of these men than they did about Davis or Rogan.

The situation repeated in the 2000 voting. With Buzzy Bavasi's resignation and the death of Pee Wee Reese, there were two openings on the panel. They were replaced, respectively, by former executive John McHale (born in 1921) and Hank Aaron (1934). The committee failed to elect any player from the main group of eligibles but did enshrine former Negro leaguer Norman "Turkey" Stearnes, who retired as a player in 1940, and nineteenth-century second baseman Bid McPhee, whose career spanned 1882–99. McHale was not yet old enough to vote when Stearnes hung up his spikes, and Aaron was a kid in first grade.

If none of the VC members were old enough to have any real expertise about the careers of Davis, Willis, Hulbert, Hanlon, McPhee and others, what made them any more qualified to judge their merits than another ex-player who was forty-five years old instead, or an active player who was twenty-six? More seriously, how were any of these esteemed "elders" intrinsically better suited to pass judgment on any of those candidates than a baseball historian or statistician of any age? After all, if there is no one around old enough to know anything meaningful about a man, the merits of his specific credentials become a matter of (1) separating the historical truth from the folklore about his career and (2) comparing his available statistics to those of any others under consideration, to the other players of his period, and to men who played at his specific position, regardless of era. Arguably, baseball historians are equally or better suited to do the former task, and statisticians are certainly better qualified for the latter.

The age of the committee members is not the VC's only time-related problem. Unavoidably, most of its inductees are old men too, and many of them have already been embalmed. Table 16 comprises a Hall of Fame actuarial, comparing the number of men elected by the BBWAA since 1936 (all of them as players) and by the committee since 1953 (including players only), the ages of the youngest and oldest men chosen by each group, the number of men who fell within various age ranges at the time of their election, their average age at the time of selection, the number of inductees who were living or dead at the time of their election, and the average number of years they had to wait between their retirements as players and selection for Cooperstown.

TABLE 16
HALL OF FAME ACTUARIAL

Actuarial Factor	BBWAA	Vets
Number Elected	93	68
Age of Youngest Inductee	36	61
Age of Oldest Inductee	70	140
Number, Ages 36–49	56	0
Number, Ages 50–59	29	0
Number, Ages 60–69	7	20
Number, Ages 70–79	1	29
Number, Age 80 or More	0	19
Average Age at Induction	49.5	80.7
Number Living	87	47
Number Dead	6	21
Avg. Wait after Retirement	9.6	43.4

Historically, 60 percent of the men elected by the BBWAA are younger than fifty at the time of their selection, while an even larger majority of those chosen by the Veterans Committee (71 percent) are age seventy or more. The writers' youngest inductee was Lou Gehrig, elected at age thirty-six; its oldest was Cy Young, chosen at seventy. The youngest men tabbed by the VC for their careers as players were Lloyd Waner, George Kell and Orlando Cepeda, all of whom were sixty-one; its oldest player chosen was Bid McPhee, who would've been 140 years old if he'd still been breathing at the time of his 2000 election. In all, the BBWAA has elected only eight men over the age of fifty-nine. The Vets have yet to pick anyone that young, but have chosen thirteen would-be centenarians, none of whom were alive for the post-ceremony photos. About 31 percent of the VC's player selections were dead at the time of their election, whereas only 7 percent of the men tabbed by the BBWAA have not been around to give their induction speeches. Excluding Negro leaguers, if Table 16 also included the data for the VC inductees chosen for their non-playing achievements, the panel's totals there would be skewed even further into geriatric and morbid extremes: although the ages of those men add only one year to the VC's average at induction, almost half of them were dead at the time they were chosen; and, the oldest man ever elected to Cooperstown, William Hulbert, would've been 163 when he was enshrined in 1995.

Of course, none of the data in Table 16 is surprising, given the separate eligibility rules for the Hall of Fame's two sets of electors. The BBWAA chooses only players, presumably the men whose credentials are impeccable, and starts voting on each of them five years after their retirement. In contrast, although the rules have been changed several times since 1953, the Veterans Committee is currently prohibited from considering anyone whose BBWAA eligibility has not been expired for at least three years. Because eligibility for the writers' ballot lasts a maximum of fifteen years, the VC cannot weigh the credentials of any player who has not been retired for twenty-three seasons. Using a different approach, the 185 players elected to Cooperstown through 2000 had an average career length of 17.6 seasons. So, if they got to the majors at age twenty-one, and retired at about thirty-seven or eight, then the ones who were not elected by the BBWAA must usually wait until they are about sixty before they become eligible for the VC process.

These actuarial circumstances inject a tremendous amount of pressure into the Hall of Fame selection process, little of which is ever felt by the BBWAA (because it is not the Hall's court of last resort), and almost all of which falls upon the Veterans Committee (because it is). Understandably, men who believe they deserve HOF recognition do not want to die before they've been inducted; and, as a result, the VC members feel some obligation to select candidates who are still available to enjoy the reward. That pressure is increased by the fact that living honorees draw more spectators to the induction ceremony than dead ones do, so there's a built-in economic motive too.

Arguable examples of that pressure are evident from the beginning of, and throughout, the VC process. Its first two player selections in 1953 were both alive at the time — Bobby Wallace (of the .268 career batting average) and 212-career-win pitcher Charley Bender. Wallace was tabbed before fellow shortstops Monte Ward (elected in 1964) and George Davis (1998), both of whom were already dead in 1953 but had better subjective credentials than Wallace did (although Ward's are muddled by the fact he spent the first six years of his career as a pitcher). Bender was chosen at least a decade ahead of four different three-hundred-plus-win hurlers that were also dead in 1953 — John Clarkson, Tim Keefe, Pud Galvin and Mickey Welch. Later examples include, but are not limited to, the elections of living outfielders Elmer Flick (1963) and Earle Combs (1970) ahead of Sam Thompson (who died in 1922 and was enshrined in 1974).

Regardless of its kind intentions (or financial motivation), the impulse to induct living men who can appreciate and enjoy their honor ahead of dead men who cannot attend the ceremony corrupts the Veterans Committee process because it compromises the panel's primary purpose — to correct oversights in the BBWAA voting. An oversight is an oversight. If a man deserves to be in Cooperstown but was not chosen by the BBWAA, the fact that he is dead does not diminish or erase the level of that injustice. If anything, it should be a motive for hastening his election, because — in any venue — justice delayed is never justice served.

One of the VC's 1998 inductees, George Davis, is a case in point. Davis died in 1940 at age seventy, just four years after the Hall of Fame process began. Somehow, he never got a vote from the OTC1 in 1936 or from the BBWAA before 1939. Whether or not that absence of support caused him any anguish during the last four years of his life, after 1940 he was no longer around to blow his own cornet; until very recently, there was no one else playing it for him either; and, for most of the Hall's first sixty years, he was a very good, but largely forgotten ballplayer from around the turn of the century. In all, seventeen other shortstops were enshrined at Cooperstown ahead of Davis, seven by the BBWAA (including Ernie Banks, who actually played more games during his career at first base, but is listed as a shortstop on the HOF roster) and ten by the veterans panel or one of its predecessors. But a thoughtful look at Davis's career statistics in the context of his time shows that he was a more-deserving candidate than several of the shortstops enshrined much earlier by the VC or its progenitors (certainly better than Dave Bancroft, Phil Rizzuto, Joe Tinker or Bobby Wallace), and just as deserving as some of the men from the same position elected by the scribes (Luis Aparicio and Rabbit Maranville, at minimum). The selection of living but inferior players ahead of him was statistically unjustifiable, and the fact that he slipped through the selection process without getting elected for over sixty years is another indictment of the system's lack of objective standards.

Despite all this, there has been one positive effect from the Veterans Committee's formation. Its removal from the OTC2's dual responsibility to serve as Hall of Fame trustees allowed for (gradual, if not immediate) clarification of the separate jurisdictions of the committee and the BBWAA and over time has at least eliminated disputes between the Hall's two elective organs regarding who is eligible for consideration by either panel (but not necessarily who should be). In the best of worlds, that would've ended further friction between the VC and the writers.

But it hasn't worked out that way. Over the first four decades of the VC's tenure the BBWAA became increasingly annoyed by the widespread perception — among the writers and Church-of-Baseball faithful, alike — that the committee was lowering the Hall's overall standards by electing the scribes' rejects. Some of the writers' agitation may have resulted from ongoing unhappiness over having to share their privileged franchise with another organ. After all, over time the VC and its predecessors have

George Davis, shown here with the White Sox around 1908, compiled better over-all career statistics than many of the eighteen other shortstops who've been elected to Cooperstown. But Davis never received a Hall of Fame vote from the BBWAA, and he was not enshrined until 1998 — almost ninety years after he retired and nearly sixty years after his death — when no one on the Veterans Committee that elected him had any firsthand observational knowledge of his skills. (Photograph from *The Sporting News*)

chosen sixty-three more Cooperstown members than the BBWAA; and, no doubt, there are many among the scribes who feel the committee's jurisdiction always should've been limited to consideration of men who served in non-playing capacities. But the VC shares fault for the schism, because it's also certain that its susceptibility to cronyism and politicking, and its preference for the living over the dead, have prompted the elections of many men whose presence among the Cooperstown roster have lowered the institution's undefined standards over time.

Again, none of that might've happened if the OTC1 had fulfilled its initial mandate (thereby setting nominal, albeit informal standards for nineteenth-century inductees) and if the BBWAA itself had not failed to elect several deserving twentieth-century players like Sam Crawford. So, both organs share responsibility for lowering Cooperstown's standards, and the ongoing schism between them has been a pot-and-black-kettle dispute.

Unfortunately, that ongoing conflict came to a head in the early 1990s, at the same time that the Hall's trustees and electors were forced to confront the ugliest and most divisive eligibility issue in the Shrine's history. Even worse, because politics inevitably determined the outcome, the compromise that resulted not only denied the prospect of Hall of Fame status to one of baseball's all-time greats, but radically altered the selection process in a manner that — barring subsequent changes — assures inadequate representation among the HOF roster for all major-league players since World War II.

8

Regardless of the Verdict of Juries

Jackson, Cicotte, Williams, Gandil, Risberg, Felsch, McMullin and Weaver. Boyer, Kuenn, Lolich, Maris, Mazeroski, Oliva, Santo, Tiant and Wills. Although they sound like the names of two grossly over-partnered, ambulance-chasing law firms, they are just two lists of ballplayers separated by time. All of the first group, the eight Chicago Black Sox who conspired to throw the 1919 World Series, last appeared in the majors in 1920. The significance of the second bunch will take a while to clarify, but among the latter, the first to reach the Show (Harvey Kuenn) began his career in 1952, and the last to retire (Luis Tiant) left it three decades later. They are connected historically, however, by two threads—one comprised of shame and embarrassment, the other of expedient stupidity—tied together by a guy called Charlie Hustle.

Although they were acquitted in a 1921 court of law, we all know that at least six of the Black Sox were guilty, nonetheless. After all, their trial took place in Chicago, in the early days of Prohibition and Al Capone, when many city officials were available at a reasonable price to anyone possessing sufficient cash or a political IOU. So it's not surprising that signed confessions disappeared, key witnesses were never forced to testify, the defendants behaved throughout the trial as though they were guests of honor at a speakeasy celebration, or that after the verdict the eight players actually partied in the same private club as the jurors.

Kenesaw Mountain Landis practiced law in Chicago as early as 1891 and—after his appointment by Teddy Roosevelt—served as a federal judge

119

there during 1905–20. He knew how the city worked. Within the scope of his jurist's wisdom, he also knew what was best for baseball, even when the game's owners didn't. So, when the short-lived (1914–15) Federal League's antitrust suit against Organized Baseball was assigned to his court in 1915, he simply stalled any ruling—giving the game's owners time to work out a settlement with the FL brass that obviated any legal decision. Some might claim that Landis's inaction represented nothing more than judicial prudence; maybe it was. But, only the truly naive—the Gomer Pyles of the world—could also believe that it had no connection to his appointment as baseball commissioner in November 1920, just two months after the Black Sox first made nationwide headlines.

Landis was anything but naive, and he also knew that the Black Sox were guilty—in his mind all of them. Some of that attitude must've come from his knowledge of how Chicago worked. But his stance as commissioner regarding the accused players also evolved from the fact that he was born too late to serve his true calling. As evidenced by the harsh sentences he'd given to World War I pacifists and leftists of the Bolshevik era, he should've been a hanging judge in the Old West, like Roy Bean, the only law west of the Pecos (although Landis probably never kept a portrait of Lilly Langtry on the wall of his chambers). So, it's also not surprising that—on the day after the Black Sox were acquitted—Chicago newspapers carried the instant edict of baseball's new czar:

> Regardless of the verdict of juries, no player who throws a ballgame, no player that undertakes or promises to throw a ballgame, no player that sits in conference with a bunch of crooked players and gamblers where the ways and means of throwing a game are discussed and does not promptly tell his club about it, will ever play professional baseball.

The message was clear. Under Landis, justice (or retribution) would be swift and due process irrelevant. Of course, the old gent could still be politely, if disingenuously, civil: months later, when Buck Weaver first entered Landis's office to plead his (relative) innocence and petition for reinstatement to the game, the judge displayed a warm demeanor, invited Buck to sit comfortably, and offered the Black Sox third sacker a chaw of tobacco. One-on-one, Landis even sounded sympathetic to Weaver's plea, but gave him no direct answer. Soon after Buck left, the man named for an 1864 Civil War battle in Georgia gave his formal response as commissioner to the press: "Birds of a feather flock together. Men associating with gamblers and crooks could expect no leniency." In other words, hang 'em high boys, and don't waste much good rope.

Banishments were not new to baseball. Four players with the National League's second-place Louisville franchise — Bill Craver, Jim Devlin, George Hall and Al Nichols — had been barred from the sport following a game-fixing scandal in 1877, the circuit's second year in existence, and NL umpire Dick Higham, a former player, was also dismissed for shady actions in 1882. But, as evidenced by the 402-error career of first baseman Hal Chase, who was accused by his New York Highlanders manager George Stallings of throwing games as early as 1910, any deterrent effect from those blacklistings was gone by then, perhaps much sooner.

But the Black Sox were really just Act Two of a three-part drama that began soon after their 1919 series loss to Cincinnati, months before their fix first made headlines or Landis took office. Act One took place during the 1919–20 offseason, while rumors of the thrown series spread among baseball people and journalists. The well-traveled Chase, two of his Giants teammates — pitcher Jean Dubuc and third baseman Heinie Zimmerman (a near-triple crown winner for the Cubs of 1912) — and Cubbie outfielder Lee Magee all were quietly released by their teams and soon found they could no longer interest any other clubs in their services. They all had been suspected of involvement in Chase's game-fixing (although Dubuc was allowed to return to the majors as a coach for Detroit in 1930–31, still on Kenesaw's watch). Among them, only Magee was combative enough to fight his obvious blacklisting, and he sued the Cubs, the National League and its president John Heydler. The civil trial, which ended before the series fix ever made the papers, revealed that Magee and Chase had both bet against their own teams during 1919, so the jury ruled against Magee.

The crookedness in baseball had gained its first major exposure. But it also was obvious from the method of the four players' fates that the baseball owners' preference was to hide the dirtiness in the game as much as possible — for reasons of economics, if nothing else. As the 1920 campaign progressed, with Babe Ruth on his way to a record fifty-four-homer season, and the Yankees, Indians and White Sox waging a three-way battle for the American League pennant, attendance soared and no one wanted to jeopardize the motion of turnstiles. In August, however, the game received two more blows: Cleveland shortstop Ray Chapman died just hours after his beaning by the Yanks' Carl Mays at the Polo Grounds on the sixteenth; and then, on the thirty-first, Chicago president Bill Veeck, Sr., received a telegram from Detroit prior to a game between his also-ran Cubs and the more-hapless Phillies indicating thousands of dollars had been wagered that Chicago would lose that day behind its scheduled pitcher Claude Hendrix. Veeck and manager Fred Mitchell decided to go with future Hall of Famer Grover Alexander instead, offering Alex a $500 bonus if he won the game and never again mentioned the incident. The Cubs lost, nonetheless, and by 4 September, after an anonymous letter was received by the Chicago *Herald and Examiner*, news of the attempted fix had gone public.

The Cubs-Phillies incident prompted grand jury proceedings in Chicago, at which the presiding judge, Charles MacDonald, recommended investigation of the rumors that the previous year's World Series, involving the other Chicago team, had also been thrown. Baseball could no longer ignore its ultimate embarrassment or sweep it under the rug. The owners mutually agreed in secret to clean their house (although, no doubt, reluctantly), and Landis was hired in November to serve as the game's high-profile maid service, with absolute authority — an omnipotent Mr. Clean.

The judge's first exercise of that power came in March 1921, five months before the Black Sox verdict, when he issued a lifetime banishment to Phillies first sacker Gene Paulette for consorting with gamblers. About the same time, he barred Giants outfielder Benny Kauff, who had been the Federal circuit's biggest star before it folded. Kauff, who owned an auto dealership with his half-brother, had been arrested and charged with receiving stolen cars, and — in predictable necktie-party fashion — Landis decreed that the indictment itself evidenced Benny's probable guilt. Kauff was later acquitted and petitioned for reinstatement, but Landis turned him down (so much for due process, again). In June of that year Landis also banned Reds pitcher Ray Fisher for life, not for any gambling misdeed, but simply because he had violated his reserve-clause contract by negotiating with an "outlaw" team that wasn't part of Organized Baseball (so much for individual economic freedom as well; one is grateful that Curt Flood didn't play during the Landis era too).

The commissioner's dictatorial actions, along with the banishments of the nineteenth century, set ample precedent for his decision on the Black Sox, which was announced on 3 August 1921. By the end of the 1925 season, six other men — second sacker Joe Gedeon, outfielder Jimmy O'Connell, pitchers Phil Douglas, Claude Hendrix and Hubert "Dutch" Leonard (whose career had included a record-low 0.96 earned run average in 1914), along with coach Cozy Dolan (a former player) — also had been blacklisted for alleged betting involvements. In addition, four former big leaguers — Babe Borton, Gene Dale, Harl Maggert and Tom Seaton — were also banned for similar suspicions.

But again, the owners' attempt to quietly blacklist Chase and his pals in 1920 had evidenced their preferred response to scandal; and, by the end of Landis's McCarthy-like purge, which occurred at the same time that

American government was shaken by the Teapot Dome embarrassments to the administrations of presidents Warren Harding and Calvin Coolidge, baseball moguls and fans alike were no doubt just as tired of scandal in general as later generations of Americans grew weary of hearing about Watergate, the Iran-Contra affair, Monica Lewinsky and cigars. So there had to be fears among much of the game's leadership that the sport — like a tired, battered boxer in the late rounds — could not withstand many more blows.

The curtain rose on Act Three in November 1926, when Ty Cobb was released as manager by Detroit and, a month later, Tris Speaker resigned as Cleveland's skipper, supposedly to enter private business. At the time, Tigers owner Frank Navin justified Cobb's dismissal with claims that the Detroit team was demoralized under his leadership — a valid reason for letting any pilot go, but also one that, given Cobb's personality, might've been equally true in any of his six years as skipper. Speaker's resignation was harder to fathom, however, because the thirty-eight-year-old player-manager had batted .304, with 164 hits and 86 RBI that season, hardly evidence that his baseball skills were in decline. Also, the Indians had gone 88–66 in 1926, finishing second to the Yankees by just three games, and in Speaker's eight years as Cleveland pilot the club had won one pennant, finished second and third twice each, and posted .543 winning percentage (the Tigers had been 79–75 in 1926, but finished in sixth place, twelve games behind New York).

The closely timed departures of the two immortals raised another red flag, prompting speculation by sportswriters. Just before Christmas, Landis was compelled to announce that both men had been "permitted to resign" after allegations by former Tigers hurler Dutch Leonard — banned after the 1925 season — that the three of them, along with Cleveland's Smoky Joe Wood (by then retired and coaching baseball at Yale), had conspired to fix a Detroit-Tribe game on 25 September 1919 and had placed bets on the contest's outcome (Speaker was the Indians' manager that year, but Cobb did not become the Tigers' skipper until 1921). As substantiating evidence, Leonard had given American League president Ban Johnson letters he'd written to Cobb and Wood, explaining their winnings on the wagers, and Johnson had passed the letters to Landis. In making the announcement, Landis obfuscated that the incident had not come up before because "none of the men involved is now associated with baseball," and indicated that his ruling on the matter would follow during the winter.

Soon, Black Sox shortstop Swede Risberg asserted in a published interview from Minnesota that Cobb and other Detroit players had also agreed, at the price of $1,100 (about $45 from each Chicago player), to throw two doubleheaders to help the (then still White) Sox clinch the 1917 pennant, and banished first sacker Chick Gandil chimed in from California to back up Risberg's story, admitting that he had personally collected the money from each of his teammates and served as the Tigers' paymaster. Risberg even claimed that Sox management, including pilot Pants Rowland and owner Charles Comiskey, had known about that fix. Beyond those two, the claim also implicated, by innuendo, Chicago players like Eddie Collins and Ray Schalk (two of the supposedly honest heroes of the 1919 series scandal), along with Red Faber (who was injured and didn't pitch in the tainted fall classic), each of whom — like Cobb, Speaker and Comiskey — were later elected to Cooperstown.

Once all of this hit the fan, Landis was compelled to hold hearings on the matter. About thirty players from the 1917 Tigers and White Sox appeared before the commissioner in early January 1927. With Risberg and Gandil in attendance, they admitted that Detroit players had received money from the Sox in 1917 but claimed — in unison, and despite the fact the Tigers had lost all four games of the two doubleheaders in question — that the money was actually a grateful reward to the Bengals for having defeated Boston, Chicago's closest pennant contender, in a separate late-season series. A week later, after a couple of team owners had sworn that the practice was common, Landis announced his finding that the money had been a "gift fund ... an act of impropriety ... but not an act of criminality," and ruled that everyone involved was exonerated. He also decreed that, henceforth, there would be a five-year statute of limitations on all baseball offenses.

Without doubt, Ban Johnson, at least, had believed Leonard's allegation and felt as early as September 1926 that there was ample evidence to warrant Cobb and Speaker's banishments. After the story broke, the AL president even asserted that neither man would ever play in the circuit again while he was in charge. That almost proved true, but not as Johnson had intended it: Cobb and Speaker both played in the league in 1927–28; but Johnson — who had feuded constantly with several owners and criticized Landis's handling of the affair — was forced out as AL president in July 1927.

But, Leonard's letters to Cobb and Wood contained no clear linkage between the wagers discussed and the 1919 contest in question. In turn, Cobb denied having thrown any game, ever, and claimed that Dutch's charges were motivated by anger over the pitcher's release from the club. In turn, Speaker denied any knowledge of the incident, noting that he had never received any letter from the hurler and was not even mentioned in either of those provided by Leonard as evidence. So, because Leonard had also refused to come from California for a formal hearing on the matter, Johnson had honored a request by the two living legends to resign from baseball without one, in order to spare their families — and, more importantly, the game itself — any embarrassment.

Predictably, when Landis's ruling on the 1917 Chicago-Detroit "gift" left Cobb and Speaker hanging on Leonard's allegation, they both rescinded their resignations and hired attorneys. In late January Landis held another hearing, the result of which (given his recently decreed statute of limitations) was a foregone conclusion — both were acquitted. The decision pleased the public, whose incredulity about the charges was typified by humorist Will Rogers, who quipped that if Cobb and Speaker had "been selling out all these years, I would like to have seen them when they wasn't selling."

Today, no one who ever knew the whole truth about Act Three remains alive, allowing only for speculation. Perhaps, as some contend, Leonard's allegation was entirely contrived, due — as Cobb argued — to personal animosity for Detroit's pilot. But, if that was Dutch's motive, why did he also implicate Speaker and Wood, unless he hoped they might crack under pressure and admit to roles in a real incident? Risberg and Gandil's claims also can be seen as two "birds of a feather" standing up for another from the same flock (Leonard), with a concocted story motivated by five years of resentment for their own banishments and a desire to restore some of their sullied credibility.

But, Gandil is known to have instigated the World Series fix among the Black Sox players, so it's obvious that he, at least, was never slow-witted, and it would not have taken him five years to dream up such a lie — which had no direct bearing on Leonard's charge. If Chick was a total slime, it's just as likely he would've told his fable in 1921, at the time of his own exile, for the very same motive — like a child caught in the act, who attempts to justify inappropriate behavior by claiming someone else who wasn't caught did it too, and also should be punished. Beyond all that, historian Harold Seymour also has demonstrated that Ban Johnson was aware that the doubleheaders may have been fixed as early as October 1919; that catcher Ray Schalk had discussed the Chicago-Detroit payoff with Landis in 1921; and that Black Sox center fielder Happy Felsch had made allegations identical to those by Risberg and Gandil in a 1922 suit against Charles Comiskey.

Given self-preservation as the players' motives, the most curious actor in the drama was Landis. The fact that he went public with the story, while Johnson was apparently trying to keep it quiet, at first seems consistent with the actions of both men before and after the Black Sox revelations.

But, throughout the hearings of January 1927, Landis behaved as though all of the charges had been unexpected news to him — and that was clearly not the case. The judge's stiff sentences of war-era leftists and heavy-handed treatments of Benny Kauff and Ray Fisher indicate Landis may have been even more autocratic and judgmental than his gambling banishments appear. So, there's no doubt that, absent another motive, he was capable of being just as harsh to Cobb and Speaker, regardless of their status as living legends. But Landis exonerated both, allowing them to continue their careers, albeit with different clubs: Cobb went to the A's for 1927–28; Speaker moved to Washington for 1927 then joined the Georgia Peach in Philly the following year, both men's last in the majors. Oddly, however, neither Cobb nor Speaker — both of whom were under forty and (in the latter's case, at least) should've been desirable as skippers to some team or another — ever managed again.

On the other hand, Landis's handling of the Federal League suit and face-to-face demeanor with Buck Weaver also demonstrated that the judge was fully capable of duplicity, whenever it met his needs. In that light, his most telling comment during the affair was an offhand complaint that "Won't these ... damn things that happened before I came into baseball ever stop coming up?" — clearly an indication of his exasperation with the ongoing scandals and an obvious motive for adopting his conveniently five-year statute of limitations sixty-two months after he took office.

Above all else, it's hard to comprehend why, if they were as innocent as Landis's verdict implied, and upon their initial confrontation by Johnson, it was that Cobb and Speaker — especially someone as combative as the former — would've agreed at first to resign so meekly without a fight or some kind of due process. So, it seems possible that a substantial portion of the Leonard-Risberg-Gandil accusations were true; that the commissioner, along with many owners, believed the game could not survive another Black Sox–magnitude embarrassment, especially one involving such high-profile players; and that a deal was cut with Cobb and Speaker that allowed them to continue their playing careers (only) and spared baseball another major humiliation.

All of this has serious implications for the Hall of Fame. If, as Leonard alleged, Cobb and Speaker had any involvement in throwing or betting on the 1919 game, or were aware of a plot to do so without telling their respective club officials, then — by the standards of Landis's 1921 Black Sox edict and the contents of the Hall's 1945 morality clause — they should have been banned from baseball and later barred from Cooperstown, just like Joe Jackson and the other Black Sox. Also, if the Risberg-Gandil-Felsch story had any truth to it, and Cobb, Collins, Schalk, Faber or (even) Charles

Comiskey had any knowledge of the fixed doubleheaders, then consistency also demands that the same treatment should've applied to them as well. Beyond that, the commissioner's 1927 statute of limitations, enacted chiefly for the judge's convenience, is a lame rationale for letting anyone off the hook — except, perhaps, Speaker (because he was not mentioned in Leonard's letters, and it's curious that Dutch would've had the foresight to save copies of those written to Cobb and Wood but not the "Gray Eagle"). All of the alleged transgressions took place during 1917–19; and, although the Black Sox were "caught" in 1921, it's also clear that Landis knew (from Ray Schalk) that the doubleheaders may have been fixed during that same year. In that light, the fates of the Black Sox and other banished players seem less like justice than haphazard, or selective, retribution — and just as subjective as the Cooperstown selection process.

Pete Rose was not yet born when Landis issued his Black Sox edict in 1921, and Ty Cobb had collected only 3053 of his 4189 career hits. Rose didn't enter life until April 1941, in Cincinnati. At the time, Landis was still commissioner; Cobb, Speaker, Eddie Collins and Charles Comiskey were already Hall of Famers (the latter posthumously); and Bart Giamatti was probably still too young to have read Dante, or certainly Machiavelli. All of the Black Sox and Hal Chase, too, were still alive and serving out their lifetime exiles (Joe Jackson, only fifty-one at the time, might've still been playing sandlot ball somewhere in South Carolina).

By the time Rose got to the majors in 1963, Giamatti was in college, engrossed by Renaissance literature; Cobb, Speaker, Landis, Chase, Jackson, Weaver, Leonard, Fred McMullin and Lefty Williams were all dead; Happy Felsch had only a year to live; and Chick Gandil had nine. Eddie Cicotte was also alive, and would survive through May 1969 — long enough to see some of Pete's first 1109 hits on television, if he still cared to watch baseball.

By 1963, Eddie's son, also a pitcher, had already come and gone from the Show. Al Cicotte was in the majors for five of the seasons during 1957–62, mostly in the American League, but spent 1961 with St. Louis. He career record was 10–13, in no way similar to his father's 208–149, and Al obviously played all of his career on the level. But, it's almost a shame we never got to savor — if only long after the fact — the historic irony of Pete Rose batting, at least once, against a Cicotte.

In early 1989, when Giamatti became the atypical selection to succeed Peter Ueberroth as baseball's seventh commissioner, Rose had been retired as an active player for two full seasons, already had his 4256 hits stored — like a promissory note — in the BBWAA vote bank, and had managed his hometown Reds to a second-place finish in the National League's

Central Division the previous season, Pete's fifth year as skipper. At that point, Rose had a career ledger of 353–307 (.535) as manager, and Giamatti had already been chain-smoking for more than two decades.

By the time the 1989 season began, it appeared from reports in the media that Rose had his own addiction. The spectre of Pete's investigation for gambling hung above the Reds all summer, causing the team's preseason title hopes to evaporate amid a 59–66 record under Rose's understandably distracted leadership. When Giamatti finally announced the results of baseball's inquiry—occurring, ironically, at about the same point in the season that Pete's former Cincinnati teammate Johnny Bench was inducted at Cooperstown—the clap of Pete's negotiated departure from the game fell upon the Church of Baseball like the sound of a dropped Hall of Fame plaque shattering on the empty museum's floor at midnight. Hell, one even expected Schotzie to tug with its teeth at the stirrup of Rose's uniform pants and—mouth moving like the talking Bassett hound Cleo from the 1950s Jackie Cooper sitcom *The People's Choice*—tearfully implore "Say it ain't so, Pete. Say it ain't so."

But perhaps it was, some of it anyway—although we'll probably never know just how much, because baseball once again tried to obfuscate as much of the Rose affair as possible. From the moment of its announcement by Giamatti, the absurd settlement, under which Rose supposedly agreed to leave baseball voluntarily only if the full results of the investigation were kept secret and he was never publicly accused of betting on ball games, sounded as dumb as a Norm Crosby word-play routine—much like Ban Johnson's arrangement with Cobb and Speaker and nothing like the honorable agreement you'd expect to have been negotiated by a former Ivy League chancellor. When Giamatti let slip that baseball had proof Rose had gambled on its games, the likable commissioner—who, to that point, had seemed concerned about nothing but the best interests of the sport and its fans—came across (even if accidentally) just as two-faced as Landis had been with Buck Weaver in the twenties. Even worse, it was hard to believe that "Charlie Hustle"—who had never made a stupid play on the field in twenty-four seasons, nor seemingly taken an ill-advised swing in a record 14,053 at-bats—was actually arrogant enough to believe the public would buy his protestations of choir-boy innocence in light of his agreement to leave the sport that everyone presumed, from long observation of his personality, was more important to him than anything else.

It wasn't just that Pete Rose lived and breathed for baseball. Clearly, the game had the same obsessive importance for Rose—maybe more—as public attention does to fitness guru Richard Simmons, or do all the playmate-counting notches that Hugh Hefner has cut into his bedpost over time. More than that, anyone who saw Rose barrel headfirst into catcher Ray Fosse to score the winning run in the twelfth inning of the 1970 all-star game, essentially knocking Fosse into a back-up career as color commentator, or can recall the snide, cocky, combative grin on Pete's lips as he crept ever closer to home plate, daring Mickey Rivers to bunt on him during the 1976 World Series, has no doubt that winning, at any cost, by whatever means, was Rose's primary reason for living.

And beyond even that, Pete's pursuit of Cobb's career-hit record, dominated as it was by his self-absorbed awareness of the event's statistical minutia and historic significance, convinced many who saw him play during the last few seasons of his career that accomplishment of the goal was nothing less than his all-consuming moment of self-validation. So, subjectively, it went way beyond the limits of credibility for most people to accept that — even if Pete had bet on ball games — his drive to win and competitive arrogance would've ever allowed him to bet against himself, as player or manager; and, as a result, emotionally and objectively it was impossible to believe that a warrior so well-versed in the game's history, and so possessed by all of those needs, could've risked their ultimate fulfillment, and his rightful place in baseball's Valhalla, for a mere compulsion to wager.

Nonetheless, Pete went into limbo, immediately reduced to hocking his bats and other paraphernalia on obscure cable channels, simply to pay his attorney fees — or maybe, as many suspected, his gambling debts. In doing so, he quickly became a pathetic, self-drawn caricature of his obsession with Cobb's record and the butt of joking derision (e.g., "These are the sweat socks I wore for hit number 4192. We're taking bids at 1-800-EVEN-BET."). More sadly, Giamatti — whom fans had quickly embraced, with good reason, for his potential to gently heal the many other ills afflicting baseball at the time — collapsed and died from a cigarette- and stress-induced coronary outside his Manhattan office just days after Rose's banishment. Obviously, the kindly academic with encyclopedic knowledge of Machiavelli did not have the heart — either figuratively or literally — to apply the Italian writer's philosophy as commissioner and live comfortably with the results.

Rose was due to become eligible for Cooperstown in 1992. But, the year before, the Hall of Fame trustees announced their intention to bar Pete from the ballot, because he was on baseball's ineligible list, and for as long as he remains there. The trustees insisted that if the evidence collected by attorney-investigator John Dowd was accurate, then Rose had clearly failed the requirements of "integrity" and "character" included in the Hall's 1945 morality clause and deserved no less than the same HOF exile imposed upon Jackson, Cicotte, Weaver, Chase, et al.

But the trustees' intent did not sit well with the BBWAA, many of whose members no doubt felt the same incredulity about Rose's gambling as had the public at large when the story broke two years earlier. Also, and perhaps more significant than any real advocacy for Pete, some writers— possibly many — must've resented being told who they could or could not vote for, beyond the eligibility requirements already in place. Once again, they apparently had forgotten that their role as the Hall's primary electorate was an extended privilege. But, the scribes' irritation was also predictable — recall that Jackson got two votes in 1946, after he was indirectly barred from HOF consideration. So a debate ensued, during which Rose inevitably became synonymous with Shoeless Joe, and both men were labeled by some as victims.

Three main points were made in Rose's favor. Each of them had emotional appeal in the 1990s, an era containing even greater moral ambivalence than the Lost Generation of the 1920s— when, in contrast, precious little forgiveness was extended to Shoeless Joe. But two of the arguments were too simplistic, and the third was scuttled by Pete's behavior, although it had more merit.

First, and predictable from the secrecy involved in Rose's negotiated settlement, Pete's fans claimed that there was no clear proof that Charlie Hustle had ever bet on baseball games. So, given that fact, the quality of Rose's career performance offered no more indication he could've bet against his own team than Jackson's home run, .375 batting average and errorless play evidenced any intent on his part to throw the 1919 series. And, to a statistician, Pete's record as manager also lacked any credible evidence of game-fixing: his 412–373 final ledger as a skipper represented almost eighteen more wins over the equivalent of about five full seasons than was statistically likely given the number of runs his teams scored and allowed, and his average of about 3.7 wins per season above that expectancy was remarkably high for any pilot, especially one who might've been throwing ball games to win wagers. But, the simplistic argument regarding Rose's performance overlooked three facts: Jackson definitely took the gamblers' payoff money for the 1919 fall classic; Rose's subsequent tax-evasion trial offered public evidence of his connection with gamblers; and — under the language of Landis's 1921 edict and the temporary exiles of several former players who have worked for various casinos— both of those indiscretions have been interpreted in the past as sufficient grounds for a man's banishment, at least temporarily, whether or not he played on the level.

It also was noted that, above all else, the Hall of Fame is intended to honor achievement on the field and that sainthood is no prerequisite for membership. In that light, it's obvious that Cobb the racist and Babe Ruth the womanizer would've never passed muster with the Pope or Mother Teresa but got into Cooperstown solely for their prowess as players. But that premise also ignored the fact that baseball has no rules prohibiting bigotry or philandering, but does have written proscriptions — deemed necessary to assure the sport's integrity — against betting on games and consorting with gamblers.

The final point, the Bill W. Defense, had somewhat more merit — provided that Rose never bet against his own team. By the 1990s, compulsive gambling was correctly recognized as an addictive disease, like alcoholism and drug addiction. Pete's defenders argued that, since baseball had repeatedly forgiven players like Steve Howe for their drug problems, fairness also dictated that there had to be room in Cooperstown, next to boozers like Grover Alexander and Hack Wilson (among others), for an otherwise deserving compulsive gambler. Unfortunately, as the founder of Alcoholics Anonymous would've pointed out, it's impossible to help anyone who will not admit their problem. Rose unwaveringly insisted that he had no gambling addiction, so the strength of this argument was undermined by Pete's attitude; and, although there is ample cause for compassion regarding his apparent level of emotional denial, his refusal to admit the problem left no room for allowances.

But, the issue of whether Rose deserves to be in Cooperstown was not the only legacy of his banishment from the game. Beyond the possible injustice of the fact that Pete and Shoeless Joe were outside, while Cobb, Speaker and other potential miscreants were in, the very worst aspect of the Rose affair was the peace negotiated between the Hall of Fame trustees and the BBWAA to resolve their conflict over Charlie Hustle.

9

The Sixty-Percent Non-solution

As noted earlier, the BBWAA has complained for years that the Veterans Committee is allowed to select too many of the writers' rejects, contributing to what many perceive as the Hall of Fame's continued slide toward mediocrity. As the debate about Pete Rose's Cooperstown eligibility became increasingly intractable, the complaint was raised again, very loudly.

Logically, there was no real connection between the two issues, and the scribes' bluster had to be a bluff, because they weren't about to discard their voting privilege altogether in protest. But, it worked nonetheless, as — for the sake of expedience on Rose (i.e., getting him barred from the Hall of Fame ballot) — the trustees tossed the writers a very big, compensatory bone. In terms of overall fairness, it was the stupidest decision in the Hall's long history of dumb mistakes.

By tradition, the VC meets to vote in Florida every March, during spring training. As of 2000 the panel included Hall of Fame players Yogi Berra, Juan Marichal, Stan Musial, Ted Williams and Hank Aaron, plus former team executives Joe Brown, Hank Peters and John McHale, past National League president Bill White, ex–Negro league first baseman Buck O'Neil, and media reps Bob Broeg, Ken Coleman, Jerome Holtzman, Leonard Koppett and Allen Lewis — a total of fifteen members.

Among players passed over by the BBWAA, the committee currently may consider (1) any man who meets the ten-year service requirement and whose major-league career began before 1946 or (2) men whose careers began after that date, have been retired for at least twenty-three years and — under a rule instituted in 1991 as part of the Rose compromise — *have received at least 60 percent support in any BBWAA election.* For several years prior to 1991, the panel had been limited to considering only those post–1945 players with one hundred votes or more in any BBWAA election, and when the new rule was enacted, all of the men who met that earlier proviso were grandfathered into the VC-eligible group as well.

On the surface, all of that sounds fair. After all, as the performance of the OTC2 in the 1940s showed, the two elective organs should have separate and clearly defined jurisdictions. Logic would also seem to dictate that any legitimate Hall of Famer should be able to muster 60 percent support from the writers, even if they failed to elect him, right?

Dead wrong. Through 2000, only seven players who've been chosen by the Veterans Committee or one of its predecessors have ever received as much as 60 percent support in any BBWAA election, and most of the rest never came close (the seven included Jim Bunning, Orlando Cepeda, Frank Chance, Johnny Evers, Nellie Fox, Enos Slaughter and Rube Waddell, although manager Miller Huggins did it too). Through the same date, among the ninety-two players tabbed by the VC overall, only twenty-three of them ever received as much as 40 percent support from the writers on any ballot, and the average high-support score among the entire group is just 25 percent. What's more, sixty-eight of the ninety-two never got as many as one-hundred votes in any year of the scribes' voting, with their highest individual totals ever averaging only forty-three votes.

There are a couple ways to interpret those numbers. It's obvious that through much of their history the veterans committees have inducted a lot of men who got relatively poor support from the BBWAA. On one hand, it may be (as many writers contend) that most of these men are illegitimate Hall of Famers — true errors of selection, whose memberships at Cooperstown taint the VC process, specifically, and the HOF roster, in general. The men inducted by the VC and its predecessors include most of the more dubious Cooperstown selections ever — Dave Bancroft, Rick Ferrell, Elmer Flick, Chick Hafey, Jesse Haines, George Kelly, Fred Lindstrom, Rube Marquard, Tommy McCarthy, Joe Tinker, Lloyd Waner and Ross Youngs — to name a dozen who never received anything close to a hundred votes or 60 percent support. No doubt, the trustees' sensitivity to complaints about those and other selections, plus a desire to avoid such criticism in the future, motivated their willingness to include the 60 percent requirement in the 1991 compromise about Rose's eligibility.

But, the list of low-support inductees also includes a roughly equal number of the VC and its predecessors' very best choices for Cooperstown.

Cap Anson, Dan Brouthers, Mordecai Brown, Buck Ewing and Eddie Plank all were chosen by forerunners of the current veterans panel, while Roger Connor, Sam Crawford, George Davis, Billy Hamilton, Johnny Mize, Sam Thompson and Monte Ward have been inducted since 1953. None of those men ever received higher than the 51.3 percent support achieved by Anson and Ewing in the 1936 OTC1 voting; Mize is the only one among the group who ever earned more than one hundred votes in any HOF election; and, as noted earlier, Davis and Thompson never got a single vote from any BBWAA elector, ever.

What's more, through 1999, only three other men besides those noted above had ever received at least 60 percent support from the BBWAA and had not yet been chosen for Cooperstown. But, two of them —catcher Carlton Fisk and first baseman Tony Perez — were elected by the scribes in 2000, leaving former Brooklyn first sacker Gil Hodges as the only man who currently qualifies for consideration under the 60 percent rule.

Hodges retired as a player in 1963. But, his big-league career began with two at-bats for the 1943 Dodgers— so he fits (barely) into the pre–1946 group and would be eligible for the VC's consideration even it he hadn't attained highs of 242 votes in 1979 or 63.4 percent support in 1983. As a result, absolutely no one currently qualifies under the 60 percent restriction.

Every other post–1945 player eligible for the Veterans Committee voting as of 2000 had to be grandfathered in as a beneficiary of the previous one-hundred-vote requirement. When the rules were changed in 1991, only eleven postwar players had ever met that standard, and two of them were the now-enshrined Bunning (a high of 317 votes in 1988) and Fox (295 in 1985). Table 17 lists the other nine men, who comprised the second list of players at the beginning of the previous chapter. It also notes the last year in which they received votes from the BBWAA (Last w/Votes), their last year of eligibility in the writers' balloting (Last Elig), their highest vote (High Vote) and support-percentage (High Pct) ever received, and the average vote (Avg Vote) and support-percentages (Avg Pct) they earned in all of their BBWAA elections.

TABLE 17
POST-1945 PLAYERS ELIGIBLE FOR
VC CONSIDERATION AS OF 2000

Player	Pos	Last w/Votes	Last Elig	High Vote	High Pct	Avg Vote	Avg Pct
Ken Boyer	3B	1994	1994	109	25.6	55.7	13.2
Harvey Kuenn	OF	1991	1991	168	39.4	100.1	24.3

Player	Pos	Last w/Votes	Last Elig	High Vote	High Pct	Avg Vote	Avg Pct
Mickey Lolich	SP	1999	1999	109	25.6	48.9	11.3
Roger Maris	OF	1988	1988	184	43.2	108.8	27.1
Bill Mazeroski	2B	1992	1992	182	42.3	88.3	20.9
Tony Oliva	OF	1996	1996	202	47.4	142.5	33.1
Ron Santo	3B	1998	1998	204	43.1	116.6	26.1
Luis Tiant	SP	2000	2002	132	31.0	59.2	13.0
Maury Wills	SS	1992	1992	166	40.6	112.0	27.3

Among these nine, only Luis Tiant (italicized) is still eligible for the BBWAA voting. He will remain on the ballot through 2002, provided he doesn't fall below the 5 percent cutoff. But it's clear from his vote history that he will not be elected by the writers (he received fifty-three votes and 10.7 percent in 1999 and eighty-six votes for 17.2 percent in 2000). Mickey Lolich's BBWAA eligibility expired in 1999, and he will not be eligible for VC consideration until 2003. Ron Santo's last year on the writers' ballot was 1998, so he will not be under the committee's purview until 2002.

That leaves six post–1945 players from Table 17 — Boyer, Kuenn, Maris, Mazeroski, Oliva and Wills — plus Orlando Cepeda, who were eligible for Veterans Committee consideration in 1999. But, Maris was dropped from the VC's final ballot in 1999, despite the fact that the 1998 home-run exploits of Mark McGwire and Sammy Sosa raised expectations about his possible election. Among the others, only Cepeda (the panel's 1999 inductee), Mazeroski, and Dom DiMaggio (from the pre–1946 group) were listed as leading candidates in most of the print media's rumor-fed speculation before and after the 1999 voting.

So apparently, except for Mazeroski, the HOF prospects of the five other men from Table 17 were all rather dim by 2000. The poorest BBWAA vote- and percentage-high numbers among that group belong to former Cardinals third sacker Ken Boyer. But, nonetheless, his highest vote total (109) is better than the largest amount received by fifty-six of the ninety-two players already elected by the veterans committees, and his highest support level (25.6 percent) is greater than that earned by thirty-eight of them. In comparison, Dom DiMaggio's best-ever performance in the writers' balloting was only forty-three votes, for just 11.3 percent support in 1973. So, based solely on their BBWAA performance, all of the men in Table 17 appear to be better Hall of Fame candidates than many of the players chosen by the veterans panel in the past and have much better credentials than the man listed in the media as the VC's leading pre–1946 candidate of 1999.

The significance of all this is that, because of the Pete Rose compromise, as of 2000, and until someone else receives 60 percent support without getting elected by the writers, the nine men listed in Table 17 are the only post–1945 players who can ever be considered by the Veterans Committee at any time in the future. *Every other player whose career began after the end of World War II and was not elected during his period on the BBWAA ballot is no longer eligible for Cooperstown.*

That leaves a lot of good men outside, looking in. The list of postwar players who do not meet the VC's current eligibility requirements, and whose terms on the BBWAA ballot had expired by 2000, includes one-time MVPs Dick Allen, Don Baylor, George Bell, Vida Blue, Jeff Burroughs, George Foster, Dick Groat, Willie Hernandez, Elston Howard, Jackie Jensen, Fred Lynn, Denny McLain, Thurman Munson, Don Newcombe, Boog Powell, Al Rosen, Bobby Shantz, Joe Torre and Zoilo Versalles, plus Cy Young Award winners Dean Chance, Mike Cuellar, John Denny, Mike Flanagan, Randy Jones, Vernon Law, Jim Lonborg, Sparky Lyle, Mike Marshall, Mike McCormick, Jim Perry, Mike Scott, Steve Stone, Rick Sutcliffe, Bob Turley, Pete Vuckovich and Bob Welch. They are part of a group that also includes, but is not limited to, Buddy Bell, Bobby Bonds, Bob Boone, Bill Buckner, Lew Burdette, Bert Campaneris, Cesar Cedeno, Ron Cey, Jack Clark, Rocky Colavito, Alvin Dark, Darrell Evans, Dwight Evans, Elroy Face, Curt Flood, Bobby Grich, Frank Howard, Dave Kingman, Ted Kluszewski, Bill Madlock, Minnie Minoso, Graig Nettles, Al Oliver, Billy Pierce, Vada Pinson, Vic Raschi, Jeff Reardon, Roy Sievers, Ted Simmons, Rusty Staub, Jim Sundberg, Kent Tekulve, Gene Tenace and Frank White. And, because their BBWAA support levels fell below five percent, several of the men on this list were dropped from the writers' ballot long before their fifteen-year eligibility had expired. Unless the rules are changed in the future — the 1946 cutoff advanced to a later date or the 60 percent requirement reduced — none of these men can ever be considered by the VC, and some of them will have received only one year of Hall of Fame consideration.

Some of those men do not deserve to be in Cooperstown. Most of them don't. But a few — Grich, Oliver, Pinson, Simmons, Torre, Darrell and Dwight Evans, for example — have better subjective or statistical credentials than the twelve men listed earlier who rank among the committee's worst selections of the past, strong evidence that the VC eligibility requirements in effect since 1991 are far too restrictive. And, many of them on the larger list are certainly better-qualified candidates than Johnny Vander Meer, who managed to get seven hundred votes in fourteen different BBWAA elections, and who — because his major-league career began before 1946 — is still eligible for VC consideration.

Ostensibly, all of this is justified by the BBWAA's position that because the veterans committees have selected too many mediocre players in the past, it's time to put a stop to those errors of selection. But the 1991 rule change cannot prevent such errors. Instead, it virtually assures that even more of them must occur. The rule sets an arbitrary time barrier, 1946, that allows the VC to continue to induct any riffraff they choose among the ten-year men who entered the majors before that date but prohibits its consideration of many candidates from the postwar era whose credentials are more viable. Dom DiMaggio might be a more legitimate Hall of Fame candidate than Rocky Colavito, Vada Pinson or Dwight Evans. But, if he is, the superior merit of his candidacy should be determined from his comparative on-field performance, not by the mere accident that his career began before 1946 while the others' did not.

Table 18 presents three lists for comparison of past BBWAA election performance to Hall of Fame status or eligibility for Veterans Committee consideration. The lefthand group includes men who played prior to 1946, received a few votes from the writers, and have been elected to Cooperstown by the VC, although they never earned as much as 10 percent support from the BBWAA. The middle group includes other VC-eligible players from the pre–1946 era who had not been inducted through 2000, but who received 10 percent support or higher from the writers at least once during their time on the ballot. The final group includes two lists of post–1945 players who have also received 10 percent support or more from the scribes: the top list features only those men from Table 17 who will be eligible for VC consideration under the current restrictions as of the year 2002 (so it excludes Mickey Lolich and any players who were still on the writers' ballot after 1999); the bottom list includes men whose BBWAA eligibility had expired prior to 2000, but can never be considered by the VC. Each man's name is accompanied by the highest support percentage he ever received in BBWAA voting.

TABLE 18
BBWAA SUPPORT-LEVEL HIGHS FOR
SELECTED HOF CANDIDATES

Pre-1946 VC-Inducted	High Pct	Pre-1946 Not Inducted	High Pct	Post-1945 VC-Eligible	High Pct
Earl Averill	5.3	Babe Adams	13.7	Ken Boyer	25.6
Jake Beckley	1.3	Phil Cavarretta	35.6	Harvey Kuenn	38.4
Jesse Burkett	1.7	Walker Cooper	14.4	Roger Maris	43.2

Pre-1946 VC-Inducted	High Pct	Pre-1946 Not Inducted	High Pct	Post-1945 VC-Eligible	High Pct
Jack Chesbro	2.2	Dom DiMaggio	11.3	Bill Mazeroski	42.3
John Clarkson	6.4	Jimmy Dykes	10.0	Tony Oliva	47.4
Sam Crawford	4.2	Joe Gordon	28.4	Ron Santo	43.1
Rick Ferrell	0.5	Hank Gowdy	35.9	Maury Wills	27.3
Elmer Flick	0.4	Mel Harder	25.4		
Jesse Haines	8.3	Tommy Henrich	20.7	*Post-1945*	*High*
Billy Hamilton	2.6	Gil Hodges	63.4	*VC-Ineligible*	*Pct*
Harry Hooper	3.0	Johnny Kling	10.0	Dick Allen	18.9
Travis Jackson	7.3	Duffy Lewis	13.5	Bobby Bonds	10.6
Joe Kelley	0.4	Herman Long	20.5	Lew Burdette	23.8
George Kelly	1.9	Marty Marion	40.0	Alvin Dark	18.5
Fred Lindstrom	4.4	Pepper Martin	17.3	Elroy Face	18.9
Heinie Manush	9.4	Terry Moore	11.7	Curt Flood	15.1
Kid Nichols	2.5	Lefty O'Doul	16.7	Elston Howard	20.7
Joe Sewell	8.6	Allie Reynolds	33.4	Ted Kluszewski	14.4
Bobby Wallace	2.7	Johnny Sain	34.0	Don Larsen	12.3
		J. Vander Meer	29.3	Thurman Munson	15.5
		Mickey Vernon	24.9	Don Newcombe	15.3
		Bucky Walters	23.8	Vada Pinson	15.7
		Smoky Joe Wood	18.0	Minnie Minoso	21.1
				Joe Torre	22.2

Table 18 allows for numerous comparisons that demonstrate the arbitrary injustices imposed by the VC's current eligibility restrictions. If performance in the BBWAA voting is the primary measure of a man's credentials (an assumption implied by the 60 percent support requirement), then, among the pre–1946 first basemen on these lists, Gil Hodges (not in Cooperstown) is a far more deserving candidate than was Hall of Famer George Kelly (and that contention is probably true). But, among outfielders, and by the same logic, Lefty O'Doul (whose credentials are debatable) must also be more worthy than was Sam Crawford (whose qualifications are almost impeccable). If you apply the same standards across the 1946 barrier, then the unenshrined Ken Boyer must be more qualified than HOF third baseman Fred Lindstrom (probably true, as well); Harvey Kuenn must be a better choice than fellow outfielder Billy Hamilton (definitely false); Lew Burdette, who can never be considered by the VC, must be more deserving than Johnny Sain, who still can be elected (marginally true); and Don Larsen's credentials must be almost as good as those of Babe Adams (way false). Obviously, there is no defensible logic to basing VC eligibility on BBWAA voting performance and doing so is an injustice to every good, post–1945 player who has ever fared poorly in the writers' balloting.

The arbitrary time line drawn at the end of World War II also encourages the perpetuation of one of the injustices among Hall of Fame membership that was a primary reason for the veterans panels' existence — Cooperstown's imbalanced representation for different eras of baseball history. Through 2000, the Veterans Committee had chosen 110 new Hall of Fame members—sixty-eight for their major-league playing careers and forty-two in other capacities. Regardless of what they were honored for, almost half of these men enjoyed the majority of their HOF-worthy performances during the game's Live-Ball Era. Table 19 provides a breakdown of the respective eras of major-league history that each of these selections represented. Among the column headings, NC stands for the nineteenth century (1876–1900), DB for the Dead-Ball Era (1901–19), LB for the Live-Ball period (1920–45), PW for the Postwar era (1946–60), EX for the Expansion period (1961–75), and FA for the era of Free-Agency (1976–present). Among players whose careers overlapped eras, they were assigned to the one in which they had the most major-league at-bats or innings pitched. Non-players (managers, umpires, etc., and Negro-league inductees) were assigned to whichever era they had the most years of major- or Negro-league service in the capacity for which they were elected.

TABLE 19
VETERANS COMMITTEE SELECTIONS, BY ERA (1953–2000)

Citation	NC	DB	LB	PW	EX	FA	Total
Players	13	12	32	9	2	0	68
Non-Players	4	3	18	11	3	3	42
Totals	17	15	50	20	5	3	110
Percentage	15.5	13.6	45.5	18.2	4.5	2.7	100.0

By not restricting VC eligibility among pre–1946 players, while severely limiting eligibility among players whose careers began after 1945, the committee's current rules assure only that — absent an unlikely amount of self-control by the panel — the over-representation of Live-Ball-Era inductees will increase, at the direct expense of candidates from the post-World War II time period. After all, the list of post–1945 eligibles is a fixed one, which allows the VC to choose from only nine possible candidates, while the group of pre–1946 eligibles is limited only by the ten-year service requirement. So, even if the panel enshrines all nine men from Table 17 (which now seems very unlikely), they eventually will be forced to fall back on the earlier generation of candidates—unless someone else among post–1945 players qualifies in the meantime.

In the short-term, the latter prospect is doubtful. Among players on the BBWAA ballot in 2000, the five best scores among unelected candidates were posted by outfielder Jim Rice (51.5 percent support), catcher Gary Carter (49.7 percent), relief pitchers Bruce Sutter (38.5) and Goose Gossage (33.3), and first baseman Steve Garvey (32.1). The 2000 voting marked the first time that Gossage was on the ballot, so there's no way to confidently assess whether his support is likely to rise or fall in the future. Garvey's first year eligible was 1993, when he netted 41.6 percent support; and, presuming he is not elected by the scribes (or does not fall below the five percent cutoff), he will be eligible for VC consideration in 2013. But through 2000, Steve had never again equaled his first-year level of support, and his two most recent scores represented the lowest percentages he'd received in eight years on the ballot. Rice (whose first year of VC eligibility would be 2011), Sutter (2012) and Carter (2016) each earned their highest support levels to date in the 2000 voting, so only the former appears to have a realistic chance at 60 percent approval anytime soon.

But, given the candidates that will become eligible for the writers' voting in the first five years of the twenty-first century, the chances that any of those five will ever attain 60 percent approval are even more problematic. Dave Winfield (eligible in 2001), Eddie Murray (2003), Paul Molitor (2004) and Wade Boggs (2005) all have surpassed at least one of the scribes' de facto criteria for batters. The list of new eligibles in 2001 also includes Don Mattingly and Kirby Puckett; 2002 will see Ozzie Smith and Andre Dawson added to the ballot; Ryne Sandberg and Fernando Valenzuela will join them in 2003; and Dennis Eckersley will be eligible in 2004. Smith and Sandberg are likely to join Winfield, Murray, Molitor and Boggs as certain (if not first-year) BBWAA selections; most, if not all, of these men could push Rice, Carter, Sutter, Gossage and Garvey further down the list; and, by the time that happens, other de facto candidates still active in 2000 — like Cal Ripken, Jr., and Tony Gwynn — may become eligible for the ballot, along with five-time Cy Young winner Roger Clemens and career stolen-base leader Rickey Henderson.

Over time, the unavoidable result of all this must be that — relative to the players who came after 1945 — the pre–1946 candidates from the middle section of Table 16 (or others from the same era, with even weaker elective credentials) will have a long-term advantage in the VC voting, if only by force of their numbers and the absurd dichotomy in the eligibility criteria. And, because most of them represent the Live-Ball Era, that can only exacerbate the representative imbalance among the Hall of Fame roster. But even worse, perpetuation of the 1991 rule change also assures that — barring a substantial increase in the number of men elected annually by the BBWAA — representation for the postwar eras of baseball history can never achieve (or likely even approach) proportionality to that for earlier periods.

Clearly, all of the eligible post–1945 players need help from the EEOC — Equal Enshrinement Opportunity Commission. But, that's precisely what the Veterans Committee is supposed to be. Under the present rules, it is not now and never again can be.

Beyond that, the 60 percent standard is also just as arbitrary as the Hall of Fame's ten-year service requirement. And, like all of Cooperstown's previous eligibility refinements, it also does less to define what a Hall of Famer is than what he is not (someone who failed to get 60 percent support from the BBWAA). But, if 60 percent is a meaningful standard, it would've made more sense — within the context of preventing errors of selection — to simply lower the support level required for election by the writers from 75 percent to the smaller figure, and then do away with the Veterans Committee altogether. No doubt, the HOF trustees were unwilling to do that in 1991, if it was suggested at all. But, it's obvious that the 60 percent figure was merely a product of compromise and has no special sanctity on its own merit (why not 50 percent, 40, or even 25 — the latter being the most just and logical number because it represents the average high for VC inductees to date?). As is, due to the BBWAA's 75 percent standard for election, anyone receiving only 60 percent is a priori a "reject," too; and there is nothing to prevent the scribes from using that argument at a later date to get their way on some other issue of contention.

Making all of this appear even more unfair is the impression that the Veterans Committee, like its counterpart of the 1940s, may interpret and apply its eligibility rules in whatever manner suits its whim and political expedience. The VC's 1998 inductees were supposedly limited to one man from each of four categories — (1) someone from before 1920, (2) someone from the Negro leagues, (3) a manager, umpire or executive and (4) a player who met its current eligibility restrictions. George Davis fit the first criteria, and Bullet Joe Rogan, the second. The panel's other two 1998 inductees were former executive Lee MacPhail from category three and ex–American League outfielder Larry Doby, presumably the qualifier from the last group.

Doby was the first African American to play in the American League. His career in the Show began with Cleveland in July 1947, three months after Jackie Robinson entered the majors, and it ended in 1959. Larry became eligible for the BBWAA voting in 1965, but there was no election that year, so his first appearance on the ballot was in 1966, when he received seven votes for 2.3 percent support. In 1967 the writers used the two-tiered preliminary- and runoff-vote format mentioned in Chapter 4. On the first of those ballots, Doby earned ten votes, for 3.4 percent support, and (along with Bobby Thomson) was the lowest-ranked qualifier for the runoff. On that second ballot, Larry got just one vote, for 0.3 percent support. Although his eligibility extended through 1979, he never received another vote from the writers. So, technically, Doby did not meet either of the VC's 1998 eligibility criteria, because his big-league career did not begin until after 1945, and he had never earned one hundred votes or 60 percent support from the writers.

Larry played right field for the Indians in their pennant-winning year of 1948, was Cleveland's regular center fielder for the next seven seasons, and played the latter position regularly for two more years with the White Sox, so he was a lineup fixture for ten of his thirteen big-league seasons. During that period (1948–57), he twice led the AL in home runs and topped the circuit once each in runs scored, RBI, slugging and on-base percentages. He finished among the top ten in MVP voting twice, as runner-up to Yogi Berra when the Indians won the pennant again in 1954 and eighth behind Phil Rizzuto in 1950. Doby was named to the league's all-star team seven times—more than any other AL outfielder in that period except Ted Williams (nine times)—but was a starter in the game only once (1950). Over that decade, Williams led with a half-dozen starts, followed by Mickey Mantle (five starts, six all-star squads), Dom DiMaggio (three starts, four teams), Al Kaline and Hank Bauer (three starts, three squads apiece) and Hoot Evers (two starts, two teams). Nine other AL flychasers were named to multiple all-star teams during the decade — Minnie Minoso (five squads, one start), Joe DiMaggio, Tommy Henrich and Vic Wertz (three teams, one start each), Dale Mitchell (two squads, one start), and Jackie Jensen, Roy Sievers, Jimmy Piersall and Charlie Maxwell (two teams, no starts).

The AL's first echelon of outfielders during the period that Doby was a regular — Joe DiMaggio, Williams, Mantle and Kaline — all possess indisputable HOF credentials and are already in the Hall. Arguably, Doby ranks with Minoso, Henrich, Bauer, Wertz, Evers and Dom DiMaggio as the best among the circuit's second tier of flychasers from that era. Henrich, whose career spanned 1937–50, really belongs to an earlier generation of players; and, although Wertz placed among the top ten in MVP voting four times during the 1948–57 decade (twice as a first baseman), he never led the league in any offensive category. Bauer and Evers both topped the circuit in triples once, but Bauer's best MVP showing during that period was only an eighth-place finish in 1955, and Evers's highest was eleventh-best in 1950. Dom DiMaggio topped the league in runs scored twice and triples and stolen bases once each during his career, but he never placed among the top ten MVP candidates during Doby's decade as a regular. Only Minoso approached or surpassed Doby's overall career achievement. Minnie never placed higher than fourth in MVP voting, but he did so three times during Doby's decade (1951 and 1953–54) and also finished eighth once (1957). Minoso also led the league in a batting category nine times during his career — three times each in triples and stolen bases, plus once apiece in hits, doubles and slugging percentage. Subjectively, given Doby's larger number of all-star appearances and historic significance as the AL's first African American, his HOF credentials are about equal to Minoso's, and, if better, not by much.

All of this indicates that Doby's Hall of Fame credentials are good. But, were they good enough for the committee to justify circumventing its own eligibility rules, as it did with Addie Joss's election in 1978, or like its predecessor had done in 1945–46? Doby began his career as a second baseman for the Negro-league Newark Eagles in 1942. Given his failure to achieve 60 percent support from the BBWAA, the only way his eligibility could be justified by the VC in 1998 was to include him among those men whose careers began before 1946, and the panel apparently did that by extending the start of his "major-league" service back to the beginning of his Negro-league career in 1942.

Judging by Doby's skills and historical significance, his Cooperstown membership is subjectively justifiable, and the mere fact of his election deserves no special criticism, given the lesser credentials of some other VC inductees. But, the manner in which Doby was chosen — by rationalizing circumvention of the eligibility guidelines in order to give special treatment to a player of historical importance — suggests that the committee feels no obligation to adhere to its own rules and that it is willing to extend any favoritism it deems justifiable. As such, the action set a bad example — although, no doubt with the best intentions.

But even worse, no amount of favoritism (or cronyism) by the committee can ever compensate for the long-term injustices that must ensue among the Hall of Fame roster as a result of the 60 percent-support requirement imposed as part of the Pete Rose compromise. Baseball's long-existent penchant for obfuscation virtually assures that we will never know all of the facts regarding the game-fixing incidents reported in 1926 or about Charlie Hustle's gambling. Perhaps Ty Cobb and Tris Speaker's indiscretions, if any, were insufficient to justify criticism of their Hall of Fame status, and maybe Rose (and Joe Jackson) should be barred from Cooperstown. But, although it must've seemed expedient at the time, the price paid by the trustees in 1991 to assure Pete's ineligibility was exorbitant beyond all reason: it denies too many other men of his generation, and later ones, their rights to fair and adequate evaluation of their Hall of Fame credentials; and, by preventing them from receiving the full verdict of both of Cooperstown's juries, it serves as one more indictment of the Hall of Fame's refusal to adopt any objective standards.

As for Rose, anyone who knows Pete's accomplishments as a player and has read the Dowd Report with a nonpartisan attitude cannot avoid ambivalence about his exclusion from the Hall of Fame. Without doubt, Rose's on-field achievements are worthy of Cooperstown, and it's possible that his transgressions, if any, were less than that of Shoeless Joe (perhaps even Cobb and Speaker). Beyond the statements of witnesses whose actions and testamentary motives were less than innocent in their own right, the evidence presented by Dowd is all circumstantial. But the type and weight of it also makes Pete's stonewall denial since his banishment seem anything but forthright and lends no credibility to his demeanor during the infamous pre-game interview at the 1999 World Series. In that light, and whatever the truth may be, it seems a far greater injustice that, as a result of Rose's predicament and the absurd compromise it engendered, others like Curt Flood, Minnie Minoso and many of their contemporaries— whose on-field credentials are nowhere the equal of Charlie Hustle's, but who had unquestionably positive impacts on their sport — can never again be considered for HOF membership than it does that Rose is left outside, looking in.

10

The Fickle Finger of Fate

Mickey Lolich won 217 games in a sixteen-year career (1963–79) spent mostly with the Tigers. Lolich surpassed twenty victories twice in his career, winning twenty-five games in 1971 and twenty-two more in 1972. In the first of those two seasons he led the American League in wins, strikeouts, innings pitched and complete games, to finish second behind Vida Blue in the Cy Young voting. He was also the hero of Detroit's 1968 World Series victory over the Cardinals, winning three games in the fall classic and going the distance to beat Hall of Famer Bob Gibson 4–1 in the seventh game. When he retired, Mickey's 2832 strikeouts ranked seventh-best, all-time. He was a very good pitcher whose Hall of Fame candidacy had two major flaws: he also lost 191 games, for a winning percentage of just .532; and, in the three other seasons that he led his team in victories, he posted losing records of 14–19 (1970), 16–21 (1974) and 12–18 (1975) for some bad ball clubs.

Lolich's BBWAA eligibility began in 1985, when he got seventy-eight of a possible 396 votes, for 19.7 percent support that was good enough to place fourteenth among the thirty-six men with votes that year. In 1986 he gained eight more votes and climbed to 20.2 percent; two years later 109 scribes voted for him, equal to 25.6 percent approval. After that, his candidacy fizzled, dropping to forty-seven votes and 10.5 percent in 1989; and, thereafter, he never received more than forty-five votes. In 1994–95 he came close to being dropped from the ballot, earning just 5.1 and 5.7 percent support in those years. But he climbed back to seven percent in 1996 and hung on the ballot through 1999, his last year of eligibility, when he earned just twenty-six votes for 5.2 percent.

Overall, Lolich received 733 votes in the fifteen years he was on the BBWAA ballot, for an average of about 11 percent support per try. During 1985–99, there were a total of 6,677 front-door electors. As a result, Lolich earned the dubious honor of being (among men who've received votes on at least ten ballots) the most often rejected candidate in the history of Cooperstown elections—as his name was omitted from 5,944 ballots over his fifteen-year eligibility.

An even greater sense of frustration, had he lived to experience it all, would've been felt by former Dodgers first baseman Gil Hodges, who holds the all-time record for most votes received without gaining election. Gil's Cooperstown eligibility began in 1969, when he got 82 of a possible 341 votes, for 24 percent support. His percentage doubled to 48.3 in 1970 and rose to an even 50 percent the next year before declining to 40.7 percent in 1972. Hodges died in April of that year; and, beginning with 1973, he earned 50 percent support or higher in ten of his last eleven years on the ballot, nine of them consecutive (1973–81). Gil's highest support percentage came in 1983, his last year eligible, when 63.4 percent of the scribes voted for him, and he also earned 60.1 percent on two other ballots (1976 and 1981). Overall, Hodges received 3,010 votes, an average of 201 per ballot, including a high of 242 in 1979.

Among the ranks of the most frustrated Cooperstown candidates ever, Lolich and Hodges are joined by some very good players, most of whom were Mickey's contemporaries. Table 20 lists the men who had received the most votes without ever being elected, and those who—like Lolich—had the highest number of ballot rejections (Omit) through the 2000 voting. The number of ballots on which each man received votes (Bal) is also noted. Except for Hodges, all of the men on both lists began their careers after 1945; and, because expansion has caused a dramatic increase in the number of HOF electors, both lists are dominated by players active after 1961, the year of the majors' first expansion. Three of the unelected players with the most votes to date—Steve Garvey, Jim Kaat and Jim Rice (italicized)—were still eligible for the writers' voting as of 2001. Marty Marion is the only other man with more than a thousand votes (1,010) who has not been elected, and only six other candidates— Elston Howard, Luis Tiant, Dick Allen, Bobby Thomson, Mickey Vernon and Lew Burdette —have surpassed five thousand rejections. The men on both lists were all good players, and some of those on the right side of the table may have Cooperstown credentials that are equal to or better than some on the left.

TABLE 20
MOST-FRUSTRATED HOF
CANDIDACIES, THROUGH 2000

Most Votes	Votes	Bal	Omit	Most Rejections	Omit	Bal	Votes
Gil Hodges	3010	15	2648	Mickey Lolich	5944	15	733
Tony Oliva	2138	15	4286	Vada Pinson	5904	15	519
Ron Santo	1749	15	4816	Curt Flood	5885	15	541
Maury Wills	1680	15	4532	Thurman Munson	5868	15	487
Roger Maris	1632	15	4311	Joe Torre	5788	15	795
Harvey Kuenn	1502	15	4662	Minnie Minoso	5665	15	957
Steve Garvey	1385	8	2365	Don Larsen	5451	15	492
Bill Mazeroski	1324	15	4888	Elroy Face	5437	15	671
Jim Kaat	1217	12	4299	Ken Boyer	5410	15	836
Jim Rice	1087	6	1785	Don Newcombe	5340	16	311

In one sense, the BBWAA electors are similar to Supreme Court justices. The writers apply subjective selection standards that range along a spectrum from narrow to broad in the same way that jurists vary from "strict" constitutional constructionists like William Rehnquist to "liberals" like William O. Douglas. So, although the scribes are prohibited from voting for more than ten candidates per ballot, many of them, exercising their subjective option, vote for less.

During the period 1936–2000, including the Old-Timers Committee election of 1936 and runoff ballots of 1946, 1949, 1964 and 1967 (i.e., every ballot for which there are published records available), there were sixty-one different HOF elections involving a total of 19,734 voters. If every elector had voted for ten men each time, a total of 197,340 votes would've been cast. But the total number of votes received in these elections was 145,778, or 73.9 percent of all those possible. So just over one-quarter of all the available votes have gone unused over the years, when individual electors felt there were not ten men on the ballot worthy of the Cooperstown honor.

There's nothing inherently wrong about leaving blank spots on the ballot, but their impact is significant. In any given year those uncast votes reduce the chances that any particular player will be elected. When Nellie Fox missed enshrinement by two votes in 1985, there were 396 electors, requiring 297 votes for selection. But only 2,918 (or 73.7 percent) of the 3,960 possible votes were cast that year, so the participating writers passed on 1,042 separate opportunities to support anyone who was eligible and on upwards of 747 chances to give Fox the two more votes he needed (that

Former Dodgers first baseman Gil Hodges holds the unenviable distinction of having received more votes for Cooperstown than any other man who had not been elected through the 2000 voting. Hodges earned a total of 3010 BBWAA votes, and topped 50 percent support in ten of his fifteen years on the writers' ballot. But his best-ever showing — 63.4 percent support in 1983 — was still forty-four votes less than needed for election. (Photograph from *The Sporting News*)

is, the 1,042 blank spots minus Nellie's 295 votes—although, because we don't know how many of the electors who voted for Fox listed fewer than ten names on their ballots, the number was undoubtedly smaller than 747). Similarly, in 1994 when Orlando Cepeda's 335 votes missed election by 7, only 2,894 of a possible 4,550 votes were cast. So the writers left 1,656 spaces blank and potentially rejected Cepeda as many as 1,321 separate times. When viewed in terms of uncast votes, the BBWAA failures of Fox, Cepeda and other near-miss candidates appear as far bigger rejections than when merely isolating the number of votes by which they missed election.

But, before examining the uncast votes a little closer, it's instructive to identify the general parameters of Cooperstown voting. Table 21 provides combined descriptive statistics for all of the sixty-one HOF elections held through 2000. The all-time highs, lows and the overall means for each parameter are identified, along with the various years in which they occurred. On average (the boldfaced "Means" column on the right), each ballot has included about 324 voters and required 243 votes for election. Typically, about fifty-three candidates receive support in each election, but—because that average is impacted by year-to-year holdovers—the total number of men who've actually earned votes through 2000 was just 747, not the 3,264 you'd get by multiplying 53.5 times 61. Beyond that, the fifty-three men of the per-ballot average have typically received about sixty votes apiece, for a mean support of just over 17 percent. Normally, most of the candidates receive less than 10 percent support, but the overall average is higher because of the numerical impact of the handful of men who earn relatively high support percentages.

TABLE 21
BBWAA ELECTION STATISTICS, 1936–2000

Ballot Parameter	High	Year(s)	Low	Year(s)	Mean
Number of Electors	499	2000	78	1936*	323.5
Total Votes Possible	4990	2000	780	1936*	3235.1
Total Votes Cast	3364	1999	374	1936*	2389.8
Percentage of Votes Cast	100.6	1945	39.2	1967#	76.2
Minimum Needed to Elect	375	2000	59	1936*	242.9
Men with Votes	152	1958	20	1949#	53.9
High Ind. Vote Total	491	1999	40	1936*	272.0
Mean Ind. Vote Total	134.6	1999	6.6	1936*	59.6
Median Ind. Vote Total	104	1984	2	1936*	35.6
High Ind. Percentage	98.8	1992	51.1	1958	82.7

Ballot Parameter	High	Year(s)	Low	Year(s)	Mean
Mean Ind. Percentage	27.8	1984	5.9	1958	17.1
Median Ind. Percentage	25.9	1984	1.1	1938	9.8
Total Number Elected	5	1936	0	several	1.5
BBWAA Electees on Ballot	22	1936	1	1988	7.4
VC Electees on Ballot	44	1939	0	several	14.2
Hall of Famers on Ballot	56	1939	2	1998	21.6
Pct HOFers on Ballot	100.0	1946&49#	6.7	1988/2000	37.8

Note: Asterisk indicates 1936 OTC ballot; pound sign indicates runoff election(s).

Some of the data in Table 21 is curious and reflects the basis for part of the criticism presented in earlier chapters regarding the electors' erratic behavior and the arbitrariness of the selection process in general. For example, in 1945 there were fifteen more votes cast (2,495) than the 248 electors were allowed (2,480), so the overall percentage of votes cast equated to 100.6 — indicating a refusal of some voters to abide by the ten-man limitation. That disregard for the regulations may have been somewhat justified, however, given that the 1945 ballot contained fifty-four eventual Hall of Famers. But, oddly, no one was elected that year despite the decisions of some voters to ignore the rules (first baseman Frank Chance topped the ballot with 72.2 percent support), and it was the only time in the history of the BBWAA franchise that more votes have been cast than permitted. You might expect that the same thing would've happened in 1939, because a record fifty-six future Hall of Famers received votes that year, but it didn't.

At the opposite extreme of enthusiasm, only 1,198 of a possible 3,060 votes were cast in the 1967 runoff election, producing an all-time low for percentage of votes cast (39.2 percent), despite the fact that more than half of the men on that ballot (eighteen out of thirty-one) are now Hall of Famers. You'd also expect that the presence of so many viable candidates would've generated a higher percentage of votes in 1967, but it didn't.

As noted in Chapter 4, there have been four runoff elections in BBWAA voting history. The first two were prompted, primarily, because the large number of men eligible at the time made it extremely difficult to elect anyone, but why the writers returned to the format two decades later is anyone's guess. Regardless, by prior decree, only one man was allowed to be elected in each of those four runoffs; and, beyond the Alphonse-Gaston injustices discussed in Chapter 4, there is another obvious reason why this two-tiered process has been abandoned twice.

All four runoff elections are notable for the voters' apparent lack of enthusiasm for the candidates on each ballot — or, perhaps, for the runoff process itself. The 1967 runoff not only produced an all-time low for the percentage of votes cast, but less than half of the possible ballot slots were filled in two of the other three runoffs as well, and only 45.1 percent of all possible votes were cast in those four elections combined. Yet, each runoff ballot was loaded with future Hall of Famers: as noted above, there were eighteen in 1967; two-thirds of the thirty qualifiers for the 1964 runoff have since been elected to the Hall; and every candidate who qualified for either the 1946 or 1949 runoffs is now on the Cooperstown roster (hence the 100 percent scores earned by those two years under the Percentage of Hall of Famers on Ballot category in Table 21). In all, 77 percent of all the candidates on the four runoff ballots were men who are now in Cooperstown.

In that light, the data in Table 21 also demonstrates the fickleness of the BBWAA electors. On average, each of the sixty-one Cooperstown ballots has included 21.6 future Hall of Famers, of which 7.4 are eventually chosen by the writers. But, typically, only 1.5 of those men are elected by the scribes in a given year. So, they annually pass over about six men who — for unexplained, and no doubt various, reasons — they later deem worthy of election even though they were not perceived as such in that particular year (leaving an average of fourteen others on each ballot who are elected much later by the VC). All of that is consistent with the fact (noted in Chapter 5) that men who are elected by the writers sometime after their first year on the ballot require more than seven elections to be chosen. It's also predictable in that, each year, every man's credentials are weighed by each voter relative to a slightly different set of candidates. But, it doesn't explain the erratic fluctuations in support received by many men during their periods of eligibility.

Table 7 in Chapter 3 evidenced how the support levels for Lou Boudreau, Marty Marion, Pee Wee Reese and Phil Rizzuto bobbed up and down inconsistently during the late 1960s, like brightly painted horses on a slow-moving carousel. That example was not atypical. The tendency for individual support levels to fluctuate from year to year was evident in the first five HOF elections of 1936–42 and has continued ever since — even when measured solely among men who are eventually elected by the BBWAA. Table 22 gives three such examples from different eras. Each of them provides the support percentages and ordinal rankings of five men who were elected at some point by the writers, and each example evidences considerable fluctuation among the support levels for each candidate over the five-ballot periods covered. The table also indicates the year in which each candidate was elected by the writers (Year); and, if that year is included in the table, the support percentages and ordinal rankings are noted in boldface.

TABLE 22
TYPICAL FLUCTUATIONS IN INDIVIDUAL BBWAA VOTE HISTORIES OVER TIME

Player	1936	Ord	1937	Ord	1938	Ord	1939	Ord	1942	Ord	Year
Rogers Hornsby	46.5	9	26.4	12	17.6	16	64.0	5	**78.1**	**1**	1942
George Sisler	34.1	11	52.7	7	68.3	2	**85.5**	**1**	—	—	1939
Eddie Collins	26.5	12	57.2	5	66.8	4	**77.5**	**2**	—	—	1939
Grover Alexander	24.3	14	62.2	4	**90.9**	**1**	—	—	—	—	1938
Willie Keeler	17.7	17	57.2	6	67.6	3	**75.3**	**3**	—	—	1939

Player	1950	Ord	1951	Ord	1952	Ord	1953	Ord	1954	Ord	Year
Hank Greenberg	38.6	10	29.6	12	32.1	11	30.3	11	38.5	8	1956
Gabby Hartnett	32.5	11	25.2	13	32.9	10	39.4	10	60.0	7	1955
Dazzy Vance	31.3	12	31.0	11	44.9	8	56.8	6	62.7	6	1955
Ted Lyons	25.3	13	31.4	10	43.2	9	52.7	7	67.5	5	1955
Joe Cronin	19.9	14	19.5	14	20.5	13	26.1	12	33.7	9	1956

Player	1981	Ord	1982	Ord	1983	Ord	1984	Ord	1985	Ord	Year
Don Drysdale	60.6	2	56.3	6	64.7	6	**78.6**	**3**	—	—	1984
Harmon Killebrew	59.6	4	59.4	4	71.9	3	**83.3**	**2**	—	—	1984
Hoyt Wilhelm	59.4	5	57.0	5	65.0	5	72.1	4	**83.6**	**1**	1985
Juan Marichal	58.1	6	73.7	3	**83.7**	**2**	—	—	—	—	1983
Luis Aparicio	12.0	18	42.0	8	67.4	4	**84.8**	**1**	—	—	1984

In the first example, Rogers Hornsby's erratic scores are attributable, in part, to the fact that he was still an active player in 1936–37. In the first year of voting, with no restrictions on who the electors could support, Hornsby and eight other active players received votes (Mickey Cochrane, Jimmie Foxx, Frankie Frisch, Lou Gehrig, Lefty Grove, Al Simmons, Bill Terry and Pie Traynor). But active players were no longer eligible in 1937 (in theory, anyway), so all of them — except Hornsby, for some reason — received no votes. Why Hornsby got any at all in that second year, while the others did not, is a mystery: although serving as manager for the Browns, he had 56 at-bats as a part-time player; Cochrane (98 at-bats), Frisch (32) and Traynor (12) also served as player-managers of the Tigers,

Cardinals and Pirates, respectively that year (Cochrane left the job at mid-season); and, although Terry was also managing, he had retired as a player after 1936. So, if anything, you'd think that Terry would've been the only one to get support in 1937, not Hornsby.

But, none of that does anything to explain why Grover Alexander improved from fourteenth place and just 24.3 percent support in 1936 to first place and 90.9 percent in 1938. Granted that seven of the men above him in the 1936 election (Ty Cobb, Babe Ruth, Honus Wagner, Christy Mathewson, Walter Johnson, Nap Lajoie, Tris Speaker and Cy Young) were elected by the writers in 1936–37, but Alexander still climbed past six other men from the 1936 list and more than tripled his support level in just two years of voting. So, apparently, Alex seemed like a much better candidate to a large number of voters after those other eight men were elected. It's as though many voters suddenly realized, "Oh, I forgot about Alex!"

Among the five men listed in the second group, Hank Greenberg was easily the support-percentage leader in 1950, and Joe Cronin was last among them. Yet, somehow, Gabby Hartnett, Dazzy Vance and Ted Lyons had all jumped past Greenberg by 1952; and, although the three men played musical chairs with their ordinal positions, all of them were elected in 1955, ahead of Greenberg, who followed the next year. During the same period, Cronin's support percentages and ordinal position increased slowly but gradually through 1954, then he somehow more than doubled his support over the next two ballots and was elected with Greenberg in 1956.

In the final example, in the three ballots for 1981–83, Juan Marichal climbed from fourth best among the men listed to earn election in the last of those years. Don Drysdale went from first among the same group to fourth and fifth on the two succeeding ballots and climbed back to third (good enough for induction) in the fourth election shown. At the same time Hoyt Wilhelm, who was third among the group in 1981, fell to fourth and stayed there until he was elected in 1985. But the most dramatic fluctuation belongs to Luis Aparicio, who went from 12 percent support in 1981 to 84.8 in 1984, not only joining Drysdale and Harmon Killebrew among the 1984 inductees, but actually topping both of their final scores in the process.

The bottom line for Table 22 is that unless a man is elected in his first year of eligibility, there is often no true consensus among the BBWAA voters about the quality of his credentials until the year of his election. Because all of the men listed above were elected by the writers, the fluctuations shown offer no evidence that the passage of time enhances or solidifies most voters' perspectives on a given man's credentials—for, if it did, you'd expect each man's scores to rise steadily toward his election, decline toward oblivion or remain static. But, they often don't do that, so it's dangerous to isolate any man's specific-year score as indicative of his true credentials relative to anyone else who also is not elected. With that in mind, Table 22 offers further evidence that the BBWAA's 5 percent-support rule discussed in Chapter 4 imposes injustice.

Beyond all that, and coupled with the inherent difficulty in achieving 75 percent support, the uncast votes also have contributed to a perpetual backlog of relatively legitimate candidates who—although their composition changes gradually from year to year—must await disposition of their Hall of Fame fates. This backlog began to accumulate at the beginning of HOF voting in 1936, when 2,605 (or 85.7 percent) of a possible 3,040 votes were cast in the BBWAA and OTC1 elections combined, meaning there were a total of 435 blank spaces on the ballots that year. Of the ninety-five men who received votes in either of the 1936 elections, sixty-one of them —or 64.2 percent from the two ballots combined—were enshrined through 2000 (the writers eventually elected twenty-two of them, and the various veterans committees subsequently tabbed thirty-nine more). So given what we know now, there was already a backlog of fifty-six unenshrined Hall of Famers after the first five men were chosen in that initial year of voting.

This Cooperstown waiting list was most imposing during the first three decades of voting. Some backlog was unavoidable at the time, because the electors had to weigh the credentials of virtually every man who had played major-league baseball from 1876 through almost World War II, and they were still in the early stages of defining the subjective and or de facto precedents regarding exactly what credentials indicated that a man was worthy of the HOF honor. As a result, and coupled with the lack of any eligibility limits in the early years of the balloting, from 1936 through the 1960 election—after which expansion began to alter the composition of the BBWAA—there were seven occasions when more than one hundred different candidates earned votes, topped by 1958 when an all-time high of 152 men received support from the writers, including thirty-seven who eventually were enshrined (although no one was elected by the BBWAA that year). Excluding the runoff elections of 1946 and 1949, when the number of names on the ballot was limited by decree, an average of 88.8 men earned votes in each of the twenty elections held during the 1936–60 period, including 43.2 eventual Hall of Famers per ballot, but only 1.7 were enshrined per election. Of course, the backlog didn't actually increase by that 41.5 man difference per year, because many who received votes in each election were holdovers from previous years. But, because a few more men who were eligible by 1960 may be elected by the Veterans Committee in the future, it's fair to argue that there were still about forty such future Hall of Famers left unenshrined after the 1960 election.

In the years since 1960, with the fifteen-year eligibility window, the screening committee and 5 percent-support rules in place for some or nearly all of that time, the average number of men receiving votes in non-runoff elections has declined to 37.4 per year, the typical number of Hall of Famers on each ballot has dipped to 9.8, and the average number elected has dropped marginally to just under 1.5. So the backlog has shrunk, due in part to changes in the eligibility structure — although the average number of Hall of Famers per ballot during the post–1960 period must increase over time, as Cooperstown's two elective organs continue to choose new members.

The weight of these backlog numbers implies that, regardless of the narrow subjective standards applied by the BBWAA's most finicky voters, there always has been a surplus of viable — if not unquestionably worthy — candidates eligible for election. The voting records also indicate that, historically, the liberal constructionists have comprised a solid majority among the writers. After all, there undoubtedly have been many instances when various electors voted for no more than two, three, or maybe a half-dozen candidates in a given year. So, because 74 percent of all possible votes have been cast to date, for each elector who listed only three men on the ballot, three others must have named an average of nine, and a large majority of the voters must've filled out most of their ballots over the years for the overall proportion of actual votes cast to be as large as it has been to date.

The BBWAA voting history also indicates that the number of ballot spots left empty has increased significantly over the years. Excluding runoff elections, the empty ballot slots during the 1936–60 period represented just 9.1 percent of the total possible votes, so the typical elector of that era listed about nine names on each ballot. For the years 1962–2000 the proportion of empty spaces increased to 30.5 percent, with the average elector voting for about seven men. But during 1991–2000 alone, the number of empty spots rose to 39.7 percent of the possible vote total, so each elector typically named only six candidates during the last decade.

Coupled with the trend toward a larger number of first-year electees, those numbers imply that although recent BBWAA voters have had no difficulty identifying obvious Hall of Famers, their prevailing mindset is to reject (i.e., not vote for) most marginal candidates and leave those men's fates to the Veterans Committee. But, given the narrow eligibility rules currently applied by the VC (at the scribes' own insistence), many of those rejected cannot now qualify for the committee's consideration. As a result, the backlog must inevitably increase, as will the amount of political pressure on the VC's members. In turn, the Frankie Frisch–style cronyism and pro-Phil Rizzuto–type politicking are almost certain to have a bigger influence on the committee's future decisions.

The weight of these numbers also indicates that the rule limiting BBWAA electors to voting for a maximum of ten candidates is, and always has been, unnecessary. On the surface, elimination of this restriction might seem likely to open Cooperstown's front door to a prospective flood tide of second- or even third-rate Hall of Famers. But, as long as a substantial portion of the BBWAA electors choose not to vote for the maximum — again, traditionally about one-fourth of them, but recently much more — the number of men elected in a given year cannot rise significantly, even if a few electors vote for as many as fifteen or twenty candidates. In the past, absence of this rule might've prevented the current embarrassment of having eight men who've been elected to Cooperstown by the veterans committees but never received a single BBWAA vote and thereby enhanced — albeit marginally — the credibility of both elective processes.

Given the current, 60 percent-support minimum required for post–1945 players to be eligible for VC consideration, the credibility of the selection process is also damaged by the contrasting totals of men elected earlier by the various veterans panels who received relatively low BBWAA support and of those who thus far have been rejected by the process despite higher levels of support from the writers. Table 23 provides the range distributions for the highest support percentages ever achieved by every man who received votes in any HOF election through 2000, with the data separated into four categories: (1) men elected in their first year of BBWAA eligibility, (2) men chosen subsequently by the writers, (3) candidates elected by the veterans committees (including sixteen men who received votes from the writers and were later enshrined for non-playing capacities), and (4) men who were never elected at all. Among them, exactly one-hundred — or just 13.4 percent of the 747 men with votes — have earned the 60 percent support currently required to make post–1945 players eligible for VC consideration. All but nine of those hundred were elected by the BBWAA; eight of those remaining nine — including manager Miller Huggins, who earned 63.9 percent on the 1946 preliminary ballot — were later enshrined by one of the veterans panels; and the only man left who was not elected through 2000 is Gil Hodges, whose career began before 1946.

But, note also that the number of men elected by the veterans committees after BBWAA support-level highs of less than 20 percent (forty-six in all) is larger than the number of unelected candidates with support-level highs between 20 and 59.9 percent (a total of thirty-six). Among the first group, only two—outfielder Larry Doby and manager Leo Durocher—were chosen for major-league accomplishments that occurred after 1945; and, as noted in Chapter 9, Doby's election fudged a bit on the VC's present eligibility requirements (Satchel Paige, who played in the bigs after 1945, also received support but was enshrined for his Negro-league career, most of which occurred prior to that year).

TABLE 23
Range, Highest BBWAA Support
Levels Attained by All Men with Votes

Players w/Votes (percentage)	≥ 90	≥ 80	≥ 70	≥ 60	≥ 50	≥ 40	≥ 30	≥ 20	≥ 10	< 10	*Total*
BBWAA, 1st Year	20	11	3	0	0	0	0	0	0	0	34
BBWAA, After 1st	0	30	27	0	0	0	0	1*	0	0	58
Vets Committees	0	0	4	4	9	9	14	14	14	32	100
Unelected	0	0	0	1	1	8	8	18	27	492	555
Totals	20	41	34	5	10	17	22	33	41	524	747

Note: Asterisk denotes the 22.6 percent support earned by Lou Gehrig in the 1936 BBWAA voting. Gehrig was enshrined in a special election in 1939, but his support level for that ballot (at least 75 percent) is unknown.

Given the number of ballot spots normally left blank by the writers, it's unlikely that—absent the ten-candidate vote limitation—the scribes would've elected anyone else over time, except maybe Hodges and the eight men chosen by the VC who received 60 percent support or more. But, the rule's absence from the start of HOF balloting would have allowed many of the men who have not come close to election to earn maximum support levels that were higher than the ones they actually received. In turn, that would have accomplished two things to enhance the credibility of the overall selection process: many of the veterans panels' most dubious, low-support selections might, in hindsight, appear more credible now (at least, based on their vote histories), and—far more important—it would not be quite so difficult for the post–1945 players to qualify for VC consideration.

Of course, an increase in the number of candidates eligible for Veterans Committee consideration would not please those who believe that

Cooperstown is already tainted by the admission of too many mediocre players. But it would be consistent with the apparent mindset of the voting majority over the course of BBWAA election history, and it might also help to eliminate one of the apparent flaws in the current Hall of Fame roster — the fact that the present Cooperstown membership appears grossly disproportionate by historical era.

11
Proportional Bias

Although there is disagreement among baseball historians regarding the precise cutoff dates, major-league history is usually divided into six periods of unequal length — the nineteenth-century (1876–1900), plus the Dead-Ball (1901–19), Live-Ball (1920–45), Postwar Integration (1946–60), Expansion (1961–75), and Free-Agent (since 1976) Eras. Although trends from consecutive periods have overlapped, each of these eras nonetheless reflect distinct developments in either the style of play, the demography of major-league rosters, or the economic conditions prevalent in the game. A seventh era, distinguished by a new economics, further expansion and the predominance of offense over pitching, probably began with the 1995 season, in the aftermath of the costly, season-ending players strike of 1994. But, as only a few years have elapsed since then, it also can be treated — for now — as an extension of the Free-Agent Era.

Because of differences in the number of seasons played, plus how many leagues and teams were in existence at the time, the number of players from each era who meet the Hall of Fame's ten-year service requirement — or who received HOF votes for short-term careers before the rule was instituted — varies considerably, with a large plurality having played since the beginning of the Expansion Era in 1961. Table 24 examines by era the number of eligible players (El Plyrs) who had met those requirements through 1994 (again, the last season they could be active and still be on the HOF ballot by 2000), including those who remained active after that date but had ten years of service by the end of that season. It also gives the percentage of the overall total represented by each historical period (Era Pct), the number of players from each era elected by the BBWAA and veterans committees through 2000, the total number of Hall of Fame players from each period to that date (HOF Total), and the percentage of all Cooperstown players that number represents (HOF Pct). Finally, it provides the number of players (Ideal Tot) and the plus-or-minus variation (Era Var) from that total which should've been elected from each era if every period of baseball history currently had representation proportional to the number of eligibles it produced.

TABLE 24
HOF-ELIGIBLE PLAYERS BY ERA, NUMBER ELECTED, AND ERA VARIATION

Era	Era Years	El Plyrs	Era Pct	By BBWAA	By VC	HOF Total	HOF Pct	Ideal Total	Era Var
19th Century	1876–00	197	8.6	1	25	26	14.1	16	+10
Dead-Ball	1901–19	267	11.6	9	24	33	17.8	21	+12
Live-Ball	**1920–45**	**458**	**20.0**	**30**	**32**	**62**	**33.5**	**37**	**+25**
Postwar	1946–60	301	13.1	15	9	24	13.0	24	—
Expansion	1961–75	458	20.0	27	2	29	15.7	37	-8
Free-Agent	1976–94	614	26.8	11	0	11	5.9	50	-39
Totals		*2295*	*100.1*	*93*	*92*	*185*	*100.0*	*185*	*0*

Note: For this comparison, pitchers were assigned to the era in which they had the most major-league innings pitched, while non-pitchers were placed in the era in which they had the most major-league at-bats. The variation from 100 percent resulted from rounding.

As evidenced by Table 24, and expanding on the data given in Table 19 (Chapter 9), the Live-Ball Era of major-league history has been favored by electors from the BBWAA and veterans committees alike. With sixty-two representatives, comprising over one-third of Cooperstown's overall player roster, the era has twenty-five more than would be appropriate if an equal-sized HOF membership was distributed proportional to the number of eligible candidates from each historical period.

This apparent favoritism resulted for several reasons. To begin with, the Live-Ball Era is regarded by many as baseball's Golden Age. Dominated by Babe Ruth, the period marked the ascendancy of the home-run hitter as an American cultural hero, brought a profound alteration in the way the game was (and has continued to be) played, and acquired a mythic aura in the process. The Hall of Fame's creation and early elections occurred during the period, and many of the first electors were the sports-writing contemporaries of Live-Ball heroes—who owed much of their own success to describing those players' exploits. So it figures that three of the first five inductees—Ruth, Cobb and Johnson (the latter two of whom were mainly dead-ballers) and two-thirds of the top fifteen men in the 1936 BBWAA balloting were guys who played significant, if not majority, portions of their careers during the Live-Ball Era. And, given that the 1936 electors were not restricted to voting for retired players, it's no surprise that three more of that year's top fifteen vote-getters (Rogers Hornsby, Mickey Cochrane and Lou Gehrig) were Live-Ball players still active at the time.

Also, the Live-Ball Era lasted long enough — twenty-six seasons— to encompass two separate ten-year generations of HOF candidates, and then some. So, many players like Hank Greenberg, Joe Medwick and Joe DiMaggio are synonymous with part of the period even though they were barely, or not at all, contemporary with earlier men like Ruth, Cobb and Johnson; and, because their careers lasted beyond the end of the Live-Ball Era, they also extended the period in which players from that era were under consideration by the electors. Even after establishment of the BBWAA's fifteen-year eligibility window, the very length of the Live-Ball Era itself assured that players from that period were eligible for front-door consideration into the late 1960s, when guys like Medwick and Red Ruffing were elected; and, given the structure of Veterans-Committee eligibility, this also extended the period in which players from the era dominated its selection process.

Despite all that, in terms of raw numbers, the voters' apparent favoritism for Live-Ball players is logically indefensible. The present composition of the Cooperstown roster imposes a subjective judgment that more than one-third of the greatest players in baseball history performed during a period which comprised only one-fifth of its overall duration to date. It also requires an acceptance that, although both eras produced the same number of eligible candidates in Table 24, the sixty-second-best Live-Ball player (hypothetically, Fred Lindstrom or Jesse Haines) was better, or at least more deserving of the Cooperstown honor, than the twenty-ninth-best man from the Expansion period (Bill Mazeroski, Roger Maris or Ron Santo, for example). That premise is valid only if you believe that the earlier period's overall quality of play was at least twice that of the latter's.

But, even if you accept that premise, the current distribution of HOF membership also requires a belief that the least-qualified Live-Ball Hall of Famer also was better than the twelfth-best player from the Free-Agent Era, and that the quality of play in the 1920–45 period was roughly five times better than it has been since 1976. That contention sinks faster than the Battleship *Arizona* went down at Pearl Harbor: major-league baseball in the Live-Ball Era was a "whites-only" game, involving only an occasional player born outside the United States, using facilities, equipment and training methods that were inferior to their modern counterparts; the Free-Agent Era has included the best players from virtually every race and continent, drawn from a much larger population base which more than compensates for any comparative dilution of talent that may have resulted from its expanded number of teams. Find someone who believes that Lindstrom or Haines was a better player than as-yet-unenshrined Free-Agent candidates like Eddie Murray or Roger Clemens, and you can probably sell them, sight-unseen, an ocean-front condo in Amarillo.

But, because the Hall of Fame selection procedure is inherently focused on the past, at any given point in time its structure imposes that there always will be an imbalance of representation favoring earlier eras. Active or very recent players are not eligible for BBWAA consideration, and the Veterans Committee process includes a built-in, twenty-three-year delay from the moment of each candidate's retirement. So, the number of men in Cooperstown from relatively recent eras can never be proportional to those from earlier periods, and the number of VC electees from recent times must always be smaller than those chosen by the writers.

Although the Live-Ball Era's Cooperstown representation is disproportional in terms of raw numbers, when compared to the overall number of eligible players it produced, its membership ratio is not grossly inconsistent with those accrued by the two earlier periods of major-league history. The sixty-two Live-Ball members represent 13.5 percent of the 458 eligible players produced by that era. In comparison, the twenty-six nineteenth-century members comprise 13.2 percent of the eligibles from that period, and the thirty-three men from Dead-Ball times include 12.4 percent of the eligible players from 1901–19. Overall, the first three eras of big-league history average almost exactly 13 percent representation in Cooperstown; and, if that standard is applied to the 458 Live-Ball eligibles, then the period should have sixty men in the Hall. So, it can also be argued that the sixty-two current Live-Ball members represent only two more than the number to which the era is entitled and that the apparent raw-number bias favoring men from that period is, in part, a statistical mirage.

Applying the precedent of a 13 percent representational average to the number of men eligible from the three most recent historical periods allows for an estimate of the Hall of Fame's likely numerical composition at some distant point in the future (say, roughly fifty years from now), when selections of players from all six eras may have ended, providing a more coherent picture of what proportional representation would imply regarding the overall HOF roster. Table 25 presents such a projection, based also on the premise that the Free-Agent Era ended after the 1994 season (i.e., ignoring any men like Mark McGwire, who played in their tenth major-league season sometime after 1994). It includes the number of years for each of baseball's historical eras (Era Yrs), the percentage of big-league history represented by those years (Pct Yrs), the projected number of Hall of Fame members for each era (Proj Tot), the ratio of eligible players from each era which that total represents (% In HOF), the percentage of overall Cooperstown membership that projection would represent (HOF Pct), and the variation between the projection and the number of HOF members from each era as of 2000. Note that the third and fourth columns in Table 25 necessarily repeat data from the previous table.

TABLE 25
PROJECTED COOPERSTOWN ERA TOTALS, USING 13.0 PERCENT STANDARD

Era	Era Yrs	Pct Yrs	El Plyrs	Era Pct	Proj Tot	% In HOF	HOF Pct	1999 Var
19th Century	25	21.0	197	8.6	26	13.2	8.7	0
Dead-Ball	19	16.0	267	11.6	33	12.4	11.0	0
Live-Ball	26	21.8	458	20.0	62	13.5	20.7	0
Postwar	15	12.6	301	13.1	39	13.0	13.0	+15
Expansion	15	12.6	458	20.0	60	13.0	20.0	+31
Free-Agent	19	16.0	614	26.8	80	13.0	26.7	+69
Totals	*119*	*100.0*	*2295*	*100.1*	*300*	*78.1*	*100.1*	*+115*

So relatively proportional representation by era fifty years hence would require the election of 115 new members in that period, including fifteen more players from the Postwar, thirty-one from the Expansion and sixty-nine from the Free-Agent Eras. Given the precedent of 185 players elected in Cooperstown's first sixty-three years (or 2.9 per year) a total of 115 new ones over the next five decades represents slightly more than two new inductees per year and is (therefore) probably less than the number that will actually be chosen.

Existence of the Veterans Committee and its predecessors are evidence that proportionality among the HOF roster is and always has been deemed desirable, and Table 25 indicates that it easily can be achieved within the bounds of voting tradition. Of course, to do so would also require the unlikely prospects that no more players be elected from any of baseball's first three historical eras and that the VC's current eligibility restrictions be sufficiently liberalized to assure fair representation for the Postwar, Expansion and Free-Agent Eras.

But the Hall of Fame roster is also imbalanced positionally. Table 26 provides a tabulation of the same set of Hall of Fame eligibles measured in Table 24. With two exceptions noted below the table, each man is assigned to the position he played most often in the majors. Through 2000, the disproportional representation by position favored outfielders, shortstops, first and second basemen, to the detriment of catchers, pitchers and third basemen.

TABLE 26
HOF-ELIGIBLE PLAYERS BY POSITION,
NUMBER ELECTED, AND VARIATION

Position	Elgbl Plyrs	Elgbl Pct	By BBWAA	By VC	HOF Total	HOF Pct	Ideal Total	Pos Var
Pitcher	813	35.4	32	26	58	31.4	65	-7
Catcher	271	11.8	7	5	12	6.5	22	-10
First Base	152	6.6	8	9	17	9.2	12	+5
Second Base	166	7.2	8	7	15	8.1	13	+2
Shortstop	181	7.9	8	11	19	10.3	15	+4
Third Base	158	6.9	5	4	9	4.9	13	-4
Outfield	554	24.1	25	30	55	29.7	45	+10
Totals	2295	99.9	93	92	185	100.1	185	0

Note: Although Rod Carew and Ernie Banks are listed on the Hall of Fame roster as a second baseman and shortstop, respectively, they both played more games at first base during their careers. For the purposes of this table, they were included at the position of their HOF citations.

For most of the twentieth century, which comprises about 80 percent of major-league history, big-league teams carried twenty-five-man rosters over the majority of each season (except for September, when they are expanded). On average, and in very rough estimation, at any given time each of these rosters included nine or ten pitchers, two or three catchers, and about two men for each of the other seven positions—except, perhaps, first base, where a reserve outfielder often serves as the backup. From that general habit, and assuming (counterintuitively) a relatively equal probability of career-limiting injury for each position, the estimated proportion of men who could be expected to meet the Hall of Fame's ten-year eligibility requirement from each position would be pitchers, 38 percent (at an average of 9.5 per roster); catchers, 10 percent (average of 2.5 per team); first basemen, 6 percent (1.5 per club); second basemen, shortstops and third basemen, 8 percent each (two per position for each roster); and outfielders, 22 percent (about 5.5 per team). These estimates are very similar to the numbers found in the "Elgbl Pct" column of Table 26, and it's plausible that—much as anything but random chance—the variances reflect differences caused by the smaller rosters prevalent during much of the nineteenth century. With both sets of figures in mind, it's also arguable that the number of men elected to Cooperstown representing each position should, therefore, reflect the relative proportions evident in these numbers. After all, each position is equally vital to any team's success, right?

Maybe not. One possible cause of the Hall's positional imbalance is the fact that some spots on the baseball diamond are harder to play defensively than others. Ignoring pitchers, from whom good fielding is a bonus rather than a must, the other positions—catcher, the four infielders, and the three distinct outfield spots—can be displayed on a linear scale which, from left to right, expresses the relative, decreasing degree of difficulty (and, in most cases, the amount of athleticism) inherent to each position's defensive play. This scale, shown below, is known as the "defensive spectrum."

$$C - SS - 2B - CF - 3B - RF - LF - 1B$$

There is considerable disagreement regarding the propriety of including catchers on this scale, and where exactly the position should be placed along it, if included. Even the most casual baseball fan knows that, generally, catchers tend to have round, squat bodies (many are even chubby). Also, the overall level of athleticism required to play the position is in no way as evident as the quickness of hand and foot or the graceful agility needed to play either of the middle-infield positions which follow catcher immediately along the line above, and most men who don the tools of ignorance are nowhere as swift afoot as the pokiest of most other fielders. Intuitively, and by most of the visual evidence, catchers should reside at the far right of the defensive spectrum, not the left.

But catchers play the most physically and mentally demanding position on the baseball field. To begin with, they have to wear all that protective gear, which adds to the amount of weight they must move on every play—each of which begins from an uncomfortable squat that also slows their reaction time. They go into and out of this squat on virtually every pitch, even if only to toss the ball back to the mound after the batter has taken, missed or fouled-off a pitch, exacting a heavy toll on their ankles and knees. Despite the large, padded mitts they use, every pitch thrown their way is the potential cause of a broken knuckle, finger or hand, each foul tip by the batter a broken toe waiting to happen, and catchers can even have their elbows shattered by wildly swung baseball bats. Their risk of injury is higher on every pitch than any other position on the diamond, and that is why most major-league clubs carry two reserve backstops on their roster instead of the lone back-up they have for most of the other positions.

Beyond that, catchers are also required to move around as much, or even more, on each defensive play than fielders at the other positions—as, unless there are runners in scoring position, each is expected to lug himself and most of his gear part way down the baseline to back up first base on most balls hit fair. Catchers are also required to possess a rifle arm capable of firing bullets from their low squat with pinpoint accuracy that nip runners who lean too far off first on pitchouts, or that travel 127.3 feet to second base in a near-arcless trajectory during attempted steals.

Finally, catchers are also required to be "in the game" mentally far more than any other position. They must know the strengths and weaknesses of opposing batters as well or better than the pitcher does; they must be in sync with their battery mate on the selection of each pitch; because of the possibility of steals, bunts and hit-and-run plays, they must follow the pitch count, number of outs and status of baserunners more closely than anyone else on the diamond; and they must help position the other fielders on each pitch, appropriate to the number of outs, the count and type of pitch being thrown, and the tendencies of each batter. So, there is as much—perhaps more—reason to place catchers on the far left of the defensive spectrum as anywhere else along it.

Reasons for the left-to-right placements of the other positions along the defensive spectrum are far more obvious. Shortstops need a greater amount of range and better throwing arms than second basemen, but both positions—because of the agility vital to turning double plays—require more acrobatic athleticism than any other spot on the diamond. Center fielders need not be quite so agile, but must be swift runners capable of covering larger amounts of territory than their fellow outfielders and must have strong arms for the throw from deep center field. Third basemen also need strong arms, very quick reflexes and considerable acrobatic ability, but are not required to defend nearly as much space as the middle fielders behind the pitcher. Right field is tougher than left, mainly because of the long throw required from the foul line in the outfield corner to third base. Left fielders should have some speed and be able to make a good throw to home plate, but their toss to third base is shorter than that of the other outfielders. First base requires agile feet, good hands and some acrobatics, but on the whole is less demanding than any of the other positions.

Given all of that, the positional imbalance among the Cooperstown roster might reflect a built-in bias among the voters favoring the more difficult defensive positions. But, even a cursory look at the Hall of Fame totals in Table 26 deflates that theory. By the numbers above, catchers are the most under-represented position on the HOF roster; and, of the two middle-infield spots that are next in line for degree of difficulty, only shortstop has an excess of members large enough that part of it might be attributable to bias favoring defensive skill. Also, among the fifty-five outfielders in the Hall, and based on their Cooperstown positional citations, center field — the hardest of the three, defensively — has only sixteen representatives, the fewest of the separate fly-chasing positions, and left field, the easiest, has more (eighteen, compared to twenty-one right fielders). Finally, first basemen, occupying the least-demanding defensive position, have far more members than third basemen, whose need for comparatively superior fielding skills is evidenced by the position's nickname, "the hot corner." In fact, if Ernie Banks and Rod Carew are added to the list of first sackers in Cooperstown, then first base has nineteen Hall of Famers, a total surpassing that of shortstops (with Banks removed) and second only to right fielders among the eight positions.

Approached another way, there are only a handful of Hall of Famers about whom it can be plausibly argued that defensive skill was truly significant to their elections: catchers Ray Schalk and Rick Ferrell, first baseman Frank Chance, second sackers Bid McPhee and Johnny Evers, shortstops Luis Aparicio, Dave Bancroft, Rabbit Maranville, Joe Tinker and Phil Rizzuto, third baseman Brooks Robinson, and outfielders Richie Ashburn and Max Carey. But, although the offensive statistics of several of these men are below average among the Hall of Famers at their respective positions, there are other factors relevant to some of their elections which mitigate any probability that they were enshrined primarily for their defense. Although Chance, Evers and Tinker all were chosen in 1946 by the OTC2, in part for their undeserved reputation as a premier double-play combination, Chance also had a lengthy and successful career as a manager (he skippered the 1906 Cubs that set the all-time record for regular-season games won) and he was certainly not regarded as the defensive equal of Hal Chase, the shady contemporary who received more votes than Chance in the first HOF balloting. Evers (1914), Rizzuto (1950) and Robinson (1964) were one-time MVPs, which also boosted their Cooperstown credentials; and, although Brooks was widely believed to have been the best-ever defensive player at third base at the time of his retirement, his career production in home runs and RBI are comparable to the best offensive players at his position. Based on their fielding stats, Ashburn and Carey (along with Tris Speaker) were arguably the best defensive outfielders of all time, but Ashburn was a two-time batting champ who also led his league in hits on three occasions and on-base average four times, and Carey was a ten-time leader in stolen bases. Similarly, Aparicio led his circuit in stolen bases in each of his first nine seasons in the majors and — despite a poor career on-base average of just .313 — was regarded, along with Maury Wills and Lou Brock, as one of the premier leadoff hitters of his era.

All of that leaves only Schalk, Ferrell, McPhee, Bancroft, Tinker and Maranville — two catchers, a second baseman and three shortstops — as men who were possibly elected for their defense. In that small group, McPhee had the most career homers (53) and runs batted in (1067); Ferrell, the highest career batting average (.281). Among the 185 players elected through 2000, each of those numbers are inferior to the means among HOF members as a whole and among the Cooperstown players from those three positions. So there may be a slight tendency among the voters to reward fielding excellence among catchers, shortstops and second basemen — the three most difficult positions on the defensive spectrum. If so, the tendency is much stronger within the Veterans Committee as all but Maranville are VC selections.

But, if only six of the Hall's 127 non-pitchers (about 5 percent of them) can be isolated as possible defensive selections, that's scant evidence of pro-fielding bias of any kind among the voters. Instead, that low total supports the argument that the Cooperstown fates of non-pitchers are predominantly decided by their offensive skills and any positional bias among the Hall of Fame roster has resulted primarily from differences in batting statistics.

Table 27 provides the mean career values for a select group of batting stats among Hall of Fame members (excluding men elected for non-playing capacities) at each position through the 2000 voting. It gives the number of players elected at each position (Tot), followed by the average career figure among that group for the de facto categories hits (H) and home runs (HR), plus total bases (TB), runs scored (R), runs batted in (RBI), stolen bases (SB), batting (BA), slugging (SA) and on-base averages (OBA). The highest average for each category is boldfaced; and separate averages are also provided for outfielders as a whole and all 127 men combined.

TABLE 27
AVERAGE CAREER BATTING STATISTICS BY POSITION, HOF PLAYERS THROUGH 2000

Position	Tot	H	HR	TB	R	RBI	SB	BA	SA	OBA
Catcher	12	1746	187	2739	890	995	97	.287	.445	.365
First Base	17	2320	**273**	3787	1317	**1415**	149	.310	**.506**	.388
Second Base	15	2503	123	3534	1372	1076	295	.305	.434	.381
Shortstop	19	2283	101	3193	1203	1041	263	.288	.401	.357
Third Base	9	2290	227	3564	1192	1210	133	.294	.453	.361
Left Field	18	**2598**	244	**4056**	1450	1349	223	.315	.493	.387
Center Field	16	2444	208	3727	1449	1161	**313**	**.317**	.485	**.396**
Right Field	21	2548	249	3980	**1464**	1318	235	.312	.480	.388
(Outfield)	*(55)*	*(2534)*	*(235)*	*(3931)*	*(1455)*	*(1283)*	*(254)*	*(.314)*	*(.486)*	*(.390)*
Overall	*127*	*2372*	*202*	*3616*	*1317*	*1207*	*223*	*.305*	*.463*	*.379*

It's easy to see from the data in Table 27 why there is a proportional excess of outfielders and first basemen in Cooperstown, as one of those posts has the highest positional mean among Hall of Fame members for each of the nine batting stats listed. First sackers lead in home runs, RBI and slugging average, and one or the other of the three outfield positions owns leadership in each of the other categories. As a whole, scores for first basemen are above or equal to the Cooperstown average in all but two of the stats (hits and stolen bases); the means for the outfielders as a group are above the average in all of them; and so are the scores for each separate outfield position — with the exception that center fielders have a below-average mark for runs batted in.

As for the other positions, Hall of Fame second basemen are above the Cooperstown average in four of the nine offensive categories (hits, runs scored, stolen bases and on-base average), while third sackers are above the mean in only two of them (home runs and runs batted in), and shortstops in just one (stolen bases). As a group, catchers comprise the low end of Cooperstown offensive performance, as the averages for the twelve backstops enshrined through 2000 are below the Hall of Fame mean in every batting statistic.

Table 28 gives the positional averages among all players eligible for Cooperstown through 2000 for the same stats included in Table 27, with leadership for each category boldfaced again. The individual outfield assignments (left, center or right) are based on the positional citations that appear in "The Teams and Their Players" section of the Macmillan *Baseball Encyclopedia*, with each outfielder placed at the position where he had the most seasonal listings.

TABLE 28
Average Career Batting Stats by Position, All HOF-Eligible Players

Position	Tot	H	HR	TB	R	RBI	SB	BA	SA	OBA
Catcher	271	777	53	1111	332	372	31	.252	.354	.319
First Base	152	**1469**	**139**	**2249**	742	**766**	92	.279	**.425**	.349
Second Base	166	1299	55	1773	669	509	132	.266	.361	.333
Shortstop	181	1236	47	1669	612	489	119	.257	.344	.319
Third Base	158	1285	91	1865	658	587	101	.265	.380	.331
Left Field	197	1350	114	2035	714	643	134	**.281**	.421	**.350**
Center Field	173	1396	93	2082	**764**	582	**172**	.279	.401	.346
Right Field	184	1389	128	2124	734	671	115	.279	.422	.349
(Outfield)	*(554)*	*(1377)*	*(112)*	*(2061)*	*(736)*	*(634)*	*(140)*	*(.279)*	*(.415)*	*(.348)*
Overall	*2295*	*1242*	*88*	*1807*	*632*	*563*	*107*	*.269*	*.387*	*.336*

Note that the relative differences among the batting means in Table 28 are generally consistent with (although predictably inferior to) the positional averages among Hall of Famers given in the previous table. But, more important in terms of any positional bias, both sets of batting averages are also indicative of the relative importance of hitting and fielding ability at each position, from left to right, along the defensive spectrum. If the eight positions on that spectrum are grouped according to their composite totals for the number of categories in which they exceed the overall Cooperstown batting means in Table 27, then the relative degree of difficulty along that linear measure can be identified by three distinct clusters of positions: group one, including catchers and shortstops only, exceeds the Hall of Fame average in just one batting category, combined (stolen bases by shortstops); group two, second basemen, center fielders and third basemen combined, exceeds the HOF means in a total of fourteen categories; and group three, right and left fielders, plus first basemen exceeds the average in a total of twenty-three.

Similarly, with regard to Table 28, catchers and shortstops combine to exceed the averages among all Cooperstown-eligible players in only one category (again, stolen bases by shortstops). The group including center fielders, second and third basemen surpass the overall batting means for Table 28 in seventeen categories. And the first basemen plus left and right fielders exceed the overall averages for HOF-eligible players in twenty-six.

So the two positions at the far left of the defensive spectrum clearly have the most negative impact on offensive production, with the next three in order having considerably less but still more than the last three on the right. And the order of the spectrum confirms why catcher, shortstop and second base are the only positions at which it is possible to identify Hall of Fame members who may have been chosen for their fielding prowess. Not only do the more difficult defensive positions exact a heavy toll on batting performance, but baseball managers are also traditionally required — by practical necessity — to sacrifice offensive production at the more difficult fielding positions (notably catcher and shortstop) in order to solidify their team's overall defensive play. So, the lower batting norms by players at the more difficult defensive spots are preordained by the rigors of the positions themselves and by the philosophies which govern decisions about who plays them regularly.

But, as noted in Chapter 2, defensive statistics can be misleading, and may obfuscate a true picture of the relative fielding skills among players examined as a group. In contrast, batting stats are less ambiguous and, therefore, more useful as tools to identify outstanding career performance. So it's clear that superior offensive statistics drive the Cooperstown elections of non-pitchers: the surplus of first basemen and outfielders on the HOF roster is primarily attributable to the gaudy batting stats accrued by men at those positions; and the shortage of catchers is caused by the fact that the rigors of the post exact a greater toll on offensive performance (even more than shortstop) than can be compensated for in the elective process by the subjective evaluation of fielding skills.

Beyond the shortage of catchers, and as indicated in Table 26, there appears to be a significant deficit in the appropriate number of pitchers elected to Cooperstown through 2000. Table 29 provides the career averages for starters and relievers among Hall of Fame members and all HOF-eligible hurlers, using the same inclusion criteria applied in Table 24. The data includes the number of men from each position (Tot), plus the means for games won (GW), winning percentage (Pct), earned run average (ERA), games pitched (GP), innings pitched (IP), strikeouts (SO), opponents' batting (OAV) and on-base averages (OOB), and the ratio of baserunners allowed per nine innings (Rat). Assignment of pitchers as starters or relievers is based on the role in which each hurler had the most career games pitched.

TABLE 29
AVERAGE CAREER PITCHING STATS, HOF
AND ELIGIBLE PITCHERS, THROUGH 2000

HOF Pitchers	Tot	GW	Pct	ERA	GP	IP	SO	OAV	OOB	Rat
Start Pitch	56	270	.594	2.95	578	4052	2152	.244	.300	10.83
Relief Pitch	2	129	.516	2.71	1007	1978	1455	.226	.293	10.26
Overall	58	265	.591	2.94	593	3981	2128	.244	.299	10.81
All Pitchers	Tot	GW	Pct	ERA	GP	IP	SO	OAV	OOB	Rat
Start Pitch	589	139	.525	3.56	395	2300	1118	.258	.320	11.82
Relief Pitch	224	60	.495	3.65	475	1038	613	.255	.328	12.17
Overall	813	117	.516	3.58	417	1952	979	.257	.323	11.92

The apparent shortage of pitchers in Cooperstown might be linked to the advent of relief-pitching specialization. Among the 813 pitchers eligible for Hall of Fame consideration by the year 2000, and give or take a handful of arguable cases, 224 (or 27.5 percent) of them could fairly be called career relief specialists. But, among the fifty-eight hurlers elected to the Hall through that date, only two—Hoyt Wilhelm and Rollie Fingers—were relievers.

Baseball's first true relief specialist was probably Doc Crandall, who served as a late-inning mop-up man for John McGraw's New York Giants in the years 1908–13. Crandall won 37 of his 102 career victories in relief and compiled a total of twenty-five saves over his ten-year career, most of them for the Giants (Hall of Famer Mordecai Brown had forty-nine saves during the same era, but won 210 of his 239 career victories as a starter and no doubt was enshrined for that performance).

But, Crandall never had more than a half-dozen saves in a single season (Brown's career high was thirteen in 1911). So both men's saves often may have been incidental; and, as noted in Chapter 4, the first true "closer" of significance in the present-day sense was Firpo Marberry, who toiled in the Show during 1923–36. Firpo won 53 of his 148 career victories in relief, saved 101 games, and had five different seasons with eleven saves or more (including a high of twenty-two in 1926). Marberry also led his league in games pitched in a season on six occasions; and, among all HOF-eligible pitchers, is tied with Dead-Ball-Era Giant Joe McGinnity for the all-time leadership in that category. Firpo was followed by Yankee Johnny Murphy (among several others with less success), who played during 1932–47 and won 73 of his 93 career victories in relief, saved 107 games, and led the American League in saves on four occasions (with a career high of 19 in 1939).

But, despite those pioneers, relief specialization did not blossom or gain much recognition until after World War II, when the Yankees' Joe Page saved 76 games over the five-year period 1946–50 and Philadelphia's Jim Konstanty became the first reliever to win a MVP in the last of those years. Even at that, it was not until the late 1950s that most major-league teams started to reserve a spot on their rosters for men who began their big-league careers as relievers and were not just failed or worn-out starting pitchers—guys like Elroy Face, Don Elston, Jim Brosnan, Ryne Duren, Don McMahon, Lindy McDaniel, Larry Sherry and Wilhelm (although, ironically, Hoyt was briefly a starter during the late fifties). As a result, over 80 percent of the relievers who were Cooperstown-eligible by 2000 spent all (or most) of their careers during the Expansion and or Free-Agent Eras.

When you add to all of that the fact that truly modern relief-pitching strategies did not evolve until the early years of the Free-Agent Era, it's no surprise that bullpen specialists have received little recognition from HOF electors. Among the 239 pitchers who had earned front-door votes through the 2000 election, only thirty of them can be fairly identified as relief specialists. In addition to Wilhelm and Fingers, only four of those men (Elroy Face, Sparky Lyle, Bruce Sutter and Goose Gossage) have ever received as much as 10 percent support on any BBWAA ballot, and only the latter two had ever earned as much as one hundred votes in any election. Among pioneers of the craft, Doc Crandall earned just one vote in 1947; Firpo Marberry got eleven votes (with a high of five votes and 1.9 percent support) spread over five different elections; Johnny Murphy and Jim Konstanty never received a vote, although both satisfied the ten-year service requirement; and Joe Page, whose big-league tenure lasted only eight seasons, has never been eligible for consideration.

So, given the time delay inherent to the Hall of Fame selection process, it's premature to criticize the disproportion between starting and relief pitchers among the current HOF roster. In turn, it's also obvious that the relievers' relative absence from Cooperstown to date has no relevance to the Hall's proportional shortage of pitchers as a whole.

But the Hall's pitcher deficit might also be traceable to the discrepancy between the number of de facto standards for batters and hurlers. After all, pitchers have just one de facto criteria (three hundred games won), while hitters have two (three thousand hits and five hundred homers), and one might argue that the difference makes it more difficult for moundsmen to gain election.

Through the 1999 season, a total of fifty-five men had achieved at least one of Cooperstown's de facto standards, including just twenty pitchers and thirty-five men who played other positions. Among them, a total of seven — all of them non-pitchers — were still active in the majors in 2000 or, if retired, not yet on the HOF ballot. The remaining forty-eight were all enshrined by 2000. So twenty of the Hall's fifty-eight pitchers (34.5 percent) and twenty-eight of its 127 batters (22.0 percent) were de facto qualifiers, and the higher proportion of de facto pitchers is not strong evidence that those criteria are a cause of the Shrine's pitcher shortage.

Because batting and pitching statistics represent different sets of data, they are most likely perceived by most Hall of Fame electors as non-analogous. With that in mind, and given that neither relief pitching nor the de facto standards can explain Cooperstown's relative shortage of pitchers, it's probably fair to argue that the proportional deficit of seven hurlers noted in Table 26 has resulted primarily from random chance.

Overall, and despite the offensive advantages enjoyed by outfielders and first basemen and the relative disadvantages suffered by catchers and shortstops, the same can probably be said about the disproportional representation among non-pitchers too. Table 30 provides a positional breakdown of the average support percentages earned in by all men who have received Hall of Fame votes (excluding the sixteen who were elected in non-playing capacities). Included in the data are the number of men from each position who received votes through 2000 (Tot), the average first-ballot support percentage (1Bal Pct), the average high support percentage (High Pct) and the overall average support percentage for all years on the ballot (Avg Pct) received by players at each position, along with similar information for outfielders and pitchers grouped as a whole.

TABLE 30
AVERAGE BBWAA SUPPORT
PERCENTAGES BY POSITION

Position	Tot	1Bal Pct	High Pct	Avg Pct
Catcher	69	7.9	14.5	9.5
First Base	61	7.8	18.8	12.7
Second Base	59	8.0	17.4	11.3
Shortstop	63	7.6	17.1	10.5
Third Base	55	7.9	13.0	9.6
Left Field	65	8.8	16.4	12.5
Center Field	59	7.7	16.0	10.8
Right Field	61	12.1	21.4	15.8

Position	Tot	1Bal Pct	High Pct	Avg Pct
Start Pitcher	209	9.6	18.1	12.6
Relief Pitcher	30	7.2	10.3	8.2
(OF, Overall)	(185)	(9.6)	(17.9)	(13.0)
(P, Overall)	(239)	(9.3)	(17.1)	(12.0)
Overall	*731*	*8.7*	*16.9*	*11.2*

As noted earlier, the low scores earned by relief pitchers in Table 30 are the product of their very recent emergence as a separate class of Hall of Fame candidates. The scores received by right fielders are the highest among all positions in each category and help explain why there are more men from that position in Cooperstown than any other. But, if they evidence some pro–right field bias among HOF electors, the reasons for such favoritism are obscure — as the position leads among Cooperstown members in only one offensive category from Table 27 (runs scored) and resides nowhere near the difficult end of the defensive spectrum. Also, if pitchers and outfielders are both treated as a whole and then compared to the other five positions (catcher and the four infield spots), there is little variation in the Table 30 scores: outfielders own the best first-ballot average of 9.6 percent, compared to a low of 7.6 percent by shortstops, producing a range of just 2.0 percent in that category; the range for the average high is 5.8 percent, between first basemen (18.8) and third sackers (13.0); and outfielders top the overall average with 13.0 percent, 3.5 percent higher than the low score posted by catchers (9.5 percent).

As a result, none of the data in Table 30 provides any convincing evidence of a strong bias among Hall of Fame electors for or against any position; and, if anything, it merely reinforces the overall fickleness of the HOF selection process. Like the last-minute "undecideds" in presidential elections, many Cooperstown electors — ruled by their dual reliance upon subjective and de facto standards — simply vote for candidates who look like "winners" at the given moment in time.

The 1999 BBWAA balloting was typical of that approach. Nolan Ryan, George Brett and Robin Yount, the only candidates on the ballot who had met one of Cooperstown's de facto standards, all were chosen in their first year of eligibility, while Carlton Fisk and Tony Perez, who had not equaled that achievement, were forced to wait another year. Some 1999 voters may have consciously limited their selections on a positional basis (e.g., voted for the best candidate available from each position), but they were not a majority — as six of the ten men who received the most votes were players from identical positions (pitchers Ryan and Jim Kaat, catchers Fisk and Gary Carter, and first basemen Perez and Steve Garvey). A handful of 1999 electors may even have been aware of Cooperstown's positional imbalance and have voted in some manner to correct it. But most voters, by far, supported the guys with the best subjective credentials; that the trio who owned them were a pitcher, third baseman and shortstop evidenced nothing more than random chance. No doubt, that behavior manifests among the majority for each year's ballot, with any variations of support by position dependent entirely upon the list of specific candidates available.

All the same, and with the lone exception of relief pitchers, there is no rational justification for any disproportionate positional representation among the Hall of Fame roster. Unlike representation by era, the selection process includes no built in rules or constraints which favor one position over another. Although the premise behind the defensive spectrum is logical, the scale itself is nonetheless subjective; neither it nor the positional disparities in batting statistics are sufficient reason to ignore the fact that no team can win without someone playing each position on the diamond, and doing so effectively. With that in mind, at least a relative correction of the positional imbalance is a requisite for fairness among the HOF roster, and one of the mandates of the Veterans Committee should be to do so (focusing first on the deficit of catchers and third basemen). Only the VC can correct this problem, because the random, subjective nature of the BBWAA process prevents it from accomplishing that task.

12

De Facto De Matter

With regard to Hall of Fame voting, a de facto standard should meet four essential criteria. First and most obvious, at any given point in time every man who has equaled or surpassed it and is eligible for Cooperstown election should already be enshrined. Second, regardless of the statistic or specific value involved, it should represent a level of career performance that is difficult enough to attain to preserve the achievement's relative exclusivity over time. Third, it should also be a round, easy-to-remember number—like 300 pitching wins, or 3000 hits and 500 homers for batters.

But, identifying that all of the men who meet or exceed a certain number are in the Hall doesn't automatically isolate that value as a real de facto standard, because the criterion cannot have meaning unless the electors are also conscious of some historical precedent for its application and feel some pressure—as in the Don Sutton case—to abide by it. So a true de facto standard must also be one that is widely discussed in media commentaries about HOF elections—enough, at least, so that every Cooperstown voter who is not brain-dead must be aware of it.

Through the 2000 BBWAA and Veterans Committee voting, every man in baseball history who had accumulated one of the values listed above and was eligible for HOF consideration by that date—forty-eight of them in all—had been elected to Cooperstown. Among the three categories, the most recent qualifiers to join the ballot were 1995 inductee Mike Schmidt (548 homers), plus the three 1999 electees (Ryan for wins, Brett and Yount for hits); all first-year selections.

Whether or not the Hall of Fame trustees and many of its individual electors choose to deny it, there is no disputing that 300 wins is the established de facto standard for pitchers. The number is round; only twenty hurlers in big-league history had ever reached it through the 2000 voting; all of them were enshrined by that date; and achievement of that number dominated media discussion of the Cooperstown credentials of all six 300-game winners—Gaylord Perry, Tom Seaver, Phil Niekro, Steve Carlton, Don Sutton and Nolan Ryan — to become eligible for the Hall since Perry's name was first placed on the ballot in 1989. Although Seaver, Carlton and Ryan were elected in their first years of eligibility, Perry required three ballots to gain induction; Niekro and Sutton, five apiece.

But de facto standards might change over time, and it's important to identify when 300 wins acquired that status. Table 31 traces the evolution of the de facto pitching standard through the history of the elections of the twenty hurlers who achieved it prior to the 2000 voting. The first five columns on the left give the year of each de facto pitcher selection, the Hall of Fame organ that chose them (Org), the number of ballots on which each man received votes (Bal, including the OTC1 voting of 1936), and his career wins total (Wins). The sixth column indicates the operative de facto standard in effect following each man's election, (Min) the minimum number of victories above which every eligible hurler had been elected through that date. The next column (Out) gives two numbers separated by a slash: the first is the number of 300-win pitchers eligible for election at that time who had not been enshrined through that date; the second is the number of 300-game winners at the time who were not yet eligible for election (i.e., men who were active or recently retired and not yet on the ballot). The final column (High Not In) displays the victory total and name of the eligible but unenshrined pitcher with the most career wins at that point in time.

TABLE 31
EVOLUTION OF DE FACTO
PITCHING STANDARD

Pitcher	Year	Org	Bal	Wins	Min	Out	High Not In
Walter Johnson	1936	Wri	1	417	none	9/0	511 — Young
Christy Mathewson	1936	Wri	1	373	none	9/0	511 — Young
Cy Young	1937	Wri	3*	511	373	8/0	373 — Alexander
Grover Alexander	1938	Wri	3	373	373	7/0	361 — two
Charles Radbourn	1939	OTC2	1*	309	373	6/0	361 — two
Eddie Plank	1946	OTC2	6	326	373	5/1	361 — two
Lefty Grove	1947	Wri	5	300	373	5/0	361 — two

Pitcher	Year	Org	Bal	Wins	Min	Out	High Not In
Kid Nichols	1949	OTC2	6*	361	373	4/0	361 — Galvin
John Clarkson	1963	VC	2*	328	373	3/1	361 — Galvin
Tim Keefe	1964	VC	1	342	373	2/2	361 — Galvin
Pud Galvin	1965	VC	0	361	361	1/2	307 — Welch
Early Wynn	1972	Wri	4	300	309	1/1	307 — Welch
Warren Spahn	1973	Wri	1	363	309	1/0	307 — Welch
Mickey Welch	1973	VC	0	307	300	0/0	286 — Roberts
Gaylord Perry	1991	Wri	3	314	286	0/5	284 — Mullane
Tom Seaver	1992	Wri	1	311	286	0/4	284 — Mullane
Steve Carlton	1994	Wri	1	329	286	2/1	324 — Sutton
Phil Niekro	1997	Wri	5	318	300	1/1	324 — Sutton
Don Sutton	1998	Wri	5	324	300	0/1	288 — John
Nolan Ryan	1999	Wri	1	324	300	0/0	288 — John

*Total includes votes in the 1936 Old-Timers Committee balloting. Radbourn never received a vote from the BBWAA.

As will be evident below, the BBWAA has shown more resistance to application of the 300-win standard than to either of the de facto criteria for batters. Seven of the twenty qualifiers in this category were passed over by the writers altogether and were enshrined instead by one of the veterans committees. But, except for Eddie Plank and Kid Nichols, all of the VC choices were nineteenth-century hurlers who failed to gain election by the OTC1 (or the scribes who voted in 1936–38) and, by 1939, were beyond the writers' jurisdiction. No doubt, some of the early BBWAA voters had the same doubts about the quality of the pre–1893, 300-game winners that were noted in Chapter 6. But their failure to gain much notice from those voters probably resulted, more than anything else, from the initial confusion over eligibility criteria and the likelihood that some of them simply got lost amid the huge number of eligible candidates.

Regardless, the voters' acquiescence to a 300-wins standard probably dates first to 1972–73, when the BBWAA elected Early Wynn and the Veterans Committee tabbed Mickey Welch. That's because Welch's election in the latter year (along with that of Warren Spahn by the writers) marked the first time that all of the eligible 300-game winners were on the Cooperstown roster, and the eligible unenshrined hurler with the most wins after the 1973 voting was Robin Roberts, with 286.

In 1972 Wynn was the only BBWAA-eligible 300-game winner not yet enshrined (Spahn was not on the ballot until the following year). During his last two seasons as a player (1962–63), Early had struggled trying to reach the 300-win mark. At age forty-two, he posted a 7–15 record in the first of those years, leaving him one victory short of the goal, then he lost his first two decisions of 1963 before finally gaining the elusive prize and retiring soon thereafter. Wynn became eligible for Cooperstown in 1969 and — despite his achievement — got only ninety-five votes, for just 27.9 percent support. It took Early three more years to get elected and each time he wasn't there was much written about the writers' failure to honor a 300-game winner. But, when Wynn was finally chosen in 1972, he still got only 76.0 percent support, barely enough for election.

Welch retired after the 1892 season, so all of his career decisions (307–210, .594) occurred before the mound was moved to its modern distance from the plate. In Welch's era most teams carried only three or four hurlers, and two of them usually started and finished the vast majority of games played (the others were often position players who did double duty as pitchers). So those two-man rotations earned most of a club's decisions in a season, and Mickey's high victory and loss totals are as much a function of the habits of his time as they are evidence of superior skill (and the same is true of most other hurlers from his era).

Hall of Famer Tim Keefe (342–225, .603) was Welch's teammate on two different clubs for eight of Mickey's thirteen seasons, and Welch was almost always a good but nonetheless second fiddle — a nineteenth-century Don Drysdale following Sandy Koufax. Keefe topped his circuit in a major statistical category fifteen times in his fourteen seasons; Welch did it just once, leading the NL in winning percentage in 1885; and there is little doubt that Tim was the better pitcher. Keefe's statistical superiority should not demean Welch's HOF selection any more than Koufax's should diminish Drysdale's.

But generally, Welch's other stats are inferior to those of his de facto contemporaries; his 307 wins never bought him a single vote from the OTC1 or early BBWAA electors; and it's clear that, as the last de facto pitcher of his era tabbed for enshrinement at Cooperstown, there was considerable doubt about his merits for more than three decades of voting by both organs.

Welch was also the last de facto hurler enshrined by the VC, as every 300-win pitcher to be eligible since 1973 has gained election by the writers — a clear indication of most scribes' acceptance of the standard. After Warren Spahn's election by the BBWAA that same year, and given the growth in reliance upon relief pitching, it seemed for a while that no hurler would ever again equal 300 wins. Nonetheless, Gaylord Perry reached the mark in 1982, followed in quick succession by Carlton (1983), Seaver and Niekro (1985), Sutton (1986) and Ryan (1990); and their matriculation to the exclusive club gave the scribes another chance to reject the standard, if they wished.

Resistance to Perry, Niekro and Sutton's candidacies was, however, relatively feeble (none of them ever received less than 56.9 percent support on any BBWAA ballot) and short lived. It's almost certain that all three of them were better pitchers than Mickey Welch and some of his de facto contemporaries, so — given the standard's precedent — the writers had no legitimate excuse to deny any of them. In the big picture, the scribes reverted to their old habit of electing the three hurlers with superior subjective credentials on the first ballot (Seaver, Carlton and Ryan) and making the other three sweat it out a little while, just so they would know their places in the pecking order.

Assessing the combined elective histories of de facto pitchers is complicated by their inconsistent treatment in the voting. The thirteen 300-game winners chosen by the scribes averaged just 2.7 ballots to gain election, while the nineteen other hurlers anointed by the writers through 2000 typically required 6.5 — apparently a significant edge for the de facto qualifiers.

But the comparison is not valid, because it omits the seven 300-game winners who were virtually ignored in the front-door voting and had to be enshrined by the veterans committees. As a group, those men received votes on a total of just sixteen ballots, with a per-man average of only 8.4 percent support each time — so their vote histories cannot be lumped with those of de facto pitchers tabbed by the writers.

It's also noteworthy that only six of the ten pitchers ever chosen in their first year of BBWAA eligibility have been de facto qualifiers — Mathewson, Johnson, Spahn, Seaver, Carlton and Ryan (the other four were Bob Feller, Sandy Koufax, Bob Gibson and Jim Palmer, who averaged 238 wins for their careers). Oddly, both groups averaged 91.8 percent support in their only appearances on the ballot, surprising when you consider that two of the de facto hurlers (Seaver and Ryan) are in a virtual tie for the highest support percentage ever received by anyone.

In contrast to the pitchers, achievement of the de facto totals for hits and home runs has been a definite advantage for batters facing BBWAA scrutiny.

Table 32 traces the separate evolutions of those two criteria and includes the same information for hitters in exactly the same format as the pitcher data given in the previous table. Note that, for the purposes of this table, Cap Anson is credited with 3041 hits, rather than the 2995 he is officially given now — because, until very recently, Anson was believed to have achieved the higher total.

TABLE 32
Evolution of De Facto Hits, Home-Run Standards

Career Hits	Year	Org	Bal	Hits	Min	Out	High Not In
Ty Cobb	1936	Wri	1	4189	4189	4/0	3514 — Speaker
Honus Wagner	1936	Wri	2*	3415	4189	4/0	3514 — Speaker
Nap Lajoie	1937	Wri	3*	3242	3415	2/0	3315 — Collins
Tris Speaker	1937	Wri	2	3514	3415	2/0	3315 — Collins
Eddie Collins	1939	Wri	4	3315	3315	1/0	3041 — Anson
Cap Anson	1939	OTC2	1*	3041	3041	0/0	2987 — Rice
Paul Waner	1952	Wri	7	3152	3041	0/0	2987 — Rice
Stan Musial	1969	Wri	1	3630	2987	0/0	2930 — Beckley
Roberto Clemente	1973	Wri	1	3000	2721	0/2	2705 — Cramer
Willie Mays	1979	Wri	1	3283	2721	0/1	2705 — Cramer
Al Kaline	1980	Wri	1	3007	2721	0/2	2705 — Cramer
Hank Aaron	1982	Wri	1	3771	2812	0/3	2757 — Pinson
Lou Brock	1985	Wri	1	3023	2812	0/2	2757 — Pinson
Carl Yastrzemski	1989	Wri	1	3419	2812	0/2	2757 — Pinson
Rod Carew	1991	Wri	1	3053	2812	0/1	2757 — Pinson
George Brett	1999	Wri	1	3154	2812	0/1	2757 — Pinson
Robin Yount	1999	Wri	1	3142	2812	0/1	2757 — Pinson

Career Home Runs	Year	Org	Bal	HR	Min	Out	High Not In
Babe Ruth	1936	Wri	1	714	714	0/0	378 — Gehrig
Jimmie Foxx	1951	Wri	8	534	493	0/0	288 — B. Johnson
Mel Ott	1951	Wri	4	511	493	0/0	288 — B. Johnson
Ted Williams	1966	Wri	1	521	493	0/1	369 — Kiner
Mickey Mantle	1974	Wri	1	536	475	1/5	407 — Snider
Ernie Banks	1977	Wri	1	512	475	1/4	407 — Snider
Eddie Mathews	1978	Wri	5	512	475	0/5	407 — Snider
Willie Mays	1979	Wri	1	660	475	0/4	407 — Snider
Hank Aaron	1982	Wri	1	755	475	1/1	426 — B. Williams
Frank Robinson	1982	Wri	1	586	475	1/1	426 — B. Williams
Harmon Killebrew	1984	Wri	4	573	475	0/1	426 — B. Williams
Willie McCovey	1986	Wri	1	521	475	0/1	426 — B. Williams
Reggie Jackson	1993	Wri	1	563	475	0/1	442 — Kingman
Mike Schmidt	1995	Wri	1	548	475	0/0	442 — Kingman

*Wagner, Lajoie and Anson received votes in the 1936 Old-Timers Committee election. Anson's were the only votes he ever got before his election by the OTC2.

At first glance, Table 32 seems to demonstrate that the BBWAA's acquiescence to the two de facto standards for batters occurred much earlier than that for pitchers. But some of the evidence in the table is more complicated than its face-value implication.

It appears that the BBWAA embraced the de facto hits standard relatively soon after the start of Cooperstown voting — because Anson's election by the OTC2 in 1939, only the fourth year of the Hall of Fame process, marked the first time that all of the eligible 3000-hit men were enshrined. But there wasn't much if any media discussion of that exclusive circle at the time, and the next de facto-hits man to become eligible, Paul Waner, required seven ballots to get elected (he had collected his 3000th safety in 1942). Stan Musial, the next qualifier, got his 3000th hit in 1958. At the time, *Street & Smith's Baseball*— which was probably the most widely read magazine about the sport — included an annual feature (which it still uses) called "Targets for Pitchers and Hitters," which listed the all-time batting and pitching leaders in several major statistical categories prior to the start of each season along with the active players closest to them in the rankings. Also, Musial was the first man whose achievement of 3000 hits was deemed significant enough to merit a Topps baseball card to commemorate the event (number 470 in the 1959 set). So, it's arguable that this particular charmed circle didn't gain widespread media notice until the 1950s and Musial's election in 1969 most fairly marks the writers' first real acquiescence to the standard.

The home-run standard also took longer to evolve than Table 32 seems to indicate. When Babe Ruth was elected in the first year of BBWAA voting, the Bambino was the only man in baseball history with at least 500 homers (Lou Gehrig ranked second at the time with 378). Obviously, a club with only one member is too exclusive to signify any de facto criterion.

Gehrig's career came to its tragic and abrupt halt in 1939, with Lou 7 homers shy of 500. But Jimmie Foxx achieved the milestone in 1940, and Mel Ott joined the club in 1945. For whatever reasons, Foxx needed eight ballots to get elected by the writers, and Ott required four. So the zeros in the "Out" column next to their names have little meaning in the home-run standard's evolution. Ted Williams, Mickey Mantle and Ernie Banks, the next three qualifiers to become eligible after Foxx and Ott's elections in 1951, all made Cooperstown on their initial tries. Williams was the first of them to reach the mark, in 1960, close enough to Musial's 3000th hit and its attendant hoopla that it's clear there was widespread awareness of Ted's achievement. So Williams' election in 1966 may represent the scribes' first clear acceptance of the home-run standard.

But Williams, Banks and Mantle would've been first-ballot Hall of Famers with only 499 homers each (as would've Musial with 2999 hits). And later, as Table 32 also indicates, there was some resistance to the anointments of Eddie Mathews and Harmon Killebrew, who required five and four ballots, respectively, to gain election. Mathews batted .271 for his career, Killebrew just .256, and the latter man's figure is the second lowest for any Hall of Fame non-pitcher elected through 2000 (Ray Schalk hit .253). No doubt some voters perceived that both men's achievement of the de facto standard for homers did not compensate for their lack of all-around batting prowess. Mathews earned just 32.3 percent support in his first year on the ballot and averaged 52.8 percent over the five years it took before he gained election, with 79.6 percent approval. Killebrew fared somewhat better, despite his lower batting average: he got 59.6 percent support in his first year eligible; he averaged 68.6 for each of his four ballot appearances; and 83.3 percent of the writers voted for him when he was elected. The two men's elections were six years apart, and neither man was on the ballot simultaneous with the other. It's possible that the level of resistance to the home-run standard diminished in those half-dozen years in large part because — by the late 1970s — home-run sluggers with high batting averages had become as rare as silver-certificate dollars. As evidenced by the first-ballot elections of Willie McCovey, Reggie Jackson and Mike Schmidt (who batted only .270, .262 and .267, respectively), any resistance since 1984 has been insufficient to slow the de facto train, let alone derail it. So Killebrew's election in 1984 was the moment when 500 home runs truly became an automatic entree to Cooperstown.

Regardless of when you date the BBWAA's acceptance of the two de facto criteria for batters, it's clear from Table 32 that both standards have encountered much less resistance from the writers over the years than the 300-win pitching achievement. Except for Cap Anson, whose membership is debatable, none of the de facto qualifiers for hits or home runs has had to be elected by the veterans committees; and, counting Hank Aaron and Willie Mays just once apiece, twenty-one of the twenty-nine men listed in Table 30 (or 72.4 percent of them) have been elected on the first ballot, compared to just 35 percent of the de facto hurlers.

As a group, the de facto batters' elective histories are also not as muddled as those of the pitchers. Discounting Anson, the twenty-eight other de facto batters have averaged just 2.1 ballots to gain election, while the writers' thirty-two other non-pitcher inductees typically required 7.8. The substantial difference between those numbers signals a clearcut election advantage for men with 3000 hits and or 500 homers. Also, excluding Roberto Clemente and his unknown election percentage, the nineteen de facto batters tabbed in their first year of eligibility averaged 91.0 percent support, while the five other non-pitchers chosen in their first time on the ballot (Johnny Bench, Joe Morgan, Willie Stargell, Jackie and Brooks Robinson) received a mean of 86.0 percent approval — indicative of a 5 percent de facto advantage.

Table 33 compares the support-percentage histories (including the 1936 OTC1 voting) of each group of de facto qualifiers, relative to each other and to BBWAA electees who do not meet any of the criteria. The first three data columns give the total number of men with votes for each de facto criterion (Group Total, including Cap Anson, but excluding Pud Galvin and Mickey Welch, who never got a vote from the writers) plus the average support percentages for each group on the first ballot they were eligible (1st Bal) and for all ballots on which they received votes (All Bal). The next two columns include the number of men from each group elected by the scribes (BBWAA Total) and the group's average support percentage earned upon election (Elect Pct1). The last two columns include the number from each group elected on their first ballot (1stYr Total), and their average percentage earned upon election (Elect Pct2). The italicized lines at the bottom give the averages for each group as a whole. Note that because Hank Aaron and Willie Mays met both de facto criteria for hitters, they are both included in the separate lines for 3000-hit and 500-homer batters but are counted only once apiece in the de facto totals at the bottom. Finally, the BBWAA columns do not include Roberto Clemente or Lou Gehrig.

TABLE 33
BBWAA ELECTION SUPPORT,
DE FACTO V. NON–DE FACTO MEMBERS

De Facto Type	Group Total	1st Bal	All Bal	BBWAA Total	Elect Pct1	1stYr Total	Elect Pct2
300-Game Winners	18	49.5	46.0	13	85.1	6	91.8
3000-Hit Batters	16	75.7	66.3	15	88.9	11	91.6
500-HR Batters	14	76.9	66.3	14	88.8	10	91.4
De Facto As a Whole	*46*	*64.9*	*54.8*	*40*	*87.3*	*25*	*91.2*
Non–De Facto Pitchers	19	43.4	42.8	19	83.6	4	91.8
Non–De Facto Batters	32	29.9	39.6	32	82.1	5	86.0
Non–De Facto As a Whole	*51*	*34.9*	*40.2*	*51*	*82.7*	*9*	*88.6*

The data in Table 33 evidences a 4.6 percent de facto advantage among all men chosen by the BBWAA and a 2.6 percent de facto edge for players who gain first-year election. At first those numbers seem insignificant, but keep in mind that every man chosen by the writers meets the minimum requirement of 75 percent support upon election — so the values represent a difference over the twenty-five-point spread between 75 and 100 percent (rather than 0 to 100) and are magnified by that fact. Also, there is absolutely no doubt that, generally, de facto qualification has been a substantial advantage in terms of first-year and long-term support: the de facto group as a whole has a 30 percent advantage over the BBWAA electees who do not meet one of the criteria, and their average score for all ballots is almost 15 percent higher.

As indicated by Tables 31 and 32, verification of de facto standards is complicated when at any given time there are men who have equaled or surpassed a level of statistical achievement but are currently ineligible for Hall of Fame election. For that performance level to qualify, those men's HOF credentials should be virtually indisputable.

Through the 2000 voting, seven men who had achieved one of the de facto standards for hitters were not yet eligible. They included Pete Rose (ineligible by ruling), Dave Winfield, Eddie Murray, Paul Molitor and Wade Boggs (all retired, but not on the ballot until 2001, 2003, 2004 and 2005, respectively) plus Tony Gwynn and Mark McGwire (still active). Cal Ripken, Jr., also reached 3000 hits early in the 2000 season, so he must be added as an eighth qualifier not yet enshrined.

Absent his gambling complications, there is no doubt that Rose — baseball's career leader with 4256 hits — would've been a first-year inductee in 1992, the year he was slated to join the Cooperstown ballot. Beyond Winfield's 3110 hits, Dave's career numbers surpass the Hall of Fame player averages for home runs, total bases, runs scored, RBI and stolen bases, and belie George Steinbrenner's sarcasm that — unlike Reggie Jackson — Winfield was only "Mr. May." Murray (3255 hits plus 504 homers) ranks with Hank Aaron and Willie Mays as the only men ever to achieve two de facto criteria. Eddie's other career numbers exceed the HOF average for total bases, runs scored, RBI and slugging average. Through the 1999 season, Molitor's 3319 hits were the eighth-best total ever. Paul's other stats surpass the Hall of Fame norms for home runs, total bases, runs scored, RBI, stolen bases and batting average, and his cumulative numbers would've ranked even higher had he avoided the injuries that caused him to miss about 30 percent of his team's games during five of his twenty-one seasons. Compared to the overall Cooperstown averages (and to several third basemen of his time), Boggs lacked power, accumulating only 118 homers and 1014 RBI. But he ended his career after the 1999 season with 3010 hits and a .328 batting average that was the second best among the players of his era; he won five batting titles; and his career total bases, runs scored and on-base average exceed the Hall of Fame norms.

Through the 1999 season, Tony Gwynn's power had also been relatively unimpressive (133 homers, 1104 RBI). But he had accumulated 3067 hits, the highest batting average of his era (.339), and eight batting titles (tied with Honus Wagner for the all-time National League mark and second only to Ty Cobb's twelve American League crowns). Beyond that, Tony's career numbers also surpass the Cooperstown norms for runs scored, total bases and on-base average. During the years 1996–99, Mark McGwire set major-league records for most home runs in one season (70 in 1998) plus records for two (135 in 1998–99), three (193 in 1997–99) and four (245 in 1996–99) consecutive campaigns. Through the last of those seasons, Mark's career home-run frequency (at-bats divided by homers) was 10.87, better than Babe Ruth's 11.76, and the best ever by any man with ten years of major-league service. Given that rate, if he had not missed so many games to injury during the middle of his career (he played in only 55 percent of his team's contests during 1992–96), Big Mack would've had in the neighborhood of 625 homers through 1999 (instead of the 522 he'd actually hit), which would've been the third-highest total ever. Despite a career batting average of just .265, his ongoing career numbers through 1999 already exceeded the Cooperstown norms for runs batted in, slugging and on-base averages. Through 1999, Ripken had won two MVPs, was widely regarded as one of the top three or four shortstops ever offensively, and had easily surpassed Lou Gehrig's cherished record for consecutive games played. In addition to Cal's hits, his career numbers were above the HOF average for home runs, total bases, runs scored and RBI.

Subjectively, except for Rose, and even without their de facto qualifications, there is simply no way that any of those men will not be elected to Cooperstown. Most if not all of them will be first-year selections. Molitor may encounter some first-ballot resistance, because he played in more games as a designated hitter (1174) than any other position, and no career DH has yet been elected to the Shrine. But he played three other positions effectively (third base, second and outfield); his shift to DH was intended to limit his injuries; and the weight of de facto precedent — sure to increase with the elections of Winfield and Murray ahead of him — will carry him in eventually, if not in his first year eligible. As a result, and as a group, these men's status as certain inductees confirms the identity of 3000 hits and 500 homers as de facto standards for Cooperstown.

Does Cooperstown have any other clearcut standards for batters or pitchers? Six decades of Hall of Fame selections comprise a substantial

precedent from which, it seems, some discernible statistical criteria —
beyond the de facto minimums for hits, home runs and games won —
surely must've evolved, if only by default. But, the subjective preferences
of each elector also assure that there have been anywhere from 78 to 499
different standards applied in any given election; and, unlike Ty Cobb or
Walter Johnson, many HOF players do not rank among the career leaders
in almost every possible statistic. So, recognizable HOF standards for many
statistics are as elusive as a knuckleball butterflying its way toward home
plate.

If any other standards exist, a clue to their identities should be evident in the relative degrees to which various statistics predict Hall of Fame
membership. Some stats are certain to be better forecasters than others;
and, although the predictive rates for each are dependent upon the biases
operative among HOF electors, they should reveal which statistics dominate Cooperstown election. Table 34 provides the HOF-predictive rates
for each of seventeen selected career statistics for position players and
pitchers. A majority in both lists are traditional stats which have been
available to Cooperstown voters throughout the six decades of balloting.
Because there were 127 non-pitchers and fifty-eight hurlers enshrined
through 2000, the rates are based on the number of those players who
ranked among the top one hundred career leaders for the non-pitcher variables or the top fifty for pitching (including ties for the last spot on both
lists) through 1994.

TABLE 34
SELECTED HALL OF FAME
PREDICTIVE RATES, THROUGH 2000

Rank	Pitchers	Rate	Rank	Non-Pitchers	Rate
1	Games Won	.780	1	Hits	.693
2	Shutouts	.686	2	Total Bases	.690
3	Innings Pitched	.680		Runs Scored	.690
4	Strikeouts	.620	4	Runs Batted In	.670
5	Games Started	.600	5	Doubles	.604
6	Complete Games	.460	6	Batting Average	.594
7	Ratio	.420	7	Games Played	.564
8	Years Played	.418		Triples	.564
9	Opps' On-Base Average	.407	9	Slugging Average	.505
10	Winning Percentage	.333	10	Years Played	.482
11	Earned Run Average	.308	11	On-Base Average	.481

Rank	Pitchers	Rate	Rank	Non-Pitchers	Rate
12	Games Pitched	.255	12	Walks	.440
13	Opps' Batting Average	.250	13	Home Runs	.370
14	Pennants Won	.227	14	Stolen Bases	.337
15	World Series Won	.149	15	Pennants Won	.321
16	Fielding Average	.052	16	World Series Won	.208
17	Saves	.040	17	Fielding Average	.050
	Average Predictive Rate	*.393*		*Average Predictive Rate*	*.486*

Some of the Table 34 data is predictable. Two de facto statistics, hits and games won, are the best Hall of Fame predictors for batters and pitchers, respectively. Runs scored, runs batted in and batting average also rank among the top predictors for batters; shutouts and strikeouts, traditional indicators of pitching dominance, are among the best predictors for moundsmen.

Also, and affirming the conclusions reached in the previous chapter, fielding average and the two stats most relevant to relief pitching (games pitched and saves) are poor predictors of Cooperstown election. As a group, fielding statistics all have weak predictive rates for Hall of Fame membership: for example, career marks for assists-per-game, double plays-per-game and range factor all post a score below .150 (supporting the view that defense plays a negligible role in Cooperstown selection of batters and pitchers, alike), and fielding average — the most recognizable defensive statistic — was included in the table to exemplify that trend. With only two relievers currently in the Hall, games pitched and saves cannot be expected to forecast HOF election with any meaningful frequency.

But Table 34 also includes some surprises. Career home runs, the third de facto standard (and probably the most glamorous stat in all of baseball), is also a poor predictor of Cooperstown membership overall, ranking twelfth among the batting stats included with a success rate of only 37 percent. And the predictive rates for earned run average and winning percentage, two of the most familiar statistics for hurlers, score even worse than homers. The relative predictive failures of home runs and ERA are due to the huge variations in performance norms for those two stats in different eras (most of the career leaders for home runs are Live-Ball or Expansion- through Free-Agent Era players, while the career leadership list for ERA is dominated by pitchers from the Dead-Ball period). The low score for winning percentage resulted because short-career pitchers have an advantage in that category (the longer a pitcher plays, the more likely that his winning percentage will approach .500), whereas HOF election is more dependent upon longevity (years played is a better predictor than winning percentage).

In statistical science the requirement for a valid predictor is a success rate of .667. Only seven of the statistics included in Table 34 (or, about 20 percent of them) meet that standard; only one of those (games won by pitchers) exceeds 75 percent success; and the average predictive rates for both sets of data are below .500. So 80 percent of these variables—which include the most familiar measures of batting and pitching performance—leave much to be desired as tools to forecast Cooperstown election. As a result, with the exception of games won, the data in Table 34 provides arguable evidence that there is no *strong* consensus among the electors regarding which statistics are the most valid measures of Hall of Fame credentials; and, given the subjective foundation upon which the selection process is based, that result is not surprising.

All the same, both sections of Table 34 include three other statistics (shutouts, innings pitched and strikeouts for hurlers plus total bases, runs scored and RBI for batters) which surpass, or at least approach, the standard for a valid predictor. With that in mind, it's useful to identify whether anything like a de facto criterion has evolved (or might) for one or more of those stats. Table 35 includes the highest career total in baseball history for each of those statistics (Car High), the highest-ranked eligible, but unenshrined, player through the 1999 season in each category (Highest Player Not in HOF), his career total for that variable (Car Mark), his ordinal ranking among the career leaders (Ord Rank), the number of ineligible players ahead of him on the list (Inel Abv, including players active in 2000 and those who retired since the end of the 1994 season), the number of Hall of Famers as of 2000 who were above or below him on the list (HOF Abv and HOF Bel), and the most plausible de facto standard that can be derived from the data (DF Std).

TABLE 35
PLAUSIBLE DE FACTO STANDARDS
FOR SELECTED STATISTICS

Pitchers	Car High	Highest Player Not in HOF	Car Mark	Ord Rank	Inel Abv	HOF Abv	HOF Bel	DF Std
ShO	110	Bert Blyleven	60	9	0	8	50	none
IP	7356	Bert Blyleven	4970	13	0	12	46	5000
SO	5714	Bert Blyleven	3701	3	0	2	56	none

Batters	Car High	Highest Player Not in HOF	Car Mark	Ord Rank	Inel Abv	HOF Abv	HOF Bel	DF Std
TB	6856	Dave Parker	4405	34	7	26	101	5000
R	2246	Jimmy Ryan	1642	27	4	22	105	1700
RBI	2297	Dave Parker	1493	38	5	32	95	1500

Clearly, there is no plausible de facto standard for strikeouts by pitchers. As of 2000, Nolan Ryan and Steve Carlton were the only two men ahead of Bert Blyleven on the list of career strikeout leaders. Both of them fanned more than 4000 batters, and the figure is round and easy to remember. But the number of men in that club was, for the moment, far too exclusive to give the total meaning as a de facto criterion.

Exclusivity is also a problem with shutouts. Blyleven pitched sixty of them but was not enshrined through the 2000 voting; only four men — all Hall of Famers— had as many as seventy; and that latter group is also too small to have significance. But shutouts also present even bigger dilemmas: (1) they are credited only to starting pitchers, so they are an irrelevant measure for relievers, and (2) they also require a complete game by the hurler which, due to recent relief pitching strategies, is rapidly becoming a dinosaur among baseball events. During the period 1876–1960, before the advent of modern relief pitching, the ratio of relief appearances to games started in the majors was 0.68; during 1961–90, as relief patterns evolved, it climbed to 1.58; and it rose to 2.19 in the seven-year span 1991–97, when current bullpen strategies were perfected. Commensurately, the ratio of complete games to starts declined from 0.62 in the first eighty-five years of major-league play, to 0.22 during the next thirty, and to about 0.08 in the 1990s alone — as managers altered their approach from expecting complete games most of the time, to hoping they could get one on occasion, and finally to disallowing most of them altogether, often when a shutout was in balance. As a result of all this, the ratio of shutouts to starts dropped from 0.066 over the years 1876–90 to 0.054 during the 1990s, a decline of over 22 percent. Given the refinements in relief pitching, there is no reason to anticipate that trend will soon reverse (if ever); and, as a result, shutouts will become ever more rare, and increasingly less relevant — when compared to other eras— as Hall of Fame credentials among pitchers from the Free-Agent period and beyond.

In contrast, 5000 innings pitched could someday prove to be a real de facto standard. Through 1999, all twelve men ahead of Blyleven had exceeded that total and were enshrined. But Roger Clemens, with only 3462 innings, had the highest total among not-yet-eligible pitchers through that season. Coupled with the decline in complete games and the increased frequency of relief appearances typical for the current era, that may indicate that 5000 innings already has become an unreachable standard for any pitcher in the short-term future. If so, the number would be just as meaningless as those for strikeouts and shutouts.

The most obvious de facto level for total bases is a career figure of 5000, a number achieved by only fourteen players through 1999 — all but two of whom (Eddie Murray and Dave Winfield, both certain inductees) were in Cooperstown by 2000. But, total bases also poses a problem, because the statistic gets little attention compared to several more glamorous measures of batting performance. *Total Baseball* and the Macmillan encyclopedia provide lists of career and seasonal leaders for total bases, but individual career totals are not included in either book's player registers and — for men who are not among the all-time leaders — must be calculated individually. So, although career total bases is an effective and valid predictor of Hall of Fame membership, the minimal attention paid to it by the major sources reduces any likelihood that it is, or will be, included among the batting stats most often referred to by Cooperstown electors. In that light, the stat's high predictive success is — in large part — a function of its integral relationship with career hits and home-run totals.

Runs scored also presents problems, because the most valid de facto number available through the 2000 voting (a career total of 1700) is neither as memorable nor as aesthetically pleasing as would be 1500 or 2000. Through 1999, only six men in major-league history had scored 2000 runs, while fifty-four had accumulated as many as 1500 tallies. The former group was too exclusive to be viable and included two men who were not yet eligible (Pete Rose and the still-active Rickey Henderson); while adoption of the smaller career total might create a standard that is not exclusive enough. Beyond that, the 1500-run club included four other unenshrined men assured of eventual election (Molitor, Winfield, Murray and Ripken), but it also featured five others (nineteenth-century players Jimmy Ryan, George Van Haltren, Bill Dahlen and Tom Brown plus the recently retired Tim Raines) whose prospects for election vary from slim to none. Among the first four, Van Haltren received the only Cooperstown notice, a lone vote in the 1936 OTC1 balloting; although Ryan was considered by the Veterans Committee in 2000, he was rejected in favor of Bid McPhee; and Raines's prospects are problematic at best.

All of that leaves only 1500 runs batted in as a possible, as-yet-unrecognized de facto standard. Prior to his election in 2000, Tony Perez was the only eligible player with that total not yet enshrined. The thirty-seven men above 1500 also included Eddie Murray, Dave Winfield, Andre Dawson, Cal Ripken, Jr., and Harold Baines, the latter two still active after

1999. Having reached an existent de facto total, Murray, Winfield and Ripken are certain of election; Dawson's credentials will probably pass muster too, although he may not be a first-year inductee. But Baines's presence on the list creates another problem. Baines was a competent right fielder during the first third of his career, but most of his big-league service has been spent as a designated hitter. Through 1999, Harold's age (forty) and career totals for hits (2783) and home runs (373) limited his prospects for achieving one of the recognized de facto numbers, as—most likely—he would require at least two more seasons to reach 3000 safeties and too many to achieve 500 homers. His successful candidacy, a necessity to cement 1500 RBI as a possible de facto standard, might hinge entirely upon his DH status and the degree of voter resistance encountered ahead of him by Paul Molitor.

Also, there is no clear evidence of any persistent awareness among the BBWAA voters to date that the achievement of 5000 innings or total bases or 1500 runs or RBI are significant to a man's prospects for election. Except for Tony Perez, the most recent men elected with any of those career figures—pitchers Perry, Carlton, Niekro, Sutton and Ryan plus batters Brett, Jackson, Schmidt and Yount—had all achieved one of the recognized de facto standards, and pre-voting discussion of their credentials was dominated by those numbers (along with Ryan's 5714 strikeouts). As a result, it's certain that the standards for hits, home runs and pitching victories get so much attention because they are the only ones which currently fulfill all elements of a de facto criterion's definition.

To date, the relative difficulty of achieving the de facto levels has been virtually equal for pitchers and batters alike. The twenty hurlers with 300 career wins or more represent 2.46 percent of the 813 moundmen who were HOF-eligible by the 2000 voting, while the thirty-six batters with de facto credentials (including Ripken) were equal to 2.43 percent of the 1482 eligible non-pitchers. On the surface, that seems to make the de facto numbers defensible standards of excellence by which to justify any man's election. After all, the vast majority of players on the Cooperstown roster (about 74 percent of them) never achieved one of those career totals.

On the other hand, coupled with the ever-changing norms in periodic performance, the de facto standards guarantee the eventual election of some player(s) truly undeserving of the Cooperstown honor (assuming that hasn't happened already, in Mickey Welch's case, at least). A test of that prospect may occur sometime around 2010, when Jose Canseco joins the ballot. Through 1999 Canseco was thirty-five years old, had 431 career home runs, and—barring career-ending injury (an unlikely prospect for a designated hitter)—seemed certain to join the 500-homer club before his retirement. But, absent achievement of that mark, Canseco's

Hall of Fame credentials are dubious. Jose's career stolen bases (196 through 1999) were impressive for a man six-foot-four and 240 pounds but nowhere near the top 150 totals among the stat's career leaders. He won two American League home-run crowns, but fifteen men who had equaled that feat at some time during the twentieth century were excluded from Cooperstown through the 2000 voting. He also was the AL's Most Valuable Player in 1988, but forty-five eligible past winners had not yet been elected (including two-time MVPs Roger Maris and Dale Murphy). Beyond that, as evidenced by the famous incident when Jose allowed a catchable fly ball to bounce off his head and into the stands for a homer, his play in the field was lackadaisical at times and — unlike Paul Molitor — a primary reason for his shift to DH. Despite his home-run total, whether Canseco was as good a player all-around as either Maris or Murphy is debatable, and his election on the strength of de facto precedent could be seen by many as further evidence of Cooperstown's slide toward mediocrity.

By focusing on three glamorous statistics, the emphasis placed on the de facto standards for hits, home runs and pitching victories encourages the voters of both elective organs to overlook, or at least devalue, other traditional measures of performance (total bases, runs scored and batted in for batters, and strikeouts and earned run average for pitchers, to name a few) which are also valid and important evidence of a player's abilities and achievement. It also discourages consideration of several modern statistics, most of them devised during recent decades, which may be far more accurate measures of a man's specific and overall skills (e.g., on-base average for batters and OBA allowed by hurlers).

Finally, the de facto standards — especially for home runs — also exacerbate the elective disadvantages created by differences in performance norms among baseball's various historical eras. A case in point is that of former National League outfielder Gavvy Cravath, whose career — spent mostly with the Phillies — spanned 1908–20. In all, Cravath led his league in an offensive category on fifteen occasions; he won six Dead-Ball home-run crowns, with a career high of 24 dingers in 1915, and he ended his major-league service with 119 circuit clouts, which — at the time — was the fourth-highest total in history.

Opposite: Jose Canseco had 431 career home runs through the 1999 season. At age thirty-five, barring serious injury, the designated hitter seemed assured of reaching the 500-homer, de facto standard that would guarantee his Hall of Fame election sometime around 2010. But, without that achievement, it's debatable whether the rest of Canseco's credentials would be worthy of Cooperstown recognition; his eventual election could represent the Hall's first, true de facto error of selection. (Photograph from *The Sporting News*)

With the homer explosion that followed Cravath's retirement, Gavvy disappeared from the top-fifty career leaders by 1945. In turn, he got only nine Cooperstown votes spread over five elections (1937–47). On the surface, Cravath's 119 dingers pale in comparison to Jose Canseco's 431 through 1999, and it's likely that Jose, who has led his circuit in an offensive category on only four occasions, will get thirty times more votes in his first year on the ballot than Gavvy ever did.

But statisticians use a tool called the Z Score, which measures the relative uniquity of a given numerical value in the context of a larger set of analogous numbers. The 185 Dead-Ball-Era batters who have been eligible for Cooperstown averaged only 28.5 career home runs apiece, compared to 113.2 per man among the 370 Free-Agent-Era players with ten years of major-league service through 1994. In that context, Cravath's career home run total earns a Z Score of +3.29 compared to his contemporaries, while Canseco's much larger total has a value of +3.10 when weighed against the norm for men of his era. So Cravath's achievement was more significant than Canseco's relative to the performances typical of their times, and Gavvy's home-run exploits—insignificant as they may seem today—were arguably more worthy of Cooperstown recognition.

13
Big-City Bias

Early in the 1989 season during a televised game between the Milwaukee Brewers and Chicago White Sox, a color commentator (probably Hawk Harrelson, but it doesn't really matter) raved about how, at the time, Robin Yount was the most under-recognized great player in baseball. As evidence of Yount's talents, the announcer cited that Robin had been a competent major-league regular at age twenty (a rarity); that, although Yount began his career with little evidence of superior offensive ability, through hard work and dedication he had made himself into a dangerous hitter capable of 25-homer and or 100-RBI seasons; and that he had proven his versatility by playing two difficult defensive positions (shortstop and center field) with skill and grace. The mikeman also noted that, because Yount had collected 2400-plus hits by age thirty-three, he was a cinch to join the 3000-hit club before he retired — because Robin's conditioning regimen was likely to forestall any serious injuries that might prevent him from reaching that mark.

Later, the announcer predicted that even if Yount achieved the 3000-hit mark, and despite his MVP trophy of 1982, he would have difficulty getting elected to the Hall of Fame, perhaps even be denied the honor, at least by the BBWAA. The reason, he argued, was the traditional bias among the voting writers for players from big-media cities like New York and Los Angeles and against men who spent their careers in relative backwaters like Milwaukee.

Ironically, the scribes tabbed Yount for his second Most Valuable Player at the end of that 1989 season. He won it without leading the American League in any significant offensive category and despite playing for the small-media Brewers, who finished the year with an 81–81 record that was eight games off the pace set by the AL-East champion Toronto Blue Jays and good enough for only fourth place in their division. Yount's nearest competitor in the 1989 voting was Ruben Sierra, right fielder for the small-market Texas Rangers, who had topped the circuit in RBI, slugging average, total bases and triples. Beyond those two, five of the other men among the top ten in the MVP voting that year — Cal Ripken, Jr. (Baltimore), Dennis Eckersley (Oakland), and Kirby Puckett (Minnesota), plus Bret Saberhagen and Bo Jackson (Kansas City) — were also from small-media clubs; two of the others, George Bell and Fred McGriff of Toronto, were from a big-market city which, because it is in Canada, gets small-media attention south of the border; and only one of the top ten, Rickey Henderson, played in New York or LA (but Rickey appeared in just sixty-five games for the Yankees before being traded to Oakland for the season's second half).

Also ironic, after Yount retired with 3142 hits (all of them for the Brewers), he was elected to the Hall in his first year eligible (1999). So, if Robin suffered any elective disadvantage from playing in Milwaukee for twenty seasons, it didn't manifest with sufficient force to keep him out of Cooperstown on his first try.

But noting that glosses over the fact that Yount nearly missed election in 1999. He squeaked by with only 77.5 percent approval and would not have been elected that year if just 13 of his 385 supporters had left him off their ballots. In that light, and given the significant first-ballot advantage for de facto qualifiers evidenced in Chapter 12, it's fair to assert that Robin's membership in the 3000-hit club — alone — tipped the first-year scales in his favor.

Regardless, a widespread notion persists that Hall of Fame voting is, and always has been, biased in favor of players who spent much of their careers in big-media cities, especially New York. In all, 86 of the 185 players elected to Cooperstown through the 2000 voting (46 percent) spent some time in a New York uniform during their careers (i.e., with the Yankees or Mets, the Giants or Dodgers before 1958, the BrookFeds of 1914–15, or any of their nineteenth-century Gotham predecessors); and 55 of them (about 30 percent) played in the Big Apple in five seasons or more, topped by Mel Ott who spent all twenty-two of his big-league campaigns (1926–47) with the Polo Grounds Giants.

Chicago was the game's other major media center through most of big-league history. But the Windy City's media impact was greatly diminished (if not completely eclipsed) by 1965, at the latest, after the Dodgers had moved to Los Angeles — that suburb of Tinseltown — and were joined there by the expansion Angels. Fifty-two of the Hall's 185 players spent time in some Chicago uniform, and a dozen played in LA/Anaheim. The only Hall of Famer to play in all three cities as a major leaguer was Hoyt Wilhelm, who came up with the Giants in New York (1952–56) and floated his knucklers for the White Sox (1963–68), Cubs (three games in 1970), Angels (1969) and Dodgers (1971–72). In all, twenty-seven Hall of Famers played in at least two of the three major-media cities; and, without counting any of them twice, that means 123 of the 185 players on the Cooperstown roster (just over 66 percent) played in one of the big-hype burgs at some point in their careers.

On the surface, that seems like strong validation of the complaint made by Hawk Harrelson (or whoever it was). But, as this book has harped for a dozen chapters now, surface-level observation is never sufficient because it often obscures the truth.

Accurate identification of "big-market" cities is complicated by the changes in their populations over time. Chicago, for example, was smaller than Philadelphia or Brooklyn (distinct from New York City) until the 1890 census, when it first became the nation's second most populous city, and it held that ranking until the 1960 head count, when Los Angeles surpassed it. The census takers kept separate population statistics for Brooklyn until 1950, when it was lumped with New York City as part of a new focus on urban centers rather than municipalities. So, because most Gotham papers were headquartered in Manhattan, you could argue (foolishly) that Flatbush wasn't a major media center prior to that time. And in all fairness, Philadelphia — which had the nation's second-largest population until 1890 — was probably baseball's only other big-market city prior to that long-ago date. But, by the time Hall of Fame voting began, New York and Chicago were the only true big-media cities, and they were joined by Los Angeles when the Dodgers moved west. So, for simplicity, those three will have to suffice.

Also, because so many Hall of Famers spent portions of their careers in New York, Chicago or Los Angeles, in order to assure fairness the identification of truly "big-market" players requires a strict definition. Regardless of era, one could expect that any big-city voting advantage should manifest more strongly for players who spent significant portions of their careers in one of those cities than it would for guys whose tenures there were brief. So it's probably fair to argue that, to qualify as a big-market player, a man should've spent at least half of his major-league seasons in one or more of those locales. Using that definition creates a few anomalies (Reggie Jackson spent only ten of his twenty-one seasons in New York or Anaheim and therefore gets tabbed —counterintuitively — as a small-market player), but on the whole it narrows the list of big-media Hall of Famers to those who should have most benefited, vote-wise, from their tenures in the three big cities.

As noted in Chapter 1, the members from big-media cities have never comprised a majority among the BBWAA electors but — if acting as a unit — often amounted to a block of votes sufficient to swing a marginal candidate's fate either way. During the period 1936–57, when there were still three teams in New York (plus the two in Chicago), the writers who followed those big-media teams would've comprised at least five-sixteenths (31 percent) of the front-door voters. But that assumes equal representation by franchise, and the ratio was undoubtedly higher — perhaps 40 percent — because, at any given time, there were probably more newspapers in New York or Chicago than any one of the nation's other big cities. After the Giants and Dodgers moved west at about the same time that television drove many papers out of business and expansion spread the BBWAA membership to new locales, the proportion of big-media voters must've declined some, despite the existence of six large-market clubs in Gotham, Chicago and Hollywoodland by 1962.

Assuming, on average, an equal amount of provincial bias among sportswriters of every city, all of that should've given the big-city players a measurable edge in the voting — relative to any small-market candidate — especially prior to 1958. So you might expect any big-city bias to be more evident prior to that date. Table 36 compares the elective histories of big- versus small-market players chosen by the BBWAA during three different periods: (1) 1936–57, when there were five teams in New York and Chicago combined; (2) 1958–79, which covers the era, after the Dodgers and Giants abandoned New York, of the first two tiers of major-league expansion and the gradual turnover in BBWAA membership that accompanied it (including a decade-long buffer for the members added with the 1969 expansion to qualify as voters under the writers' ten-year franchise requirement); and (3) 1980–2000, when most of that change had subsided and the BBWAA electorate acquired its present demography. The data provided includes the number of players elected by the BBWAA in each period (Tot In), the number of big- and small-market candidates as defined above (BM Tot and SM Tot), the average number of ballots it took to elect each man (Avg Bal), and the average per-ballot support percentage received per man (Avg Pct), with separate scores for the latter pair given for each of the two groupings (for this and all later tables, Roberto Clemente and Lou Gehrig, chosen in special elections, were assigned the minimum required 75 percent support for the ballot of their election). The last two columns give the average annual ratio of big- to small-city teams in the majors for each of the three voting eras (BC Rat) and the proportion of big-city players elected during each period (BCP Rat). Below the rows for each era, the same data is provided for the first two periods combined and for all voting as a whole.

TABLE 36
BIG V. SMALL-MARKET PLAYERS
ELECTED BY THE BBWAA

BBWAA Selections	Tot In	BM Tot	Avg Bal	Avg Pct	SM Tot	Avg Bal	Avg Pct	BC Rat	BCP Rat
1936–57	35	12	6.6	34.5	23	6.5	40.5	.281	.343
1958–79	23	10	5.8	41.7	13	5.4	44.5	.265	.435
1980–2000	35	9	5.8	55.0	26	1.8	76.2	.229	.257
1936–79 Only	58	22	6.2	40.4	36	6.1	42.0	.278	.379
Overall	*93*	*31*	*6.1*	*44.4*	*62*	*4.3*	*48.0*	*.272*	*.333*

If you argue that, in a perfectly random world, an equal number of Hall of Famers should be elected from each team over time, then an excess of big-market players was chosen by the BBWAA during both of the first two eras listed in Table 36. For the period 1936–79 as a whole, about 10 percent more big-city players were elected than should have been, confirming the suspicion that those men had some advantage in the early years of Cooperstown voting.

But much of that edge may not have resulted from provincial bias. Talent has never been distributed evenly in the majors, and during the period 1876–1979 teams from New York, Chicago or Los Angeles won 84 pennants, about 43 percent of the 197 possible. So, if pennant success is a valid measure of Hall of Fame credentials, then you could also argue that the 37.9 percent of big-market players elected before 1980 were about 5 percent below those cities' fair share.

Table 36 also demonstrates that on average among the players elected by the scribes during the first two eras of Cooperstown voting, small-market players required fewer ballots to gain election and earned a higher annual support percentage than their big-city counterparts. Those results are not indicative of any big-market bias at all.

Whether or not favoritism for big-city players existed among the BBWAA electors prior to 1980, the data for the most recent era of Hall of Fame voting is clearcut evidence that no big-market bias has manifested in the last couple decades. Although the ratio of big-city players elected was slightly greater than the average proportion of large-market teams, the small-locale players enjoyed a huge advantage in rapidity of election and per-ballot support. If anything, the 1980–2000 numbers seem to imply that most BBWAA voters applied an anti-big-city bias during that period.

On one level, the appearance of such a trend is predictable given the changes in the BBWAA's demography. By the mid–1980s there were twenty-six major-league teams; only six of them (23 percent) were in big-media markets; and smaller cities—Minnesota, Houston, Oakland, Atlanta, San Diego, Montreal and Dallas—had been in the club long enough for their sportswriters to acquire the HOF voting franchise. As noted in earlier chapters, the number of first-ballot electees has risen dramatically in recent BBWAA voting (twenty of the thirty-five selections since 1980 were chosen on their first try, compared to just fifteen out of fifty-eight — including Roberto Clemente — during the years 1936–79); and recent electors have tended to fill in fewer names on their ballots than was typical in earlier eras. There is no reason to doubt that the altered voter demography was one cause for those changes in approach, and it might have been accompanied by some provincial backlash against players from media-prominent locales.

But eighteen of the thirty-five selections made since 1979 were also de facto qualifiers, and only two of them — Tom Seaver and Don Sutton — met the applied definition of a big-market player. Two of the other seventeen, small marketeers Johnny Bench and Brooks Robinson, were regarded at the time of their elections as the greatest players ever at their respective positions and were dead-cinch, first-ballot choices regardless of where they had played. Beyond the effects of scouting, trades or free agency, the market-size affiliations of those twenty players were the products of random chance, and their quick success in the voting resulted mainly from their statistical achievement or reputations. If you remove Bench, Robinson and the de facto qualifiers from the data for the 1980–2000 voting era, seven of the remaining fifteen players (47 percent) had big-market careers. So the apparent bias favoring small-city players during that period may be nothing more than a mirage caused by other circumstances.

If the color commentator's complaint of 1989 was at all accurate, any big-city favoritism should be evident from the start of each man's eligibility, and a hog's share of that bias should manifest among the BBWAA electors, rather than the Veterans Committee. Table 37 compares the voting histories of Hall of Famers from big- and small-media cities again. This time, the information is grouped according to whether the men were elected by the BBWAA on their first ballot eligible, after the first ballot, or by one of the veterans committees. The data provided includes the total number of big- and small-market players elected in each category (BM Tot and SM Tot), both groups' per-man averages for the number of ballots receiving votes (Avg Bal), both groups' per-man average support percentage per ballot (Avg Pct), and the ratios of big- and small-market players elected in each category (BM Rat and SM Rat). The data below each method of election includes the figures compiled by the BBWAA-elected players in either category as a whole and the overall numbers posted by all men elected through the 2000 voting.

TABLE 37
POTENTIAL BIG-CITY BIAS,
BBWAA V. VETERANS COMMITTEES

Players Elected By	BM Tot	Avg Bal	Avg Pct	SM Tot	Avg Bal	Avg Pct	BM Rat	SM Rat
BBWAA, Ballot 1	7	1.0	88.7	28	1.0	88.5	.200	.800
BBWAA, After Ballot 1	24	7.6	42.7	34	7.0	43.2	.414	.586
Veterans Committees	35	9.4	16.7	57	8.0	15.7	.380	.620
BBWAA Only	*31*	*6.1*	*44.4*	*62*	*4.3*	*48.0*	*.333*	*.667*
Overall	66	7.8	26.8	119	6.1	27.6	.357	.643

Note: Three men, Herb Pennock (BBWAA, After Ballot 1) plus VC selections Kiki Cuyler and Mike 'King' Kelly, split their careers evenly between seasons in big- and small-media cities. Pennock was assigned to the big-market group, because his best seasons and greatest fame came with the Yankees. The other two cases are more arguable: Cuyler was placed in the small-market category because, in his one season split between the two types of cities (1935), he had more games and at-bats with Cincinnati than Chicago; Kelly was also placed with the small-media group because he played more games (754) in those cities than he did in Chicago-New York. If all three men were assigned to the opposite group, their stats would not alter the results very much.

Table 37 indicates that there is no big-market advantage of any kind with regard to first-year election. Small-market players have a four-to-one edge among men elected in their first year of eligibility, and the average support percentages for big- and small-media candidates among that category are virtually identical. The seven big-market players elected on their first ballot include Babe Ruth, Christy Mathewson, Jackie Robinson and Mickey Mantle (New York), Ernie Banks (Chicago), Tom Seaver (both) and Sandy Koufax (Brooklyn-Los Angeles). All but one of those men was elected with eighty-four percent support or better; and, with so little difference between the average percentages for each group, the only man who might have gained a big-city edge sufficient to swing his election was Robinson, who was tabbed with just 77.5 percent support in 1962. In comparison, among first-year electees from small markets, two men — Lou Brock (79.5) and Robin Yount (77.5) — received less than eighty percent (i.e., marginal) support and may have benefited from some small-city edge in the voting. But, as already noted of Yount, it's much more likely that both men's de facto qualifications had a bigger impact on their elections than any city-size bias.

The ratio of big-market representation more than doubles among men elected by the writers after ballot one. So, although it contradicts expectation, it's possible that some big-city advantage manifests after a guy misses election on his first try. Along those lines, thirteen of the twenty-four big-market players among this group — Luke Appling, Yogi Berra, Roy Campanella, Bill Dickey, Joe DiMaggio, Don Drysdale, Whitey Ford, Lou Gehrig, Gabby Hartnett, Carl Hubbell, Ted Lyons, Mel Ott and Bill Terry — spent their entire careers with big-city teams. But on average, and contradicting any likelihood of big-market bias among the multiple-ballot group as a whole, the small-media players actually required fewer ballots to get elected and had a marginally better support percentage per try. And, as with the first-year electees, a larger ratio of the small-market players chosen after ballot one (eighteen of thirty-four, or 52.9 percent) were elected with less than 80 percent support than that of their big-city counterparts (nine of twenty-four, or 37.5 percent).

Comparing the BBWAA to the veterans committees, note that a higher proportion of VC inductees (38.0 percent) have been big-market players than those chosen by the writers overall (33.3 percent). That particular outcome deflates any notion that the scribes are the source of Cooperstown's reputed big-city bias. Although it doesn't take the years before 1953 into account, a possible explanation for that result may be the fact that ten of the nineteen former players who have served on the Veterans Committee to date — Berra, Campanella, Frisch, Grimes, Herman, Hoyt, Irvin, Reese, Terry and White — all had significant career connections with New York and or Chicago, and it's obvious that Frisch, Hoyt and Terry, at least (plus Berra, Campanella and White to a lesser degree) were not (or have not been) shy about electing their former buddies. Among the VC's forty-nine player selections since 1967 (the year Frisch joined the panel), nineteen of them (39 percent) have been men who spent a majority of their careers in big-media markets.

Three of the eight de facto qualifiers enshrined by veterans panels — Tim Keefe, Mickey Welch and (the debatable) Cap Anson — were big-market players, as were an equal ratio of the eight men elected by the committees who never received a BBWAA vote (Roger Connor, George Davis and Welch). That percentage (37.5) is higher than the Cooperstown average as a whole, but it probably says more about an absence of big-market bias among the voting scribes who passed on electing those men than it does about any big-city preference among the VC members over the years.

As indicated in Table 36, big-market teams have typically represented a little more than one-fourth of the franchises operative at any given moment in major-league history. In that light, the 35.7 percent of all Hall of Famers who had big-city careers seem to represent an excessive share of the Cooperstown roster. But, again, the argument for proportionality ignores the importance of scouting and trades in the distribution of Hall of Fame talent. Over the relevant course of major-league history (1876–1994) big-market teams won 98 of the 227 possible pennants (43 percent)—clear evidence that, for reasons which have no linkage to the electors' provincial biases, big-city clubs have been relatively more successful at acquiring talent. In turn, it should not be surprising that the Cooperstown roster includes a large proportion of players from those locales.

All the same, it does seem — subjectively — that small-market players dominate most published lists of Hall of Fame errors of omission and or of men who have received inadequate consideration from the Cooperstown voters. Among the thirty-nine men noted in Chapter 3 who— along with Vern Stephens and Johnny Pesky (small-city players themselves)— gained little or no attention from the BBWAA, only eight of them (Bill Dahlen, Dave Foutz, Bobby Grich, Dave Kingman, Ed Reulbach, Bob Shawkey, George Van Haltren and Hippo Vaughn) had big-market careers, and just two of those (Foutz and Vaughn) never received a single vote.

So it remains to be seen whether any big-city favoritism is evident in the vote histories of men who were not elected in a player capacity by either organ. Table 38 distills the voting statistics for those big- and small-market candidates. The 554 men measured include all but one of the Hall's sixteen managers (Joe McCarthy was never a player in the majors) plus Satchel Paige, each of whom received votes without election by the scribes and were later anointed by one of the veterans committees. But, because their vote histories are not yet complete, the table excludes fifteen players from the 2000 ballot whose eligibility carried over to 2001 (Charlie Pabor, who earned one vote in the 1936 OTC1 voting, is also left out because he never played in the modern majors). The market-size data is grouped in three categories; men with votes on eleven ballots or more, those with votes on six to ten ballots, and those with support on five ballots or less;

and includes the number of men who received votes (Tot w/V), the average number of ballots on which they received support (Avg Bal), the average per-ballot support percentage per man (Avg Pct), the ratio of big- or small-market teams typical for the group examined (City Rat), and the ratio of big- or small-city players in each grouping (Plyr Rat).

TABLE 38
BIG- AND SMALL-MARKET VOTE HISTORIES
OF UNELECTED CANDIDATES, 1936–2000

Player Group	Tot w/V	Avg Bal	Avg Pct	City Rat	Plyr Rat
Big-Market, ≥ 11 Ballots	20	13.8	13.2	.272	.417
Big-Market, 6–10 Ballots	22	7.7	3.7	.272	.344
Big-Market, 1–5 Ballots	121	1.7	1.3	.272	.274
Small-Market, ≥ 11 Ballots	28	14.3	11.3	.728	.583
Small-Market, 6–10 Ballots	42	7.7	3.5	.728	.656
Small-Market, 1–5 Ballots	321	1.8	1.3	.728	.726
All, Big-Market	163	4.0	7.0	.272	.294
All, Small-Market	391	3.3	5.0	.728	.706
Overall	554	3.5	5.6	1.000	1.000

The ratios for the two groups of big-market players with votes on six or more ballots in Table 38 exceed perfect proportionality by a considerable margin, and their average yearly support percentages are higher than those of their small-market counterparts. But, on average, the small-city players from the same two groups received votes on more ballots per man, a fact which—because none of the men in Table 38 was ever elected by the scribes—indicates more persistent long-term support for those candidates (the overall ballots-per-man average is lower for the small cities because they have more candidates among the group with votes on less than six ballots). Also keep in mind that any bias favoring big-market players evidenced in Table 38 was insufficient to get any of those men elected.

More significantly, note that the overall ratio of small-market players in Table 38 (.706) is higher than that for either of the two previous tables (.667 in Table 36, .643 in Table 37) and approaches proportional equity for that group. As a result, among the 739 players included in all three tables, 229 of them are big-market candidates (31.0 percent) while 510 of them (69.0 percent) are not, and the overall ratio of big-city players is just .038 higher than the .272 figure which perfect proportionality would require.

As demonstrated in the comments about Vern Stephens and Johnny Pesky in Chapter 3, many reasons influence whether or not a player receives any support from the writers at all, let alone enough votes to gain election. It's no doubt unfair that former Yankee middle infielders Billy Martin (one vote in 1967, before he ever managed a big-league game), Gil McDougald (thirty votes spread over nine elections, 1966–74) and Frank Crosetti (thirty votes in six ballots, 1950–68) have received Hall of Fame support when none of them was as good, subjectively or statistically, as Vern Stephens was. But for every small-market guy who was unjustly ignored in the voting, there is also someone — like Moe Berg, Marty Bergen, Joe Boley, Gates Brown, Gabby Street and Jewel Ens — who spent all or most of his career in smaller cities and received HOF support that was (and remains) basically unjustifiable. Similarly, for every small-market candidate whose absence from Cooperstown may outrage the faithful from cities like Cleveland (Mel Harder), St. Louis (Ken Boyer) or Cincinnati (Bucky Walters), there is at least one Babe Herman, Gil Hodges, Stan Hack, Ron Santo or Maury Wills who did not get elected despite distinguished careers in Brooklyn, Chicago or Los Angeles, and a truckload of former Yankees (e.g., Spud Chandler, Joe Gordon, Tommy Henrich, Charlie Keller, Roger Maris, Bob Meusel, Thurman Munson, Graig Nettles and Allie Reynolds) whose Big-Apple connections were insufficient to gain them enshrinement and whose absence from the Hall may be just as difficult for their fans to accept.

Small-market voters have always represented a majority of the BBWAA electorate (probably never less than 60 percent). So, at any given point in time, even if the big-market voters acted with unanimity, at least 58 percent of the small-city majority has been needed to augment the big media's weight in order to elect any man, regardless of his career location (i.e., the proportion of small-market voters, above the big cities' 40 percent maximum, required to achieve 75 percent approval overall). Big-market unanimity is a very unlikely prospect, as there is (and always has been) just as much likelihood of anti-New York bias — for example — among Chicago voters as of those from Cincinnati or Milwaukee.

Given the small variances in average support percentages evidenced in each of the tables above, there are only a few men (ten in all) for whom some big-market bias might have — arguably — tipped the scales in their elections, and there are twice as many about whom it might be said that a bias among the BBWAA majority favoring small-market players put them in Cooperstown. With all of the above in mind, there is no conclusive evidence in the voting history of any significant big-market bias among the BBWAA electors, and the relative success or failure of any given candidate is primarily attributable to the fickleness of a system lacking any meaningful objective standards.

14

Postseason Awards

Baseball has numerous postseason honors for players, some with more relevance to Hall of Fame election than others. The Most Valuable Player (MVP) award is the oldest and most prestigious, dating to either 1911, 1922, or 1931 — depending on how you define it. Through most of its history, the honor could be won on multiple occasions; and, as a result, the number of MVPs earned by a man has become an important aspect of his Hall of Fame credentials. Thirteen out of nineteen winners of the first two versions of the MVP, and all but two of the sixteen winners in the first decade of the current one have been enshrined at Cooperstown. Since the award's inception, only two of the eligible multiple winners — two-time recipients Roger Maris and Dale Murphy — had missed election through 2000.

The Rookie of the Year (ROY) award is the next oldest, having begun in 1947; and — like the modern MVP — the BBWAA selects its recipients (a *Sporting News* version debuted in 1946). Jackie Robinson won the initial writers' award; the first three decades of ROYs included ten players who have since been chosen for Cooperstown (seven of whom were elected in their first ballot); three later winners are certain to be enshrined when they become eligible (Eddie Murray, Mark McGwire and Cal Ripken, Jr.); and, on the whole, most of the recipients have enjoyed substantial big-league careers. But there also have been some notable duds among the selections — guys like Harry Byrd (1952), Earl Williams (1971) and Joe Charboneau (1980), who never repeated their rookie performances — and others (Herb Score, Mark Fidrych and Ken Hubbs, for example) whose careers were cut short by injuries or tragedy. So, it's a hit-and-miss award that also involves a specific moment which — unlike the MVP — cannot be repeated later in a man's career. As a result, the award has limited relevance to a man's HOF credentials relative to the MVPs.

The Cy Young Award (CYA) and Gold Glove trophies (GG) both date to the mid–1950s. The writers also select the CYAs, but Gold Glove winners are chosen under aegis of *The Sporting News*. Like the MVP, both of these honors have been around long enough to acquire a separate tradition and prestige of their own. And, because they also may be won on multiple occasions, the number of either earned by a player has significant impact on a player's Hall of Fame prospects.

So, without question, the MVP, Cy Young and Gold Glove awards have — over time — become relatively integral to discussion of any player's Cooperstown credentials. In part that's also because, although it wasn't initially intended that way, the trio have evolved to represent the three main aspects of the game itself — batting, pitching and fielding. But, like the Hall of Fame election process, the evolution of each of these honors has also had its glitches.

The concept of a Most Valuable Player award can be traced as far back as the National Association of 1875, when Boston's Deacon White was given a loving cup and some other tangible goodies by an ardent fan after leading the team to a 71–8 pennant-winning record. But there were no such awards presented during the first thirty-five years of major-league play. The first attempt at anything like it, a plan by automaker Hugh Chalmers to present a new roadster to the player from either league with the highest batting average for 1910, became a fiasco — big surprise — when the race between Detroit's Ty Cobb and Cleveland's Nap Lajoie was decided on the final day of the season amid a controversy which has not been settled to date. Cobb, who had personally written Chalmers prior to the season to express his lust for the car, began the day leading Lajoie by seven points, .383 to .376, and chose to sit out the last game to protect his advantage. Lajoie played both games of a doubleheader against the St. Louis Browns, whose manager Jack O'Connor instructed rookie third baseman Red Corriden to play deep on Nap all afternoon, thereby encouraging Lajoie to lay down seven bunt hits and go eight for eight overall to (apparently) win the auto.

Inevitably, Cobb — who could've made the greediest modern player look like a Salvation Army general by comparison — cried foul (although none of Lajoie's bunts were), and there were charges that the St. Louis pilot had conspired to assure that Nap won out over the widely detested Georgia Peach. O'Connor was fired, and American League president Ban Johnson later awarded the batting title to Cobb after discovery of a "discrepancy" in his favor among the statistical records for the season.

Chalmers gave cars to both men, trying to distance himself from the public-relations nightmare. An apparent error in the records actually was discovered in the 1980s, but it involved Cobb being credited twice for a two-for-three game at midseason, a fact which would make Lajoie the real batting champ. To date, it seems that no one knows for certain who won that 1910 batting title. *Total Baseball*, which is now the official major-league record, lists both men at .384 in its seasonal section, but its player register has Lajoie at the same number and Cobb at .383 — so even the various editors of that source do not, or cannot, agree.

Chalmers contrived a new idea for 1911 — award an auto to one man from each league chosen by the sportswriters as the "most important and useful player to his club and to the league at large." Cobb, who had to bat .420 in 1911 just to top Shoeless Joe Jackson's .408 for the batting title, won the American League car over White Sox pitcher Ed Walsh, while Cubs right fielder Wildfire Schulte nabbed the NL prize. Then, in a gesture that was uncharacteristic for Tyrus at least, both winners withdrew from consideration for the following season's honor. Over the next three years two-thirds of the awards presented were won by future Hall of Famers (Tris Speaker, Walter Johnson, Johnny Evers and Eddie Collins), but the procedure was scrapped after the 1914 campaign.

In 1922 the AL unilaterally reinstituted MVPs, whose names were initially intended to adorn the Washington, D.C. monument which, after it failed approval by Congress in 1924, later was a catalyst for the Hall of Fame concept in the mid–thirties. Predictably, the selection process for this honor was flawed in several respects, three of which drew criticism during its first couple years: once a man had won the award, he was disqualified from winning again in any future year; for some bizarre reason, player-managers were excluded from consideration; and each member of the voting panel, just one baseball writer from each of the league's eight cities, was required to vote for one player — but no more than that — from each AL team.

One result was that after Babe Ruth won the honor in 1923, he was no longer eligible, despite the fact that *Total Baseball*'s linear-weights system shows he was the best player in the league — at times by a two-to-one margin — in four of the next five seasons before the award followed the Chalmers version into extinction in 1928. The Bambino also tops the *Total Baseball* ratings for five other seasons when there were no awards, 1919–21 and 1929–30. So, although his legend doesn't need the extra accolades, instead of winning a possible ten MVPs during his career, the Babe collected just one. Also, although it wasn't seen as a problem back then, and still isn't by most current MVP electors, the AL rules established a precedent by advising voters to identify the "winning ballplayer" (yet another subjective definition) even if it meant ignoring the most obvious statistics.

The National League established its own award in 1924, and its procedure avoided most of the pitfalls in the AL's concurrent approach. So future Hall of Famer Rogers Hornsby was allowed to win two of these in 1925 and 1929, the first while serving as player-manager. But the NL version suffered its own quiet demise after the second of Rajah's honors.

The modern MVP awards voted by the BBWAA began in 1931, when the first two went to St. Louis second sacker Frankie Frisch and A's pitcher Lefty Grove, both from pennant winners. Like every other award in baseball, its biggest glitch is that there are no objective criteria for selecting MVPs and—except for the 1910 fiasco—there never have been. So predictably, over two-thirds of the awards given through 1999 (95 out of 139) have gone to players from first-place teams. Twenty-five others (18.0 percent of the trophies) have gone to men from second-place clubs and just nineteen (13.7 percent) have been doled out to players from teams even lower in the standings. Only three men have ever won the honor playing for a club with a losing record: Ernie Banks, whose consecutive MVPs in 1958–59 came when his Cubs tied for fifth place in both seasons with ledgers of 72–82 and 74–80; Andre Dawson, another Cubbie, who won in 1987 when Chicago finished last in the NL East at 76–85; and Baltimore's Cal Ripken, Jr., whose 1991 Orioles were sixth out of the seven clubs in the AL East but had the worst record ever among MVP-winner teams at 67–95.

On one hand, it's hard to believe that anyone from a losing club—let alone one that's last in the standings—can be the "most valuable" player in a league. But, it's also axiomatic that a pennant-winning club gets the season's best overall performance from its roster as a whole, regardless of any individual's heroics, and its certain that the stats of any given player on such a squad are greatly enhanced by the performances of his teammates—clearly more so than a player from a team much lower in the standings. As a result, it seems logical that the real "most valuable" player, in most instances, would and should be someone from a club that would've been nowhere near as good without him—a guy whose individual performance lifted his team to a better record than it could've otherwise expected. In that light, and absent any objective criteria, the penchant to anoint players from pennant winners—obviously endorsed by the majority of MVP electors over time—also implies that the honor would be more appropriately named the "Most Visible Winner" trophy, or something like that (although "MVW" doesn't have quite the same ring).

The Cy Young Award (CYA), which purports to honor the best overall pitching performance each season, was begun in 1956—mainly because the baseball establishment (especially Commissioner Ford Frick) perceived back then that pitchers were regularly and unfairly ignored in the annual MVP balloting. The perception was woefully unfounded. In the years prior to 1956 pitchers won fourteen of the seventy-one Most Valuable Player awards presented, about 20 percent of the overall total, and were tied with first basemen for the highest percentage of the MVP honor given to any specific position. Table 39 gives a positional breakdown of the MVPs awarded in the years 1911–55 — including the Chalmers autos, the league awards of 1922–29, and the BBWAA version of 1931 and after — along with the rounded whole-number percentages accrued by each position.

TABLE 39
MVP WINNERS BY POSITION, 1911–55

League	1B	2B	SS	3B	LF	CF	RF	C	P	Total
American	8	3	2	1	3	5	1	5	7	35
National	6	6	2	1	3	1	4	6	7	36
Total	14	9	4	2	6	6	5	11	14	71
Percentage of Total	20	13	6	3	8	8	7	15	20	100

As if that brain burp wasn't glitch enough to start with, the baseball moguls and or sportswriters immediately compounded their error by offering only one Cy Young trophy per season — forcing the presumably overlooked pitchers in each league to compete with each other for one consolation prize. This situation prevailed until 1967, when the CYA was split into American and National League versions, copying the form of the MVP.

Brooklyn's Don Newcombe won the first Cy Young Award, after leading the majors with 27 pitching victories and a .794 winning percentage in 1956. So, of course, Newcombe also won the National League MVP that season — which encourages belief that the senior circuit's non-pitchers were the players actually overlooked in the award voting that year. Since then, if anything, the existence of the Cy Young honor has made it far more difficult than before for pitchers to win the MVP (which, presumably, was not Frick's intent). The average ordinal ranking (i.e., first, second, etc.) for the highest-placed pitcher in each MVP election increased from 3.7 for all awards given through 1955 to 5.9 for the years 1956–99. Of the eighty-nine MVPs given since 1956 (including a tie for the NL award of 1979), only nine — or about 10 percent of the total, and a little more than half the amount won by hurlers during the first twenty-five years of MVP voting — have gone to pitchers, all of whom also won the CYA that year.

No pitcher has received the National League MVP since Bob Gibson in 1968, and Dennis Eckersley was the last AL hurler to win it in 1992. What's more, only eight other moundsmen have finished as high as second in the MVP voting since 1956, and Pedro Martinez, runner-up for the 1999 AL award, was the first to do it since Ron Guidry in 1978.

Over the past two decades, the predominant mindset among the BBWAA voters has become a well-publicized rationale — often justified in print on the basis that starting pitchers only play in every fourth or fifth game — that existence of the Cy Young prize should render hurlers ineligible for the MVP trophy. In turn, the latter has gradually become the ever-more-exclusive property of batsmen, who play every day. If you buy that premise, keep in mind that if the 10 percent rate of MVP pitchers since 1956 were applied to the 185 players now in Cooperstown, there would be fewer hurlers in the Hall than the number of 300-game winners enshrined to date. But, if the current attitude is going to prevail indefinitely, the most honest thing to do would be change the name of the MVP to the "Babe Ruth Award," or something similar, and formally limit the winners to non-pitchers.

In the same year that the first CYA was given, Elmer Blasco, a public relations man for Rawlings Sporting Goods, conceived an idea to reward defensive excellence — and promote sales of baseball gloves — by giving the men voted as the best fielder at each position a gold-lamé glove for the honor. Because Blasco was not a CEO like Hugh Chalmers, he had to run the concept past the corporate hierarchy for approval; and, as a result, the first Gold Glove awards were not presented until after the 1957 season.

Like its predecessors, the initial Gold Glove format also had glitches. Only one award was given for each position in 1957; so, like the Cy Young trophies of 1956–66, players from both leagues competed against each other that first year. Early on, there also was confusion about how to choose outfielders. For the first four years, selections were made on a strictly positional basis (i.e., one left fielder, one center, one right). By 1961 some non-comatose person had pointed out that a league's worst center fielder is usually better defensively than most — if not all — of its left fielders (even if his fielding average doesn't say so), and since then the awards have been given to the three men in each circuit identified as the best defensemen, regardless of their normal outfield positions.

Another problem with the Gold Gloves has been confusion about who should select recipients. The award's original voting panel included nineteen sportswriters hand-picked by J. G. Taylor Spink, publisher of *The Sporting News*. The next year, the franchise was given to the players in each league; and, as a result, winners at each position have been named for both circuits since 1958. But in 1965 the players were replaced as voters by the major-league managers and coaches combined, and that group has retained the privilege ever since.

Beyond that, the main problem with the Gold Glove process has been criticism that it rewards players for the wrong reasons. Among the major complaints, some with relative validity, there have been charges that: (1) because the season's official fielding statistics are not published until after the balloting (which takes place in September), the voters either award the honor based on reputation alone or reward the fielding leader from the previous season instead; (2) when the available unofficial stats are used, electors put too much emphasis on fielding average; (3) some voters may apply batting performance as a criterion for their choices; (4) because managers and coaches are prohibited from voting for players from their own team, they intentionally deny votes to the deserving players in closest competition with those from their club; and (5) some electors give short-shrift to the process because it distracts them during the final weeks of the pennant races.

Beyond its sponsorship of Gold Gloves, over the years *The Sporting News* (*TSN*) has also had its own versions of the MVP, Rookie of the Year and other honors. The earliest of these were its MVP awards, which began in 1929–30 — as an obvious substitute for the defunct league prizes — and lasted through 1945 (the NL still had its own award in 1929, so the periodical named an AL MVP only, and did not adopt a two-circuit format until the following year when both league honors were extinct). In the mid–1940s, *TSN* began selecting a separate "Player" and "Pitcher of the Year" for each circuit. But, due to competition from the more widely publicized BBWAA versions and the periodical's inconsistency of selection formats over time, none of those awards have gained the same widespread recognition as the scribes' versions. Also, 70 percent of the publication's MVP prizes (twenty-three of the thirty-three awards given during 1929–45) duplicated the BBWAA voting for Most Valuable Player, and a roughly equal percentage have been identical to the writer's MVP and Cy Young selections since 1956. As a result, their importance to Hall of Fame voting is debatable, with their greatest historical value relegated to those years when no corresponding BBWAA honor was given (1929–30 for the MVP awards and 1944–45 and 1948–55 when *TSN*'s Pitcher of the Year may be seen as a version of the then-nonexistent Cy Youngs).

Currently, there are other postseason awards — notably the Rolaids Relief Man/Fireman of the Year and *TSN*'s Silver Slugger trophies — but neither has much significance to HOF election as yet. The bullpen honor has been around only since the 1970s; and, in their present format, the Silver Sluggers were not given until 1980. So, although the latter may one day acquire a status similar to what the Gold Gloves imply about positional defense, neither trophy has yet had time to earn much recognition. Also, until there are more than two (or even a half-dozen) relief pitchers elected to Cooperstown, there is no reason to consider the Rolaids/Fireman award as a significant credential.

Measuring the impact of postseason honors on Hall of Fame voting is complicated by the fact that some men have won multiple awards. Through the 2000 voting, no Cooperstown member had ever won all four of the major honors (i.e., MVP, CYA, ROY and Gold Glove). But Willie Mays, Frank Robinson and Johnny Bench had all of the non-pitching prizes; Bob Gibson won the MVP, Cy Young and Gold Glove; and many HOF members and rejects received at least two of those prizes.

All the same, it's possible to estimate the voting impact of each of those honors, once again using the average support percentage received per ballot. Table 40 compares the vote histories of men who have won Most Valuable Player, Cy Young, Gold Glove and Rookie of the Year honors to those who have not. Each award is grouped separately, differentiated by frequency of selection for each, and for all winners as a whole. For each honor, the information includes the number of awards given through 1994 (Tot Awd), the number of men in each grouping who were HOF-eligible through the 2000 voting (El Tot), the number of those who were on the Cooperstown roster through 2000 (In HOF), and the percentage of eligible players elected through that date (Pct In). Following that are columns giving the number of men elected on their first time eligible (1st Bal), chosen by the scribes on a later ballot (≥2 Bal), and elected by one of the veterans panels (By VC). The final two columns give the average number of ballots on which members of each subgroup received votes (Avg Bal) and — most important — the per-ballot support percentage averaged per man (Avg Pct).

TABLE 40
AWARD-WINNER VOTE
HISTORIES THROUGH 2000

MVP Award	Tot Awd	El Tot	In HOF	Pct In	1st Bal	≥2 Bal	By VC	Avg Bal	Avg Pct
Three MVPs	8	7	7	1.000	3	4	0	3.4	58.6
Two MVPs	18	16	14	.875	8	5	1	4.2	37.3
One MVP	90	78	35	.449	14	14	7	6.2	21.9
MVPs Overall	150	101	56	.554	25	23	8	5.7	25.2
No MVP		*2067*	*129*	*.062*	*10*	*35*	*84*	*1.3*	*12.0*

Cy Young Award	Tot Awd	El Tot	In HOF	Pct In	1st Bal	≥2 Bal	By VC	Avg Bal	Avg Pct
≥Three Cy Youngs	6	4	4	1.000	4	0	0	1.0	93.5
Two Cy Youngs	4	3	2	.667	1	1	0	2.3	43.2
One Cy Young	41	29	7	.241	1	6	0	2.7	24.0
CYAs Overall	68	36	13	.361	6	7	0	2.5	28.6
No CYA		725	45	.062	4	15	26	1.3	12.3

Gold Glove Award	Tot Awd	El Tot	In HOF	Pct In	1st Bal	≥2 Bal	By VC	Avg Bal	Avg Pct
≥11 Gold Gloves	6	5	3	.800	3	0	0	4.0	28.4
6–10 Gold Gloves	28	21	6	.286	5	1	0	3.1	19.0
1–5 Gold Gloves	172	116	12	.103	9	2	1	2.6	20.1
GGs Overall	206	142	21	.148	17	3	1	2.8	20.5
No GG		2026	164	.081	18	55	91	1.4	13.4

Rookie of Year	Tot Awd	El Tot	In HOF	Pct In	1st Bal	≥2 Bal	By VC	Avg Bal	Avg Pct
ROY Winners	94	48	11	.229	7	3	1	3.3	22.1
No ROY		2120	174	.082	28	55	91	1.5	13.9

In assessing Table 40, it's important to note that the number of Hall of Famers with no awards is much larger than the total number of HOF winners of each prize. In large part, that's because there usually have been only two awards available each season, one for each league — except for the Gold Gloves, for which there normally have been nine per circuit. With almost 2200 eligible players and just 518 awards given out (in total), it's clear that most of those men cannot have won any postseason honor, including a majority of those on the Cooperstown roster. The ratio is also impacted by the limited number of years in which the awards have been given.

Beyond that, it's clear from Table 40 that achievement of postseason honors has considerable positive impact on any man's prospects for election. The ratio of Hall of Famers among award recipients is higher for each of the four honors than for the corresponding groups of non-winners, and all but the Gold Glove ratio are more than twice as large as their non-winner counterparts. The percentages also seem to indicate a hierarchy of elective importance for each of the awards. Through 2000, over half of the eligible MVPs had been elected (55.4 percent) compared to 36.1 percent of Cy Young winners, 22.9 percent of the Rookies of the Year, and just 14.8 percent of Gold Glove recipients (with the fielding award, predictably, having the least influence on success).

But, the almost 20 percent gap between the success rates for MVP and Cy Young winners is also misleading. The ratio of Hall of Famers among eligible non-winners of each award is exactly the same (6.2 percent each); the average per-ballot support percentage for Cy Young winners is actually higher, at each rung of the table, than the corresponding norm for MVP recipients; and the average support for Cy Young winners overall (28.6 percent) is also higher than the corresponding number for MVPs (25.2 percent). In that light, it's probable that (1) the higher success rate for MVPs is, much as anything, a result of the award's longer history, in which more winners have been eligible for HOF election; (2) the better support percentages posted by Cy Young winners reflect the different voting habits prevalent during the first three decades of HOF balloting compared to more recent times (notably, the increased frequency of first-ballot inductees with high support percentages in the years since 1956); and (3) the relative importance given to both awards is roughly equal in the big picture. For sake of fairness, the latter point should certainly be true in recent years, when so many among the BBWAA have refused to give pitchers equal consideration for the MVP.

Comparatively, the relative weight of each award is evidenced by the difference between the mean support percentages among winners as a whole and non-winners. On average, eligible MVP recipients have earned 13.2 percent more support than players who never won the honor. Cy Young winners have earned 16.3 percent better support than pitchers who did not receive the award. Rookies of the Year have averaged 8.2 percent more than men who did not win the freshman honor. And, trailing again, the edge for Gold Glove recipients is just 7.1 percent above those whose fielding went unrewarded. The differentials for MVP and CYA recipients are also comparable to the 14.6 percent average advantage enjoyed on all ballots by men who have attained de facto minimums for hits, home runs or games won (recall Chapter 12, Table 33), apparently indicating that both awards may be just as important to a candidate's credentials as de facto qualification.

But, in truth, they simply are not. Every eligible de facto qualifier was enshrined through 2000. In contrast, forty-five past MVPs and twenty-three Cy Young winners had not been elected by that date. The obvious difference lies in the nature of MVP and Cy Young honors, which—although just as subjective as the value placed on de facto numbers—are inevitably awards of the moment, providing no evidence of long-term achievement. As a result, twelve former MVP and CYA winners (George H. Burns, Jim Konstanty, Al Rosen, Zoilo Versalles, Dean Chance, Mike Cuellar, John Denny, Randy Jones, Mike McCormick, Steve Stone, Bob

Turley and Pete Vuckovich) never received a single HOF vote. And even multiple winners like Roger Maris, Dale Murphy and Denny McLain (the only eligible, two-time Cy recipient not yet enshrined) have so far failed to pass muster because to date their career credentials have been deemed inadequate by too many voters.

The data in Table 40 also implies, however, that achievement of three or more MVP or Cy Young awards has emerged as another of Cooperstown's de facto standards. Every eligible player with three or more of either trophy was enshrined through the 2000 voting, indicating a virtual certainty that Barry Bonds (three MVPs), Roger Clemens and Greg Maddux (five and four CYAs, respectively), each of them still active in 2000, will gain HOF election someday, even if they never attain one of the Shrine's other de facto numbers.

In contrast, the other two major awards have no effective minimum standard for induction. Only three of the five eligibles with as many as eleven Gold Gloves through 1994 had been elected, and one of them — pitcher Jim Kaat — was tied with third baseman Brooks Robinson for the all-time leadership (sixteen trophies each). Both of the unelected eligibles — Kaat and first baseman Keith Hernandez (eleven Gold Gloves) — were still on the BBWAA ballot for 2001, but their chances of future election by the writers were slim and almost none, respectively. Kaat had averaged 22 percent support through his first twelve HOF ballots, with only three years of eligibility remaining; Hernandez had received a norm of just 8.5 percent backing in his first five tries and came close to being dropped from the ballot in 1999 (earning only 6.8 percent support). The other two Hall of Famers with eleven or more Gold Gloves were outfielders Willie Mays and Roberto Clemente (twelve each). So, with one of the all-time leaders absent from Cooperstown, there is no de facto minimum for Gold Gloves; and, given the lack of importance placed on fielding performance by the voters as a whole, the absence of such a standard is not surprising. No one can win more than one Rookie of the Year award, so no de facto standard is possible — unless and until every previous winner is elected to the Shrine (and it's safe to predict that Joe Charboneau will never make it).

But the evolution of apparent de facto criteria for MVP and Cy Young honors poses all of the same problems for Hall of Fame selection as were outlined in Chapters 1 and 12 regarding the unofficial minimum standards for hits, home runs and games won. Even worse, it creates some new ones. Barring fundamental changes in human genetics and the recent philosophies governing utilization of pitchers (and ignoring the possible long-term effects of the apparently homer-friendly baseball of the 1990s), 3000 hits, 500 taters and 300 pitching victories at least approximate the historically demonstrated upper limits of athletic endurance achievable by any well-conditioned ballplayer who is not driven quite so much as Ty Cobb or Pete Rose, or penciled in as the starting pitcher as often as Cy Young or Walter Johnson. In contrast, there is far less limitation on the number of MVP or Cy Young awards a man might win in the course of a twenty-year career. No one has yet to win four MVPs, but the history of Cy Young voting just about assures that it must eventually happen: Sandy Koufax became a three-time Cy winner a decade after the award was started; Steve Carlton became the fourth man to achieve that many in 1980 then won his fourth trophy two seasons later; Greg Maddux tied that mark in 1995 then was equaled and quickly surpassed by Roger Clemens, who earned his fifth CYA in 1998.

Whatever traditions may work against such a likelihood, the upper limit of MVP and CYA honors won during a career must increase over time, implying a probable, commensurate rise in the apparent de facto standard for those honors. As each new level of success is reached, the subjective value of winning just one, two or eventually three of the awards must also diminish, comparatively demeaning the relative qualifications of those recipients and increasingly obscuring any legitimate HOF credentials possessed by men with no awards at all.

At face value, there is nothing wrong with that. Records are constantly broken, and the normal performance for every measurable statistic varies over time. So there's no reason why the upper limit of award achievement should be different, and the standards for one era could and should not be expected to apply to another.

But, the application of an open-ceiling de facto criteria for MVP and Cy Young honors can only exacerbate the problems that already plague the Cooperstown selection process regarding proportional representation by era. As was demonstrated earlier with regard to Vern Stephens, Johnny Pesky and their shortstop contemporaries, the passage of time often makes the record and reality of a moment seem more cut-and-dried than it actually was. In like manner, when viewed as a Hall of Fame credential, within their own narrow context, the five CYAs won by Roger Clemens must — in comparison — someday demean the achievements of two-time winners like Bret Saberhagen; they will dwarf the accomplishments of one-timers like Ron Guidry, Fernando Valenzuela and Orel Hershiser; and they will unavoidably reduce non-winners like the relatively well-qualified Jack Morris, Bert Blyleven, Tommy John, Jim Kaat and Dennis Martinez to the appearance of undeserving riffraff. Given the BBWAA's increased predilection to reserve the MVP for non-pitchers, whenever Barry Bonds or some other man eventually wins four of those trophies, the same thing will happen to a host of players ranging from two-time winners Roger Maris, Dale Murphy and Juan Gonzalez; once-anointed candidates like Joe Torre, Jim Rice, Dave Parker and Keith Hernandez; and the never-rewarded-but-frequently-worthy Gary Carter, Alan Trammell and Tim Raines. Along with recent voting trends favoring the election of obvious first-ballot candidates (especially de facto qualifiers), the reduction of names listed on the average ballot (to the detriment of support for men with more marginal qualifications), plus the adoption of unjustly narrow eligibility criteria for Veterans Committee consideration, this can only make it far more difficult for players from the post–1945 era to gain election to the Hall.

None of that is a problem as yet, simply because — since Yogi Berra's second-ballot election in 1972 — every eligible three-time winner of either honor (MVPs Mickey Mantle and Mike Schmidt plus CYA winners Sandy Koufax, Tom Seaver, Jim Palmer and Steve Carlton) has been a first-ballot inductee whose selection was a no-brainer requiring zero debate about the significance of their multiple awards. But, it's also inevitable that some future triple-winner will have borderline career credentials similar to Roger Maris and fail to gain (at least first-ballot) election. At that point, the argument is bound to be raised that every other three-time winner is already in Cooperstown, so there's no legitimate reason to deny him. Once that happens, the de facto status of that achievement will be set in concrete, along with all of its attendant injustices.

15

Loose Ends

Assessment of a man's Hall of Fame credentials can get complicated, because — beyond the factors measured in previous chapters— Cooperstown voters are also influenced by the achievement of individual statistical leaderships, all-star recognition and membership on teams that enjoyed regular-season and playoff success. But, while each of those items can enhance any man's credentials, it's also probable that their importance is magnified — on a case-by-case basis— for those who have not met any of the established standards in the criteria previously discussed.

As noted in Chapter 1 with regard to Babe Ruth, no debate about the relative skills of various ballplayers can avoid reference to their statistical achievements. So it follows as inevitable that no man has ever been elected to Cooperstown for his performance as a major leaguer whose selection was not based on some element of his career stats, notably his frequency at leading his league in various batting or pitching categories.

But, as evidenced in Chapter 12 (Table 34), some statistics are better predictors of Hall of Fame selection than others. In terms of seasonal leaderships, the most important and useful are necessarily those which have been around the longest, available for reference by HOF electors since the advent of Cooperstown voting. For example, there is no doubt that some modern stats, like on-base average (by batters, and allowed by pitchers), are more accurate measures of all-around performance than older devices like a hitter's batting average or a hurler's hits allowed. But OBA was not invented until the 1950s and was not added to baseball's official statistics until 1984, so it's clear that the Cooperstown electors of the 1936–60 era (at minimum) could never have used it or any seasonal leaderships in the category as Hall of Fame criteria.

With that in mind, Table 41 examines the effects on Hall of Fame voting of cumulative career totals for seasonal league leaderships in eight traditional statistical categories for batters and pitchers. The leaderships measured include hits, home runs, total bases, runs scored, RBI, stolen bases, and batting and slugging averages for hitters plus games won, winning percentage, earned run average, games pitched, innings pitched, complete games, shutouts and strikeouts for pitchers—all of them statistics which have been recorded and available for the electors' perusal since the start of Cooperstown voting (fielding statistics were omitted because of their relative lack of impact on a player's candidacy). The leaderships are lumped together, rather than measured separately for each statistic, in part for reasons of space, but also because it's obvious that all such leaderships—combined—should, in most cases, have a greater cumulative effect than any one category measured individually. (E.g., based on the data in Table 34, a man with five RBI titles will get more HOF support than one who led his circuit in stolen bases an equal number of times; but, hypothetically, so would another with three leaderships in ribbies and two in swipes.) Vertical presentation of the data in Table 41 is essentially identical to that in Table 40 in the previous chapter. The horizontal organization differs only in that the three groupings measure first the voting effects of all cumulative batting and pitching leaderships combined and below that provide breakdowns for leaderships by batters and pitchers separately. Each of the groupings also includes data for men who led their leagues fifteen times or more during their careers, those who did so on ten to fourteen occasions, players who topped their circuit five to nine times, and those who did it one to four times each. Just like Table 40, data is also given for all leaders combined and for men who never led their league at all in any of the statistics examined.

TABLE 41
EFFECTS OF CUMULATIVE SEASONAL
LEADERSHIPS ON HOF VOTING

Career Leaderships	El Tot	In HOF	Pct In	1st Bal	≥2 Bal	By VC	Avg Bal	Avg Pct
≥15 Leaderships	36	36	1.000	18	10	8	3.6	38.7
10–14 Leaderships	43	32	.744	6	13	13	5.7	29.8
5–9 Leaderships	129	41	.318	5	17	19	4.5	18.9
1–4 Leaderships	509	53	.104	6	9	38	2.4	11.3
Leaderships, Overall	717	162	.219	35	49	78	3.0	17.1
No Leaderships	1451	23	.016	0	9	14	0.8	8.7

Batting Leaderships	El Tot	In HOF	Pct In	1st Bal	≥2 Bal	By VC	Avg Bal	Avg Pct
≥15 Leaderships	17	17	1.000	10	4	3	3.2	37.6
10–14 Leaderships	27	20	.741	5	8	7	5.3	33.3
5–9 Leaderships	62	25	.403	4	10	11	4.7	20.7
1–4 Leaderships	243	42	.173	6	5	31	3.0	13.6
Leaderships, Overall	349	104	.298	25	27	52	3.5	18.6
No Leaderships	1058	23	.022	0	9	14	0.9	9.3

Pitching Leaderships	El Tot	In HOF	Pct In	1st Bal	≥2 Bal	By VC	Avg Bal	Avg Pct
≥15 Leaderships	19	19	1.000	8	6	5	3.9	39.4
10–14 Leaderships	16	12	.750	1	5	6	6.3	24.9
5–9 Leaderships	67	16	.239	1	7	8	4.2	17.0
1–4 Leaderships	266	11	.041	0	4	7	1.7	7.7
Leaderships, Overall	368	58	.155	10	22	26	2.5	15.1
No Leaderships	393	0	.000	0	0	0	0.3	3.9

Typically, the men who led their league at least once in any of the sixteen statistics measured have enjoyed an 8.4 percent advantage in per-ballot elective support over those who never won a single stat title (i.e., the difference, among Table 41's top grouping, between the average support overall and that for those with no leaderships). For batters as a group, the advantage has been 9.3 percent, while pitchers received an 11.2 percent edge. When measured separately, the higher number for pitchers (a 1.9 percent difference) may be relatively insignificant on its own. But the most curious data in the table is the fact that, although twenty-three men have been elected to Cooperstown without ownership of any major offensive title, not one pitcher has been added to the roster who failed to lead his circuit in some category at least once during his career. The causes for that result include the rarity in which players at some positions (notably catcher) lead their league in any category and the fact that there were far more non-pitchers (1407) than hurlers (761) eligible through the 2000 voting, increasing the likelihood that some untitled batters would be elected. But, all the same, the numbers indicate that — to date — it has been much more difficult for a pitcher with no statistical leaderships to get elected than it has for any hitter, even backstops.

Beyond that, it's evident that a career total of fifteen league leaderships has, over time, become the minimum standard for certain election to Cooperstown. But, under the definition supplied in Chapter 12, it's doubtful that the number qualifies as a true de facto standard, as it's very unlikely that many — if any — voters are aware of that number or its precedent.

On a stat-by-stat basis, Table 42 (below) compares the minimum career-leadership standards established through the 2000 voting for each of the sixteen statistics measured in Table 41.

In the first two data columns, it gives the name of the career leader for each category (each of them was in Cooperstown by 2000) and the number of leaderships won by that man (No. Ldr). Following that are the minimum required number of seasonal titles for each statistic at or above which every man who accomplished it was enshrined through 2000 (Min Req, bold-faced), the number of players at or above that level who were on the Cooperstown roster by that date (In HOF), the number who were bunched at the next-lowest level of achievement (Next Lev), and the number at that lower level who had not yet been elected (No. Out).

Finally, as space permits, it gives the names of any men at that next-lowest level who had not been elected through the 2000 voting (Highest Man Out) and the number of seasonal titles they won in that category.

As an example of how Table 42 works, note that Hall of Famer Ty Cobb led his league in hits on eight occasions, the all-time record. But the next man in line, Pete Rose (seven titles), was not in Cooperstown through 2000. As a result, the effective minimum requirement for hits leaderships is eight, with Cobb the only man in (hence the "one" in that column), and Rose the only man at the next-lowest level (so he, alone, represents the other two columns of data).

TABLE 42
MINIMUM LEADERSHIPS
PER AUTOMATIC ELECTION

Batters	Career Leader	No. Ldr	Min Req	In HOF	Next Lev	No. Out	Highest Man Out
Hits	T. Cobb	8	**8**	1	1	1	P. Rose, 7
Home Runs	B. Ruth	12	**8**	2	4	1	Cravath, 6
Stolen Bases	M. Carey	10	**8**	3	4	3	3 tied, 6
Total Bases	H. Aaron	8	**6**	7	5	1	J. Rice, 4
Runs Scored	B. Ruth	8	**6**	3	4	1	G. Burns, 5
Batting Avg.	T. Cobb	12	**5**	7	5	1	B. Madlock, 4
Runs Batted In	C. Anson	8	**5**	4	7	1	S. Magee, 4
Slugging Avg.	B. Ruth	13	**4**	16	7	1	D. Allen, 3

Pitchers	Career Leader	No. Ldr	Min Req	In HOF	Next Lev	No. Out	Highest Man Out
Strikeouts	W. Johnson	12	6	8	4	1	S. McDowell, 5
Winning Pct.	L. Grove	5	5	1	3	2	2 tied, 3
Comp. Games	W. Spahn	9	5	5	4	1	W. Ferrell, 4
Wins	W. Spahn	8	4	11	9	1	B. Walters, 3
Shutouts	3 tied	7	4	9	14	6	6 tied, 3
Inn. Pitched	G. Alexander	7	4	12	6	3	3 tied, 3
Earned Run Avg.	L. Grove	9	3	10	26	13	13 tied, 2
Games Pitched	2 tied	6	No Viable Minimum				F. Marberry, 6

Obviously, there is no consistency among the apparent minimum standards for career leaderships in each statistic. Batters must have a minimum of eight career titles in hits, home runs or stolen bases to be (apparently) assured of Hall of Fame election, but need no more than four slugging championships for the same guarantee.

To date, it has taken a minimum of six strikeout titles to earn certain election for any pitcher, but only three ERA leaderships provide the same assurance. Also, there is no established minimum for seasonal games-pitched leaderships at all. That's because through 1994 two men — Joe McGinnity and Firpo Marberry — were tied for the top spot with six seasonal leaderships apiece, and McGinnity was in the Hall, but Marberry was not.

The absence of consistent standards for each statistic clarifies why the cumulative total of seasonal leaderships accrued by a man is more important to his Cooperstown prospects than any number of titles in a specific category. It also assures, for now, that there can be no effective de facto standard for any particular stat. After all, it would be specious to argue that Bill Madlock belongs in the Hall because he is the only man with four batting crowns thus far excluded, when someone else could note that Gavvy Cravath won more home-run titles (six) and is not there either.

Beyond the career total of statistical leaderships, other measurements of a player's credentials include the number of times he was selected to appear in all-star games and the number of pennant- and or World Series-winning teams for which he played.

Each of these items has merit, but it's also evident that — relative to the individual achievements already discussed — they are bound to be low on the list of most electors' criteria. Table 43 measures the elective impact of each of these factors, using the same format and headings applied in Table 41.

TABLE 43
Voting Impact of All-Star Selection, World Series and Pennant Success

All-Stars	El Tot	In HOF	Pct In	1st Bal	≥2 Bal	By VC	Avg Bal	Avg Pct
≥12 All-Star Games	21	20	.952	16	3	1	2.2	58.7
8–11 All-Star Games	53	32	.604	7	15	10	7.5	29.9
4–7 All-Star Games	176	35	.199	6	21	8	4.6	17.9
1–3 All-Star Games	582	17	.029	2	7	8	1.1	8.5
All Stars Overall	832	104	.125	31	46	27	2.3	18.1
No All-Star Games	1336	81	.061	4	12	65	1.0	8.7

World Series Won	El Tot	In HOF	Pct In	1st Bal	≥2 Bal	By VC	Avg Bal	Avg Pct
≥4 World Series Won	66	20	.303	4	10	6	4.6	18.5
2–3 World Series Won	299	51	.171	11	12	28	2.9	13.6
1 World Series Won	592	59	.100	13	17	29	1.7	15.0
WS Won, Overall	957	130	.136	28	39	63	2.2	14.9
No World Series Won	1211	55	.045	7	19	29	0.9	13.0

Pennants Won	El Tot	In HOF	Pct In	1st Bal	≥2 Bal	By VC	Avg Bal	Avg Pct
≥7 Pennants Won	40	18	.450	2	10	6	6.3	23.8
4–6 Pennants Won	245	55	.224	13	11	31	3.3	14.6
1–3 Pennants Won	1188	88	.074	18	26	44	1.5	12.5
Pens. Won, Overall	1473	161	.109	33	47	81	1.9	14.1
No Pennants Won	695	24	.035	2	11	11	0.7	14.9

Because the first all-star game was not played until 1933, appearances in those contests have no relevance to the HOF prospects of men whose careers ended before (or very soon after) that date. So, absurdly, Bucky Dent has better all-star credentials (three appearances) than either Babe Ruth (two) or Honus Wagner (none)—but that hardly justifies those three votes he got in 1990. Nonetheless, the average per-ballot support percentage for men who appeared in all-star games (18.1 percent) is almost ten points higher than the norm for players who didn't (8.7 percent).

Through 1994, Hank Aaron was the all-time leader with twenty-one all-star selections, and four other Hall of Famers had at least eighteen (Willie Mays and Stan Musial with twenty; Rod Carew and Carl Yastrzemski at the lower total). Ted Williams and Pete Rose were chosen seventeen times, so Rose's ineligibility implies that the hypothetical minimum to assure election is currently eighteen, an extremely exclusive criteria. Below them, there were thirteen Hall of Famers tied with a dozen appearances each and five others with eleven. But two unenshrined men, catchers Gary Carter and Bill Freehan, also were selected on eleven occasions. Carter was still on the ballot for 2001, but Freehan's eligibility had expired, and he cannot be considered by the Veterans Committee (because he received only two votes in 1982). So, given Rose's special problems, a dozen all-star appearances is a more logical cutoff point for the all-star upper echelon in Table 43.

Beyond that, it's noteworthy that the proportion of Hall of Famers among men with no all-star appearances (6.1 percent) is almost exactly equal to the corresponding ratios of Cooperstown members who never won the MVP or Cy Young awards (6.2 percent each, from Table 40 in the previous chapter). But, except for men with three MVP trophies, the average support percentages at each frequency level for those two major awards are higher than the corresponding all-star levels shown in Table 43. So it's safe to say that a man must appear in at least a dozen all-star contests before the voting effect of his all-star selections might begin to counterbalance the absence of either major postseason honor.

Regarding postseason play, it's important to note that the modern World Series did not begin until 1903. So, to be fair to nineteenth-century players for the purposes of Table 43, the postseason competitions of the 1880s between the National League and American Association pennant winners and the NL's Temple-Cup playoffs of the following decade (which pitted its regular-season pennant winner against the second-place club) were both treated as World Series outcomes.

The postseason data in Table 43 seems to imply that the voting impact of playing for frequent pennant winners is greater than that for repeated World Series success. The ratios of Hall of Famers with four or more pennants are higher than those for the first two levels of World Series success measured, as are their average support percentages. On one hand that seems appropriate, because luck can have a greater impact on the outcome of a World Series than is likely over the course of a lengthy season, as — in theory, anyway — it's harder to get to the fall classic than to win it.

But, because the organization of the postseason data in the table is not identical, further analysis is required. Both sets of data are also skewed by the impact of players who spent large portions of their careers with the New York Yankee dynasties. Through 1994 the Yanks had won thirty-two pennants and twenty-two fall classics, far more than any other franchise. As a result, former Bronx Bombers dominate the career leaders for both categories: Yogi Berra played on the most pennant and World Series winners (fourteen and ten, respectively); the twelve HOF-eligible men with nine or more pennants were all former Yankees, as were the dozen (not identical) with seven or more World Series titles; nine of the ten who played for six World Series winners also spent most of their careers in pin-stripes; and sixteen of twenty-eight men with seven or eight pennants on their ledgers were former Yanks. So, to minimize the effects of Yankee dynasties, it's more instructive to examine the data for men with smaller career totals for each feat. Those groups also include lots of New Yorkers, but they include enough postseason "mortals" to provide a more balanced comparison.

Within those guidelines (and involving data not shown in Table 43), World Series victories have a marginally greater impact on Hall of Fame selection than an equal number of pennants won. As of 2000, there were twenty-eight HOF eligibles with four World Series victories; five of them (17.9 percent) were in Cooperstown; and each man in the group averaged 16.3 percent support per ballot. In comparison, there were 138 men with four pennants, twenty-two of them (15.9 percent) were Hall of Famers, and the group's average support was 12.6 percent. Among candidates with three wins in either category, fifteen out of eighty World Series winners were Hall of Famers (18.8 percent) compared to 27 of 220 three-time pennant winners (12.3 percent), and the average support for the fall classic group was 14.3 percent compared to 10.3 for the pennant winners. The 219 two-time World Series victors included thirty-six Cooperstown members (16.4 percent), while the 372 men with two pennants featured thirty-three Hall of Famers (8.9 percent), and the average support for the two-series winners was 13.3 percent compared to 12.2 for those with two pennants. As indicated in Table 43, 10 percent of the 592 one-time WS victors were enshrined and had an average support of 15.0 percent. In comparison (and not shown above), the 596 men with only one pennant included twenty-eight Cooperstown members (4.7 percent) and had 13.2 percent average support.

When measured as a whole, the HOF eligibles with one to four World Series victories average 14.6 percent support per ballot, and 10.3 percent of all of them are in Cooperstown. As a group, the men with one to four pennants have an average support of 12.1 percent per ballot, and 8.3 per-cent of them are Hall of Famers. As a result, in terms of voter support (and up to the lower limits of the primary beneficiaries of Yankee good fortune), each World Series victory lends about 2 percent more credence to a man's Cooperstown credentials than an equal number of pennants.

Although it has no logical correlation with overall career achievement (and, hence, any objective Hall of Fame credential), one other factor strongly influences Hall of Fame selection — the relative itineracy of a man's career. The legends, if not the abilities and achievements, of several Hall of Famers have been enhanced because they enjoyed long careers with just one franchise: Walter Johnson, who spent all of his twenty-one seasons with the Washington Senators, was the first one-team player elected to Cooperstown; among all Hall of Famers, Brooks Robinson (Orioles) and Carl Yastrzemski (Red Sox) had the longest one-franchise tenures, twenty-three seasons each; and overall, 43 of the Shrine's 185 players (23.2 percent) spent their entire careers in just one uniform. In most cases, like Ernie Banks (Cubs) and Stan Musial (Cardinals), by the middle of their careers these men were seen as the heart and soul of their ball clubs and became integral to the public's general perception of the team, in their home cities and in those of their opponents.

At the opposite end of that experience, other players earn considerable notice because they are frequently traded. Harry "Suitcase" Simpson, an outfielder of the 1950s, got his nickname because experience taught him to keep his major-league bags packed — he was traded five times (plus sold and waived once each) during his eight-year career. No doubt, the best-known (and perhaps most accomplished) man among this group was Bobo Newsom, who won 211 games and spent twenty seasons in the majors during the years 1929–53 (he had three different minor-league stints during that period). In sequence, Newsom played for the Dodgers, Cubs, Browns, Senators, Browns, Tigers, Senators, Dodgers, Browns, Senators, A's, Senators, Yankees, Giants, Senators, and finally the A's again. Bobo kept coming back to the Senators like a bad penny; by the time he retired his luggage was completely obscured by train-destination stickers; and, if Hollywood had filmed his life story, it almost certainly would've been titled *If It's Tuesday, This Must Be St. Louis.*

But the recognition given to players like Simpson and Newsom — sometimes affectionate, yet tinged with some derision — is never as reverential as that afforded to guys like Ernie Banks (they can never be known as "Mr. Cub," for instance). The mixed message inherent to that type of fame also obscures the fact that any man traded that often must have been a relatively valuable and marketable commodity throughout his career.

Table 44 examines the impact of career itineracy on HOF voting. Because the real issue involves whether a man gains any elective advantage by staying with a team throughout his career (or a disadvantage by not), the data measures how many different franchises each man played for and not how often he was traded, sold or waived — which is usually a larger number.

TABLE 44
IMPACT OF CAREER ITINERACY
ON HALL OF FAME SUPPORT

Career Itineracy	El Tot	In HOF	Pct In	1st Bal	≥2 Bal	By VC	Avg Bal	Avg Pct
One Team Only	156	43	.276	19	14	10	3.5	17.9
2–3 Teams	817	77	.094	10	27	40	1.7	14.4
4–5 Teams	837	53	.063	5	14	34	1.2	12.9
≥6 Teams	358	12	.034	1	3	8	0.8	12.0
Totals	2168	185	.085	35	58	92	1.5	14.2

As evidenced by Table 44, a man who spends his entire career with just one franchise is far more likely to be elected to Cooperstown than even one who played for only two franchises. His average support per ballot may not be much better than a guy who toiled for two or three clubs, but—in the long run—his career stability is a definite advantage, especially over guys who played for four teams or more. In addition to the forty-three men elected to Cooperstown, fifty-one others who played for just one franchise have also received votes, so about 12 percent of all men who have earned any Hall of Fame support at all (93 of 747) were one-teamers—almost double the corresponding ratio (156 out of 2168 or 7.2 percent) among HOF eligibles as a whole and triple the rate among eligible players with votes at all (62 of 1421, 4.4 percent).

At the other end of the spectrum, a player who wore as many as six major league uniforms can almost forget about entering the Shrine without a ticket. Only a dozen Hall of Famers are in that category, topped by nineteenth-century first baseman Dan Brouthers, who played for eleven different clubs. Hoyt Wilhelm, who toiled for nine different teams, is next on the list and the leader among twentieth-century players, and Steve Carlton is the only man to play for as many as six teams and still get elected on his first ballot.

Much of the favoritism shown to one-franchise players occurred during the early period of Cooperstown voting. Nineteen of the thirty-three one-teamers elected by the BBWAA (about 58 percent) were men from the Postwar Era or before, and only three of them (George Brett, Mike Schmidt and Robin Yount) were primarily identified with the Free-Agent years after 1975.

All the same, playing for just one franchise over a long career has been a definite boon to first-year election. Among Cooperstown's first five members, only Walter Johnson played for just one team (Ty Cobb, Christy Mathewson and Honus Wagner toiled for two; Babe Ruth, three). But after that, the next five first-ballot inductees—Bob Feller and Jackie Robinson (1962), Ted Williams (1966), Stan Musial (1969) and Sandy Koufax (1972)—each spent their entire careers with just one club (although Sandy's moved from Brooklyn to Tinseltown). Warren Spahn (1973) was the first man after 1936 who played for more than one club to be elected on his first try; but, even at that, all but the last of Spahnie's twenty-three seasons—which was split between the Mets and Giants—were spent with the Braves in Boston or Milwaukee. Among first-ballot winners, Spahn was followed by Mickey Mantle (1974, entire career with the Yanks), Ernie Banks (1977, all with the Cubs), Willie Mays (1979, only the last two of his twenty-two seasons spent with any team except the Giants), Al Kaline (1980, entire career with Tigers), Bob Gibson (1981, only wore a Cardinals uniform) and Hank Aaron (1982, all but the final two of twenty-three seasons spent with the Braves). So, given that all those men were primarily identified with just one club, the first truly multiple-team player elected in his first year eligible was Frank Robinson (ten seasons with the Reds, six with Baltimore, and a couple each with the Angels and Indians), who was inducted with Aaron in 1982, almost a half century after Cooperstown voting began.

No doubt, the voters' preference for one-franchise candidates was a product of a mindset fostered by the reserve-clause era, when players were bound to their clubs indefinitely and left them only at management's discretion. It's also clear that the era of free agency has eliminated much of that bias. Only a dozen of the fifty-eight players elected by the BBWAA prior to the 1980 voting (20.7 percent) had played for as many as four different teams. Since then, 34.3 percent of the scribes' selections (twelve out of thirty-five) have worn four or more different uniforms.

Ever since Nellie Fox missed election by just two votes in 1985, his last year on the BBWAA ballot (and with slightly less fanfare before then), much has been made about the fates of various candidates in their final year of eligibility. Fox set a record that year for the highest support percentage ever received without gaining election (74.5 percent); his support increased by 13.3 percent over the previous year's voting; and there is no doubt that his last-year performance was boosted by a vigorous campaign by some electors to push him over the top. In later years, similar efforts attended the final ballot appearances of Roger Maris (1988), Jim Bunning (1991), Bill Mazeroski (1992), Orlando Cepeda (1994), Tony Oliva (1996) and Ron Santo (1998) among others; and there is no doubt that similar campaigns attended the final years of eligibility for Marty Marion (1973), Phil Rizzuto (1976) and many other candidates who were on the ballot long before Fox.

In each of the cases noted above, the candidate's final-year support percentage surpassed the one received in their previous year on the ballot. Cepeda got the biggest boost among that group, jumping by 14.0 percent above his performance the previous year to a 73.6 percent figure that almost equaled Fox's frustration (although Nellie had died a decade before his near miss occurred and didn't feel it personally). But, because each of those efforts failed to get any of the men into Cooperstown through the front door, the question remains whether any of these last-chance campaigns has ever succeeded or even had a positive impact on a man's chances.

The answer is difficult to come by for several reasons. To begin with, the rules for a player's window of eligibility have been changed often over the years, and trying to determine which election represented the last year of some mens' eligibility is akin to interpreting a copy of the American corporate tax code that was written in Azerbaijani. The changes seem simple enough: through the 1945 voting, there was no back end to a man's eligibility; for the years 1946–56, his window ended twenty-five years after the date of his retirement; the cutoff was thirty years during 1956–62; and the current twenty-year limit has been in effect ever since. But there is some overlap in those dates of application, and there are a couple dozen guys who retired in the same years during the 1930s for which different limits obviously applied (e.g., Hall of Famers Kiki Cuyler, Goose Goslin and Waite Hoyt — each of them inducted by the VC — all quit after the 1938 season, but Cuyler's eligibility ended in 1960, while the other two were still on the ballot in 1962). The issue is also muddled because some men came out of retirement to appear during the World War II player shortage (although that factor didn't effect the eligibility of Cuyler, Goslin or Hoyt). As a result, the final year of eligibility is clearcut only for men who retired after 1945 (although a few of them also had their ballot terms extended after the 1991 voting).

The bottom line is that there have been only two candidates who can be identified with relative confidence as having been elected in their final year on the ballot — Red Ruffing (retired after the 1947 season, elected in 1967) and Joe Medwick (quit after 1948, elected in 1968), both of whom (apparently) fell under the current twenty-year guideline. Recall, however, that — due to the use of the preliminary- and runoff-ballot format in 1964 and '67 — both men were effectively elected twice. Ruffing earned sufficient support in the 1964 runoff to gain election under normal circumstances, but Luke Appling outpolled him in the runoff, and Red was denied induction that year by the rule limiting the runoff to one electee. There was no election in 1965, but in 1966 Ruffing placed second to first-timer Ted Williams, who was elected. In 1967, Ruffing and Medwick both tied on the preliminary vote, before Red was chosen in the runoff (in which Medwick also topped 75 percent support). Ruffing's support climbed from 68.9 percent in 1966 to 72.6 percent on the 1967 preliminary ballot and 86.9 percent in the runoff. Medwick's percentage equaled Ruffing's in the '67 preliminary vote, climbed to 81.0 percent in the runoff, and was 85.1 percent in 1968.

Beyond those two, every other last-ballot candidacy has failed. Among the 747 men who received votes from the BBWAA through the 2000 election, there were 136 whose candidacies identifiably survived through their last year of eligibility with the writers. Compared to their performance on the previous ballot, the last-year vote totals and support percentages declined for over 40 percent of these men, and only seventeen of the 136 saw their support percentage increase by as much as 10 percent in their final year on the ballot — Ray Schalk was tops with 23.6 percent, followed by Arky Vaughan (22.9) and Hal Newhouser (22.8). For the 136-man group as a whole, the average vote and support figures received in their last year on the ballot increased by only one vote and one-half of one percent, respectively, over their performances on the previous ballot. So, typically, and by inference, any overt campaigning for last-year candidates has had little success (although eleven of the seventeen whose final-ballot support increased by as much as 10 percent have been elected by the veterans committees).

There also is a widespread notion that lengthy service as a coach enhances the prospect of a man's election. The all-time record for years of service as a major-league coach (as distinguished from manager) is held by Nick Altrock, a Dead-Ball-Era pitcher who was a mentor for the Senators for forty-two years (1912–53). Altrock's career record as a hurler was just 83–75, but he received votes in seven different elections during the years 1937–60. So, because his career record was nothing special, it's probable that his longtime service as a coach explains some of that support. But, even if it does, Nick received only fifty-seven votes in all and averaged just 3.1 percent support per ballot — so his coaching service didn't buy him enough leverage to gain election by the scribes, and he has not been inducted by the veterans committees.

With a handful of possible exceptions, the same can be said of almost everyone else who had lengthy careers as coaches. Among the ninety-six men who had served as coaches for eleven years or more through 1998, only eight of them (Yogi Berra, Earle Combs, Billy Herman, George Kelly, Red Schoendienst, Al Simmons, Honus Wagner and Billy Williams) were on the Cooperstown roster by 2000. Berra, Simmons, Wagner and Williams were elected by the BBWAA, and — because their service as coaches coincided with some portion of their time on the writers' ballot — it probably had minimal impact on the scribes' perceptions of their credentials. Among the other four, all of whom were tabbed by the VC, Schoendienst had a fourteen-year career as a manager — including two pennants and one World Series victory — which obviously enhanced his credentials far more than his coaching tenure. Herman was a skipper for four seasons but never placed higher than eighth in a ten-team league, and his career winning percentage was just .408. Combs and Kelly were never pilots. So, although it didn't get them in through the front door, it's possible that the latter three's service as coaches enhanced their qualifications in the minds of the VC members who elected them.

But, historically, there has been a negative relationship between length of coaching tenure and BBWAA prospects for selection to Cooperstown. Through the 2000 voting, the average per-ballot support percentage among the forty-five men who served as coaches for sixteen years or more was just 9.1 percent; those who served as mentors for eleven to fifteen seasons averaged 14.3 percent support; and those with six to ten seasons as a coach averaged 16.8. Below that, men with one to five years averaged 13.9 percent, and those who never coached at all averaged 14.4. Beyond the Hall of Famers noted in the previous paragraph, only three other men with as many as eleven seasons as a coach — Hank Gowdy (eighteen years, 10.8 percent), Harvey Kuenn (twelve seasons, 24.2 percent) and Elston Howard (eleven years, 10.7 percent) — averaged as much as 10 percent support per ballot. So the inverse relationship between length of coaching tenure and BBWAA support indicates that, generally, service as a mentor does little or nothing to boost a man's Cooperstown prospects — at least with the voting writers.

In that light, one other aspect of Hall of Fame selection also merits discussion — the election of managers. As noted in Chapter 6, all of the pilots chosen for the Shrine have been elected by one of the veterans committees (although some of them also received votes from the BBWAA at some point). Also, the VC's current eligibility rules for managers are less exclusive than those applied for players — instead of the twenty-three-year wait after retirement required for player eligibility, pilots may be considered five seasons after their retirement or if they are retired and sixty-five years old.

Through the VC's 2000 voting, sixteen men had been chosen for Cooperstown solely for their roles as managers — Walter Alston, Sparky Anderson, Leo Durocher, Ned Hanlon, Bucky Harris, Miller Huggins, Tom Lasorda, Al Lopez, Connie Mack, Joe McCarthy, John McGraw, Bill McKechnie, Wilbert Robinson, Frank Selee, Casey Stengel and Earl Weaver.

Three of them (McCarthy, Selee and Weaver) never appeared in the major-leagues as a player. Alston played in only one game (Cardinals, 1936), Anderson in just one season (Phillies, 1959), and Lasorda in only three campaigns (Dodgers and A's, 1954–56). The others all had big-league playing careers which lasted at least ten seasons; all of them but Hanlon received support from the BBWAA voters at some point during 1936–67 (as did McCarthy); and, although most of the votes they received probably rewarded their managerial tenures, it's impossible to assess how much, if any, of that support derived from their playing skills. Sixty-five of the Hall's other members also served as pilots, including fifty-seven of the men elected as players, and in some cases—notably Frank Chance and Hughie Jennings—their memberships might be more justifiable if they had been cited for both capacities instead of just one.

As with players, there are no objective standards for election of managers, except for the ten-year service requirement (in this case, as pilots). In the absence of such standards, it's predictable that precedent has established at least one de facto criterion for managers. With the enshrinement of Sparky Anderson, every skipper with at least 2000 regular-season victories had been chosen for the Shrine (there were six others, including Mack, McGraw, Harris, McCarthy, Alston and Durocher).

As a group, managers have far fewer statistics by which to assess their Hall of Fame credentials than players do. The most familiar stats include career victories, winning percentage, years and games managed, plus the number of pennants and World Series won. To some degree, each of those statistics is influenced by longevity (even winning percentage, as the law of competitive balance dictates that the longer a man serves as a pilot, the more likely his won-lost record will approach .500). As a result, the probability of a man's enshrinement increases as much or more with length of service as it does with regular-season success: nine of the ten pilots with the most years of service and games managed were on the Cooperstown roster through 2000 compared to only five of the same number with the best career winning percentages.

In turn, the career records of Cooperstown's sixteen skippers evidence much inconsistency. Only seven of them had career winning percentages of .555 or better (the equivalent of ninety wins per each 162-game season), including the four with the shortest careers (Huggins, Lopez, Selee and Weaver); two ended their tenures as pilots with more regular-season losses than wins (Mack and Harris); and two of them won a record seven World Series apeice (McCarthy and Stengel), while two others never won a fall classic at all (Lopez and Robinson).

Unlike player selections, the enshrinement of managers is strongly correlated to postseason success. With Anderson's election, all of the seven eligible skippers with at least three World Series victories had been chosen for Cooperstown (the others were McCarthy, Stengel, Mack, Alston, Huggins and McGraw). But, for now, that number cannot be considered a de facto standard, because Joe Torre won his third fall classic in 1999, and his ultimate Hall of Fame fate is uncertain (although that victory would seem to clinch his eventual selection as a pilot).

Beyond all that, the biggest flaw in the selection of managers to date has been the application of a far less rigorous proportional standard for the enshrinement of skippers than players. The sixteen pilots in the Hall represent 2.7 percent of the 591 managers in big-league history through 1998 and 20.8 percent of the seventy-seven skippers with ten-year service or more through the same date. If equal representational standards were applied to either the 14,000-odd players who had appeared in the majors during 1876–1994, or to the 2168 men who met the eligibility requirements for tables presented earlier in this chapter, then the Cooperstown roster would include either 378 or 451 men chosen solely for their careers as players—each total more than double the 185 players who were actually enshrined. Perhaps the application of different standards for managers and players is subjectively acceptable, but the size of either proportional discrepancy is one final bit of evidence that the Cooperstown selection process always has been tainted by its lack of objective criteria.

16

Invisible Men

In the biggest disgrace in the history of professional sports, men of African (and Latin) ancestry who were too dark-skinned to be perceived as white were barred from Organized Baseball from the late 1880s until Jackie Robinson joined the Montreal Royals in 1946. For six decades that Jim Crow status quo gave people whose love for baseball was no less than that of their pale counterparts no option but to play with other men of color. In the process, this travesty turned each of them into an invisible man who, much like the title character of Ralph Ellison's race-oriented novel of the early 1950s, was ignored by a majority of the American population and was perceived unrealistically by the minority of whites who saw them play.

But the color barrier was also a tragedy for players of every race. The exclusion also prevented at least three generations of the world's greatest players from competing against the very best talent available, thereby demeaning for all posterity the performances of men in every professional league, regardless of their race.

The color barrier's evolution has been documented by numerous authors in much more detail than space affords here. But, for Hall of Fame discussion purposes, it should be noted that Jackie Robinson was not the first black man to play in the major leagues or even the first of "color" to appear in the Show during the twentieth century.

The first Afro-American known to have played baseball as a professional was John "Bud" Fowler, a native — ironically — of Cooperstown, New York, who was the second baseman for an otherwise all-white team in New Castle, Pennsylvania, in 1872. Fowler was still playing professionally in

1884, when the honor of being the first black man to appear in the majors went to someone else. With the National League and American Association already in operation, the one-season existence of the Union Association (1884) produced a third major circuit and big-league jobs for new players. One of the men who seized that chance was a Mt. Pleasant, Ohio, native and Afro-American, Moses Fleetwood Walker, who became the regular catcher for the AA's Toledo Blue Stockings after playing for the same city's Northwestern League club the previous year. After Walker's first appearance for Toledo, he was joined on the team by his brother Welday.

Welday didn't last long, appearing in only five games as a reserve outfielder and batting just .222. In contrast "Fleet," as Moses was known, appeared in forty-two games, batting .263. But, predictable for a nation which had fought a civil war over slavery less than two decades earlier, Fleet's presence with Toledo caused problems in the league, especially when the club traveled below the Mason-Dixon line. In Louisville, Walker was forced to watch his team from the stands after an opponent refused to play in the same game with him; and, prior to a contest in Richmond, Moses received a written threat that "seventy-five determined men" had sworn to take matters into their own hands if he took the field in that city. Toledo management soon bowed to the pressure of such ugliness—as, when Walker cracked a rib, his injury was used as an excuse to release him, ending his major-league tenure.

By 1887, Moses Walker and black pitcher George Stovey were both on the opening-day roster of the Newark Giants of the new International League (IL), a circuit at the highest rung of the minors. In April of that season both men played, without incident, in exhibitions against the NL's Brooklyn Bridegrooms and New York Giants. There were other blacks in the circuit: second sacker Frank Grant was a regular for Buffalo; and, early in the season, Toronto signed pitcher Robert Higgins.

But, although many white northerners still criticized the south for its treatment of Negroes, they were less enthusiastic about welcoming blacks into their mainstream. Inevitably, the Afro-Americans' presence on the same field led to hostility from some white competitors. Grant at second and Walker at home spent much of the season trying to avoid being maimed by baserunners who went out of their way to upend them. And Higgins lost his first pitching start 22–8, when his new teammates made numerous fielding and running errors to signal displeasure with his presence on the club. On 5 June 1887, Toronto manager Joe Simmons was informed that two of his players—pitcher Dug Crothers and outfielder Harry Simon—refused to appear in the team photo with Higgins.

The IL's growing racial tensions came to a head at separate locales on 14 July 1887. Newark was scheduled to play an exhibition game against the National League's defending champion Chicago White Stockings (today's Cubs), managed by star first baseman Cap Anson. The future Hall of Famer, who every authoritative source indicates was as racist or more so than Ty Cobb, refused to play the exhibition unless Walker and Stovey were barred from the game, and Newark management, faced with loss of a big payday, adhered to Cap's demand. That same day at a league meeting in Buffalo, six of the circuit's ten owners approved a resolution to deny future contracts to men of color.

Amid these problems, Stovey and Grant performed with admirable concentration and skill. The Newark pitcher led the circuit with thirty-five wins in 1887, and Grant batted .366, only fourteen points below the league leader, Newark's J. W. Coogan. The black players also contributed to the success of their respective teams: with Higgins in its rotation, Toronto won the pennant, playing .643 baseball; Grant's Buffalo club finished second at .611, only three games back; and Newark came in fourth at .602, with Fleet Walker batting .264 for the season.

Although their teams had not voted for their exclusion, the futures of the black players were a foregone conclusion. Stovey was released by Newark prior to the 1888 season, probably the only pitcher ever to suffer that fate after a thirty-five-win year (the total remains the IL's single-season record for victories). Higgins hung on with Toronto until the middle of 1888 then — fed-up with the abuse received — quit to become a barber in Memphis. Grant and Walker stayed with their clubs throughout 1888, Grant batting .326, Walker dropping to .170. But, when Grant sought a $250-a-month raise for 1889, the Bisons released him; and, although Walker hooked up with the league's Syracuse club, he retired before the 1889 season was over and became a mail clerk.

The IL's 1887 action set a precedent which, at the insistence of men like Anson, the majors and all of Organized Baseball quickly followed, and the first identifiably black player to appear in a big-league uniform also became the last one to play for any National Association of Professional Baseball Leagues affiliate until Robinson joined Montreal. Ironically, Robinson's postwar Royals were members of the same circuit in which the color barrier had first been established.

Of course, blacks continued to play baseball, and had numerous options to do so. Teams comprised entirely of Afro-Americans existed at many locales, some dating to 1862, and the first known club of all-black professionals was formed as the Babylon, Long Island, Argyle Hotel Athletics in 1885 and took the field later in the decade renamed as the Cuban

Giants. In another irony, the Giants were owned by a white businessman, Walter Cook, and even profited from racist expectations by pretending to be Hispanics in order to draw white patrons amused by their "foreign" behavior (if basketball mogul Abe Saperstein—who much later was an owner of the Negro Birmingham Black Barons—had been involved, he might've called them the Havana Globetrotters).

The first attempt at an all-black professional league came in 1887, the year of the IL's anti-colored resolution. The circuit included teams in Baltimore, Boston, Cincinnati, Louisville, New York, Philadelphia, Pittsburgh and Washington, D.C. But, several of its clubs ran into immediate financial trouble, and the league never finished its inaugural season.

All-black teams remained in existence for the next two decades, and some of the greatest stars of Negro baseball enjoyed their primes during the 1890s and Dead-Ball Era—pitcher Rube Foster and shortstop John Henry "Pop" Lloyd *aka* the Black (Honus) Wagner—were among the most notable. Many of the teams played in leagues that were not affiliated with the National Association, but others retained their independence from any circuit and competed against any and all opposition. Occasionally, they even played exhibitions against major-league clubs of the era. After one such game during the spring of 1901, Baltimore manager John McGraw reportedly attempted to add Charlie Grant (no relation to Frank), a light-skinned Afro-American infielder, to his Orioles' roster in the fledgling American League by trying to pass him off as a Cherokee named Tokahoma. But the ever vigilant and klanish Cap Anson, serving as an adviser to White Sox owner Charles Comiskey, got wind of the charade, and Comiskey raised such a fuss that the ploy had to be abandoned.

Despite the failure of McGraw's scheme, some men of "color" did appear in the majors during the years 1911–35, and the hypocrisy of the racial barrier was evident in the fact that they also played for various Negro teams before or after. All but one of these men were Cubans, and all were light-skinned enough to appear passably white. They included pitchers Jose Acosta, Pedro Dibut, Oscar Estrada and Dolf Luque, catchers Mike Gonzalez and Ricardo Torres, second baseman Ramon "Mike" Herrera, shortstop Alfredo Cabrera (a native of the Canary Islands), and outfielders Rafael Almeida, Jack Calvo, and Armando Marsans. Two of them, Gonzalez and Luque, both had major-league tenures that fulfilled the ten-year requirement for HOF consideration, after first appearing with Negro teams. Gonzalez played with the Cuban Stars (1911–14) before embarking on a seventeen-year career with the Braves, Reds, Cardinals, Giants and Cubs (1912 and 1914–32). Luque, known as "the Pride of Havana," pitched for the Cuban Stars and Long Branch, N.J., Cubans (1912–13) before posting

Known as the Pride of Havana, Cuban-born Dolf Luque pitched for the Negro-league Cuban Stars and Long Branch (New Jersey) Cubans in 1912–13 before posting a 194–179 won-lost record for four major-league teams in the years 1914–35. At the time, under baseball's hypocritical color barrier, Luque's fair-skinned appearance was acceptable in a big-league uniform, while other darker-skinned players were barred from the Show. (Photograph from *The Sporting News*)

a 194–179 record in twenty big-league campaigns with the Braves, Reds, Dodgers and Giants (1914–35). Both men also received Hall of Fame votes: Gonzalez got eight spread over five elections (1950–60); Luque netted twenty-six on nine ballots (1937–60) and probably deserved more.

But the Negro leagues as we now recall them did not begin until 1920, when Hall of Famer Rube Foster formed the first Negro National League (NNL), a circuit that initially included his Chicago American Giants plus a second franchise from the Windy City, teams in Dayton, Detroit, Indianapolis, Kansas City and St. Louis, and a club known as the Cuban Stars. The NNL's composition changed almost annually: along with Foster's Chicago team, the only two cities to remain in the league throughout its twelve seasons were Detroit and St. Louis, and in some seasons the circuit also included clubs in Birmingham, Cincinnati, Cleveland, Columbus, Memphis, Milwaukee, Nashville, Pittsburgh or Toledo.

There were six other circuits which, at various times, comprised the Negro majors. As with the original NNL, which folded in 1931 at the height of the Great Depression, membership in each of these leagues was unstable. Teams joined and quit circuits regularly, often from one season to the next, depending on their solvency, how their owners got along with the other league executives, or whether an independent schedule seemed more likely to generate greater profits. As a result, it would be cumbersome to list which teams were parts of each league at any given time. But the other six circuits included the Eastern Colored League (ECL, which operated during 1923–27), the American Negro League (ANL, 1929), the East-West (EWL) and Negro Southern Leagues (NSL, both of which existed as majors only in 1932), the second Negro National League (1933–47) and the Negro American League (NAL, 1937–60). Beyond those already mentioned, cities represented in these leagues at some time or another included Atlanta, Baltimore, Brooklyn, Harrisburg, Houston, Jacksonville, Little Rock, Louisville, Montgomery, Monroe, Newark, New York, Philadelphia, Washington, D.C., and Wilmington.

Some of the leagues' most-storied franchises included Foster's Chicago American Giants, the Cuban Stars (of New York-Harlem), a club best known as the Hilldales (Philadelphia), the Homestead Grays (Pittsburgh), the Kansas City Monarchs and the Pittsburgh Crawfords. But, when Robinson entered the majors with Brooklyn in 1947, followed quickly by Larry Doby, Roy Campanella and others, the integration of the Show sounded the Negro leagues' death knell: the second NNL folded after the 1947 season; and, although the NAL survived much longer, its talent level also was reduced significantly after the late forties as more young blacks opted for a chance at the majors.

Throughout the Negro leagues' era of glory, their players did enjoy one freedom which their white major-league counterparts lacked. Unbound by Organized Baseball's reserve clause, the best black players were relatively free to jump, in any season, to whatever club offered the most money for their services. Satchel Paige was famous for this, playing for twelve different clubs, and was no exception to the rule. Among the Negro leagues' sixteen other Hall of Famers, Oscar Charleston and Willie Wells played for fourteen different teams, Pop Lloyd for thirteen, Smokey Joe Williams for eleven, and only Monte Irvin played for just one (the Newark Eagles, 1937–48).

The Negro leagues and the all-black teams that preceded them produced at least three generations of players, the best of whose skills were unquestionably equal to those of the Hall of Famers who performed in the white majors during the same era. The most legendary were Paige and catcher Josh Gibson, the latter often called the black Babe Ruth, both of whose primes were in the 1930s.

But, although Jackie Robinson was enshrined at Cooperstown in 1962 (his first year eligible) and the BBWAA has done a credible job of honoring the best among the majors' subsequent Afro-American performers, Hall of Fame recognition was steadfastly denied to Negro-league players until almost a decade after Robinson's induction. The reluctance to enshrine any of the Negro leaguers was another testament to their relative invisibility.

Although some black-owned publications probably did it sooner, the first currently known suggestion that Negro leaguers be included at Cooperstown was made by sportswriter Jimmy Cannon in 1938. But, predictably, the idea was virtually ignored until just before Jackie Robinson retired. In September 1956 *Sporting News* publisher J. G. Taylor Spink editorialized that although Robinson's induction was a foregone conclusion, Satchel Paige — who had followed Larry Doby to the Cleveland Indians in 1948 (posting a 6–1 record at age forty-two) — was also deserving of election despite his lack of ten-year service in the majors. Paige's Negro-league career had begun in 1926 and continued through 1955, except for five seasons in the Show during the years 1948–53 — for a total of thirty years' service in one major league or another (he also pitched one scoreless inning in a game for Charley Finley's A's in 1965, at age fifty-nine). Satchel had even received a lone Hall of Fame vote from one of the writers who turned in ballots in 1951.

But, Paige's election also would've opened two cans of worms. To begin with, his major-league record, compiled mainly in relief, was just 28–31, less impressive than that of four-year major leaguer Dickie Kerr

(53–34), the honest starting hurler for the 1919 Black Sox, and not a whole lot better than that of Hub Pruett (29–48), the reliever from the 1920s whose chief claim to fame was an ability to strike out Babe Ruth. So, Satchel's enshrinement clearly could not be justified on the basis of his major-league performance and would contravene the Hall's ten-year service requirement (recall that nine-year man Addie Joss was not elected until 1978). Even worse, some thought, if Paige was chosen for his major- and Negro-league service combined, then the doors of the Shrine would then have to open for others whose service crossed over into the majors but did not fulfill the ten-year minimum in the Show; and, almost inevitably thereafter, to men who never put on a big-league uniform at all. The prevalent fear among the baseball establishment was espoused by commissioner Ford Frick in 1964, who noted that "If you make one exception, you have to make many."

Frick retired in 1965 and, after a brief tenure by former air force general William Eckert, Bowie Kuhn took over as commissioner in 1968. In the years between Spink's 1956 editorial and Kuhn's selection for baseball's top job, the civil rights movement had exposed the hypocrisy of America's racial attitudes; and Ted Williams, in his 1966 induction speech at Cooperstown, had been the first white Hall of Famer to use that podium to advocate membership for players from the Negro leagues. Soon after Kuhn became commissioner, and with support from the BBWAA, he appointed a ten-man committee to assess the Hall of Fame credentials of men who played in the invisible circuits.

But, for most of three years, the panel's mandate was a secret, because Kuhn still had to overcome much resistance among baseball's hierarchy and the Hall of Fame trustees to the notion of enshrining any Negro leaguers at all. In the end, a devil's compromise was reached in which the committee was empowered to elect nine representatives over a seven-year period, but the plaques for the men chosen would be housed in a wing at the museum apart from those who played in the majors—a separate and unequal treatment that mirrored the unconscionable segregation of the Negro leagues and players themselves.

To make things more difficult, although the Negro teams had sometimes played in major-league venues—notably Chicago's Comiskey Park (site of most of the annual Negro-league all-star games, 1933–49), Yankee Stadium in New York and Griffith Stadium in Washington, D.C.—and had often packed those ballparks when they did, the players' achievements were not as well documented as those of major leaguers. In most seasons, in order to turn a profit, Negro teams played as many or more games against non-league competition as they did against the clubs in their circuits. Many of these games—especially during the barnstorming years of the Depression—took place on the road in small towns without significant media; and, given their shoestring budgets, most of the clubs did not have an official scorekeeper. The level of segregation in American society as a whole also meant that even their league games were not generally covered by the major (white) newspapers; and, although there were black-owned papers that did report on their games in major cities, many of those sources had folded during the Depression, and most of them were long gone, along with any archives, by the late 1960s.

As a result, box scores and official statistics were not available for many of the contests played by Negro-league teams, and relatively few have surfaced in the years since the committee was formed. Although lists of league standings and leaders have subsequently been pieced together, it took years of dedicated research by many baseball historians to compile what little has survived, and most of that very incomplete record was not available to the Negro-leagues panel at the time it was formed. So the committee was forced to rely on a far greater level of subjective hearsay (and potential bias) than either the BBWAA or veterans committees have ever applied to their voting. The unprovable legends of Satchel Paige's two thousand games won and 250 no hitters and Josh Gibson's purported eight hundred home runs were certain to dominate a selection process that had little meaningful documentation to justify its results.

When Kuhn finally announced the committee's existence in February 1971, Paige was named as its first-year selection. But the commissioner was forced to acknowledge that Satchel, and the other players to follow, would not technically be Hall of Famers, and then tried to soften the situation by arguing that "the Hall of Fame isn't a building but a state of mind."

Few people were fully aware of the role the new commissioner had played in procuring even token representation for the Negro leaguers at Cooperstown, so Kuhn was quickly criticized by black and white media alike. Satchel Paige also put the "honor" in its proper perspective during his August 1971 induction speech, noting of himself in the third person that "Today baseball has turned Paige from a second-class citizen to a second-class immortal."

But, sensitive to the immediate criticism he'd received, Kuhn had already worked to redress the problem, renegotiating the initial plan for segregated housing at Cooperstown. When Paige's plaque was unveiled, it was on the wall in the main section with the other Hall of Famers, and so were those of the other Negro leaguers that followed him into the Shrine.

Sadly, after the special panel's inductions ended in 1977, it was hard to avoid the impression that the enshrinement of Negro leaguers to that date was tokenism at its worst. The nine men chosen were exactly enough — no more, no less — to comprise a solitary lineup of players from the invisible circuits; and, but for the absence of a second baseman and the inclusion of an extra outfielder-pitcher, their positional citations honored just one man for each of the spots on a baseball diamond. This token all-star team included Paige, the pitcher, inducted in 1971; Josh Gibson, catcher, and Walter "Buck" Leonard, first baseman, 1972; Monte Irvin, outfielder, 1973; James "Cool Papa" Bell, outfielder, 1974; William "Judy" Johnson, third baseman, 1975; and Oscar Charleston, outfielder, 1976; along with John Henry "Pop" Lloyd, shortstop, and Martin Dihigo, outfielder-pitcher, 1977.

Predictable criticism followed and led to approval of further Negro-league selections. Former pitcher, team owner and NNL founder Rube Foster was elected in 1981 (perhaps the token executive), and third baseman Ray Dandridge was added six years later. When they also proved insufficient to silence critics, the Veterans Committee was empowered to make some more selections, one per year during the period 1995–2000. Sequentially, those most recent choices included pitchers Leon Day and Bill Foster (Rube's brother), shortstop Willie Wells, two more hurlers, "Bullet" Joe Rogan and "Smokey" Joe Williams, and outfielder Norman "Turkey" Stearnes, bringing the total of Negro leaguers enshrined at Cooperstown to seventeen. But the clamor for further VC selections has quieted, and it remains to be seen whether the Hall has closed the book on baseball's invisible men. Realistically, the prospect for many additional choices seems diminished by establishment, in the late 1990s, of a Negro League Hall of Fame located in Kansas City — as the new museum's existence seems likely to quell any sense of urgency to add more choices at Cooperstown.

All the same, in terms of statistical proportionality, a total of seventeen Hall of Famers is clearly inadequate representation for the Negro leagues as a whole. In 1994 the Society for American Baseball Research published *The Negro Leagues Book*, which includes the most thorough — yet, no doubt, still incomplete — register of players from those circuits compiled to date. In all, the register included 4385 names of men involved with all-black teams sometime during 1862–1960, and almost one-fourth of those listed served as team or league officials (i.e., in some capacity other than players). Given the Hall's current representational standards (1.3 percent for players and 2.7 percent for managers), fairness would seem to require a roster of somewhere between forty-three (or, 1.3 percent of about

3300 players) and 118 Negro leaguers (2.7 percent of 4385) enshrined at Cooperstown — so the Hall is still at least twenty-six men short of equal treatment for blacks, and probably more.

But, the issue of appropriate proportionality is also muddled by the unavoidable fact that, although the Negro leagues represented the highest level of play available to men of color during their time, the overall quality of talent — i.e., the average skill level — in each of those circuits was never equal to that which existed in the white major leagues at any time during the years 1920–50, the Negro circuits' hey-day. That unfortunate conclusion, which might be interpreted incorrectly as racism by some, is the inescapable result of statistical analysis comparing the populations from which both environments drew their personnel.

Until the 1950s, few of the players who appeared in the major leagues were born outside of the United States; and, except for extremely rare instances of men in their late forties, all of those players ranged between fifteen and forty-four years of age. In comparison, during the three decades of existence before their talent level was depleted by integration of the majors, the Negro leagues drew most of their players from the Afro-American population in the United States and from men born in Cuba; and, with slightly more frequent exceptions, these players also came from the same age group as the whites.

The United States census data taken during the decennial measurements of 1920–60 all include separate counts for white and Negro males between the ages of fifteen and forty-four. Population figures for Cuba during those years are more difficult to obtain; but reasonable, if imperfect estimates of the totals for each of those decennial years can be made. *The World Almanac and Book of Facts* gives an overall population estimate for Cuba of 10,105,000 in 1965. From that base, a ballpark estimate of the population of Cuban males in the 15–44 age range can be projected by using the average proportions and rates of increase for white and Negro males in the United States during the decennial years 1920–60 and applying those numbers to Cuba for the same period, but in reverse (that is, by using the U.S. means for proportion and growth rate to measure the recession of Cuban male population back to 1920). Adding the Cuban figures to the appropriate census totals for American blacks creates an estimate of the primary population base from which the Negro leagues drew their talent.

Table 45 spans the decennial years 1920–50, when the Negro leagues were at their peak. It gives the appropriate white male population from the U.S. census data for each of those years (US WM 15–44), the total number of men who appeared on the major-league rosters during each of those decennial seasons (Men Maj), and the percentage of the male population between 15–44 which that represents (Pct in Majors). It also provides the official census data for Negro males aged 15–44 in the U.S. (US NM 15–44), the calculated estimates of Cuban population for the same year and age group (Cuban M 15–44), the total for both columns (Total 15–44), the number of men currently known to have appeared on all Negro-league rosters in each decennial year (Men Neg), and the percentage of the combined male populations of the two countries which that represents (Pct in Neg Lg). The last column on the right (N-Maj Ratio) shows the ratio of the percentage of males age 15–44 in the Negro leagues to those in the majors.

TABLE 45
POPULATION-BASE ESTIMATES,
MAJORS V. NEGRO LEAGUES, 1920–50

Year	US WM 15–44	Men Maj	Pct in Majors	US NM 15–44	Cuban M 15–44	Total 15–44	Men Neg	Pct in Neg Lg	N-Maj Ratio
1920	22683727	522	0.0023	2416029	1310729	3736758	456	0.0122	5.30
1930	26318244	547	0.0021	2836458	1428295	4264753	414	0.0097	4.67
1940	28344449	547	0.0019	3040580	1636924	4667504	393	0.0084	4.35
1950	29648394	583	0.0020	3244935	1711413	4956348	403	0.0081	4.12
Averages		*550*	*0.0021*				*417*	*0.0096*	*4.61*

On average, the population base for the white major leagues was about six times larger than the one for Negro circuits in each decennial year. The last column in Table 45 indicates that the number of men on Negro-league rosters during each of the decennial years 1920–50 represented a proportion of their available population base that was never less than four times larger than the corresponding one for the white majors. Even if the appropriate but unknown Cuban population has been underestimated by the same factor of four (an unlikely prospect), the relative proportion of Negro-league players to their available population base would still be twice that of the white majors— undeniable evidence that the minimum (and, therefore, average) levels of talent in the Negro circuits at each interval was more diluted than that of the Show.

Because there is no objective method by which to measure what percentage of players on Negro-league rosters possessed a level of skill equal or superior to the worst major leaguer at the time, any attempt at a precise estimation of that dilution would be spurious. But, given the ratios evident in Table 45, it seems fair to argue that the average level of talent in the Negro leagues at any given time was equal or perhaps marginally superior to that of the highest rung of the white minors.

All of this could be used by some people to argue for the adequacy of the current level of Negro-league representation at Cooperstown. But despite the implications of the population data, and unless one adopts an overtly racist presumption that the very best athletes among one race are innately more talented than the very best among another, it remains an inescapable statistical fact that — given equal coaching — the talent level among the top 1.3 to 2.7 percent of Negro leaguers must have been comparable to the same proportion of the whites on major-league rosters at any given time. So, at the level of skill implied by Hall of Fame membership, there is no acceptable way to rationalize any proportion of Negro leaguers included at Cooperstown which is less than that of their major-league counterparts, and equal treatment of both groups requires the addition, at minimum, of about two and one-half times the seventeen Negro-league inductees enshrined through 2000.

17

Hand Me That Wrench

Any errors of selection among the Hall of Fame roster as constituted through the 2000 voting are faits accomplis. Whether one believes that Roger Bresnahan, Rick Ferrell, Johnny Evers, Elmer Flick, Chick Hafey, Jesse Haines, George Kelly, Fred Lindstrom, Rube Marquard, Tommy McCarthy, Joe Tinker, Mickey Welch, Ross Youngs or any other current member has no business being honored on the same wall as Babe Ruth or Walter Johnson, the Hall's trustees are not about to rescind their memberships. So, the only way to assure long-term justice in that bad situation is to correct any true errors of omission and eliminate the causes of past errors of selection.

At present, as has been the case since the Pete Rose compromise of 1991, the most glaring injustices in the Hall of Fame selection procedure involve the Veterans Committee process. The VC held its annual meeting in Tampa, Florida, on 29 February 2000; and, like the BBWAA voting that year (described in the Introduction), the outcome evidenced almost everything that's currently wrong with the panel's process.

With fourteen committee members present at the 2000 meeting (eighty-eight-year-old former Negro leaguer Buck O'Neil was ill and did not attend), eleven votes were needed to attain the 75 percent approval required for election. According to published reports, and among the panel's main body of candidates (i.e., the BBWAA "rejects"), former Pirates second baseman Bill Mazeroski (who played during 1956–72) missed election by one vote, while eight of the members supported ex-Dodger first sacker Gil Hodges (1943–63). Other men who were considered in the voting but didn't fare as well reportedly included outfielders Dom DiMaggio

(1940–53) and Tony Oliva (1962–76), second baseman Joe Gordon (1938–50, 1942 American League MVP), and pitcher Mel Harder (1928–47). So, among those six, only Mazeroski and Oliva represented the eligible players whose big-league careers began after 1945.

It was the first time since 1993 that the panel had failed to elect anyone from the main group of eligible players, after a sequence of BBWAA "rejectee" selections that included shortstop Phil Rizzuto (1994), outfielder Richie Ashburn ('95), pitcher Jim Bunning ('96), second baseman Nellie Fox ('97), outfielder Larry Doby ('98) and first baseman Orlando Cepeda ('99). Ironically, a VC member also had been absent due to illness for the 1993 election, and the Hodges candidacy may have featured prominently in that one too. A well-circulated rumor specifies that Hodges fell one vote short of election that year, after several committee members rejected an appeal to allow fellow panelist (and Gil's former Brooklyn teammate) Roy Campanella to submit a written vote in absentia. Campanella died that June.

Apparently, the 2000 VC balloting was just as contentious, or more so. The Associated Press report on the outcome noted that the meeting had lasted five hours, much longer than normal, and that the table where the panelists debated was littered with "chewed-up pens and half-eaten cake," each an implied testament to the tension which accompanied the committee's discussion. There also was gossip that the last forty minutes of the debate had degenerated into a loud argument among three of the panelists, two of whom (a former player and a retired sportswriter) supported Hodges and another (an ex-player) who reputedly has opposed his candidacy for years.

Committee members, for whatever reasons vigilant to keep the content of their discussion secret, were typically noncommittal about the debate. VC chairman Joe Brown, a former Pirates general manager, said only that there were "so many outstanding candidates, it split the ballot." Hank Aaron, who along with former big-league executive John McHale was the committee's newest member in 2000, possibly alluded to the fractiousness when he told the Associated Press that "We hoped someone would be there [i.e., get elected], we really did. It just got too hard. Maybe next year."

Whether or not the rumors about the 1993 and 2000 VC voting are accurate, rejection of the Hodges and Mazeroski candidacies drew different reactions from the two most vested parties. Mazeroski, speaking from Bradenton, Florida, where he was serving as a spring training instructor for the Pirates, indicated that "I don't call this a big letdown. I appreciate all the support, but it just didn't happen." In contrast, a 5 March 2000 column by *New York Times* sportswriter Dave Anderson quoted Gil's widow, Joan Hodges, about her frustration over the continued absence of any public explanation from the panel as to why her late husband's candidacy has been rejected so often (by 2000, Hodges had been eligible for VC election for more than a decade). Mrs. Hodges also recalled that in 1995, when fellow National Leaguer Richie Ashburn was chosen by the panel, he had called her to apologize for getting to Cooperstown ahead of Gil, whose career began five years earlier than Ashburn's and who garnered far more votes in the BBWAA voting (3010) than the former Phillies outfielder (1119). Joan Hodges also noted her fear that repeated campaigning for Gil's cause may have poisoned his chances with some panel members but vowed to keep working for his election.

The contentiousness of the 2000 VC meeting and the disappointment it engendered may lead to some changes in the committee process. Anderson's *Times* column also pointed out that, although the Hall of Fame bylaws allow for VC members to serve no more than two consecutive terms of three-year duration, panel members Ted Williams, Stan Musial and Joe Brown had each exceeded that limit by considerable margins. But Anderson neglected to note that Yogi Berra and former NL president Bill White were appointed prior to the 1994 VC election and had both completed their supposed six-year limits after the 1999 voting. The columnist also indicated that, according to Hall of Fame chairman Ed Stack, the term limit had been established during the 1990s, and that beginning with the 2001 voting the bylaw would be enforced, to some degree at least.

Table 46 provides the complete BBWAA vote histories of all six men who were considered in the Veterans Committee's 2000 discussion. Under the candidates' names are two columns which, in vertical sequence, give the vote total (Vote) and support percentage (Pct) each man received on all ballots in which he earned support. The first line below those histories gives (in the Vote column) the total number of votes earned on all ballots and (in the Pct column) the total number of ballots from which each man's name was omitted during that period. The final line provides the whole-number average of votes received per ballot and the mean per-ballot support percentage earned by each man over his full voting history.

TABLE 46
BBWAA VOTE HISTORIES, 2000 VC CANDIDATES

Hodges		Mazeroski		DiMaggio		Gordon		Harder		Oliva	
Vote	Pct	Vote	Pct	Vote	Pct	Vote	Pct	Vote	Pct	Vote	Pct
82	24.0	23	6.1	4	1.5	1	0.4	4	2.6	63	15.2
145	48.3	36	8.3	2	1.3	1	0.4	2	1.2	75	20.1
180	50.0	33	8.6	12	6.0	4	2.1	1	0.4	124	30.8

Hodges		Mazeroski		DiMaggio		Gordon		Harder		Oliva	
Vote	*Pct*	*Vote*	*Pct*	*Vote*	*Pct*	*Vote*	*Pct*	*Vote*	*Pct*	*Vote*	*Pct*
161	40.7	38	9.5	8	2.8	11	4.1	10	4.3	114	28.8
218	57.4	28	6.8	13	3.8	11	4.1	8	3.0	154	36.2
198	54.2	48	12.8	15	5.0	4	2.5	6	2.3	160	38.7
188	51.9	74	18.4	15	4.2	30	14.9	12	4.5	202	47.4
233	60.1	87	22.0	36	9.1	1	0.4	7	4.4	135	30.1
224	58.6	100	23.5	43	11.3	31	10.3	51	25.4	142	32.0
226	59.8	125	30.3	—	—	66	22.6	14	6.2	160	36.0
242	56.0	143	33.6	—	—	13	4.2	34	11.3	175	40.7
230	59.7	134	29.9	—	—	77	27.3	52	17.8	157	37.1
241	60.1	131	29.5	—	—	97	28.4	14	4.6	158	34.7
205	49.5	142	32.0	—	—	79	26.3	—	—	149	32.3
237	63.4	182	42.3	—	—	—	—	—	—	170	36.2
3010	2648	1324	4888	148	2541	426	3211	214	2851	2138	4286
201	52.9	88	20.9	16	5.0	30	10.6	16	6.8	143	33.1

By virtue of their failure to ever receive the 75 percent approval required for BBWAA election, each of the men in Table 46 is a priori a "reject" of the scribes. In that sense, it doesn't matter that Hodges is the only one who received 60 percent support or better from the writers, that Mazeroski and Oliva never received that much and were grandfathered into their VC eligibility because they earned at least one hundred votes at some time while they were on the writers' ballot, or that DiMaggio, Gordon and Harder all had poor records in the scribes' voting relative to the other three.

The sole purpose of the veterans panel is to re-examine the merits of men passed over by the BBWAA; and, in order to do that job appropriately, the VC should have and must be given back the freedom to evaluate *everyone* who has been rejected in the writers' voting with a clean slate. Due to the wholly subjective nature of the BBWAA process, no man's vote history has any measureable correlation to the individual parts or sum of his on-field achievements. Relative to BBWAA support, you simply cannot calculate — at least with any more accuracy than the average-support comparisons used in previous chapters — the finite BBWAA value of x number of home runs, y pitching victories or z MVP awards, because they are never the same for two different candidates. Hodges got 3010 HOF votes and hit 370 homers in his career, equal to about 8.1 votes per homer. But Hank Aaron had 755 taters and received "only" 406 votes in his first-ballot election — so, arguably, each of his dingers was worth only 0.5 votes apiece. And, given that the writers voted for Rabbit Maranville 1284 times, his measly 28 homers were worth 45.9 votes each. In turn, Mel Harder won

223 ball games, equating to 0.96 votes per victory. But Johnny Vander Meer's 119 victories brought him 5.9 votes per win (700 votes), and Dickie Kerr's 53 were worth 1.4 apiece (75 votes total). Aaron and Joe Gordon were both one-time MVPs. But you can't say how much benefit either man got from his trophy, because it's impossible to isolate and accurately measure the importance of either award within the context of the support each man received let alone compare one's value to the other's.

If you could, and if there were consistent values applied in the writers' voting for each home run, pitching victory, MVP award, all-star appearance, pennant or World Series won by each player, then there might be merit in insisting that the VC should be limited to considering only those BBWAA "rejects" who received x percent support from the scribes (whether it be 60 percent or some other number). But, absent that method (or some other objectification of credentials), the VC's sixty percent support requirement for players after 1945 is nothing more than arbitrary imposition of an assumption that the BBWAA's collective wisdom is more important than the statistical (or subjective) summation of a man's actual career performance. As such, it's also an injustice imposed upon the panel and all of its possible candidates.

It's also ludicrous to set an arbitrary date on either side of which the VC's eligibility rules apply differently and with devastatingly unequal impact. The careers of all six men in Table 46 overlapped sequentially. Harder was still in the majors when (first) Gordon, then DiMaggio and Hodges made their debuts, and Hodges was still playing when Mazeroski and Oliva made their first appearances in the Show. Gil had seventy-nine at-bats before Harder left the majors (two in 1943, the other seventy-seven didn't come until 1947, Harder's last season). In comparison, Hodges had 2578 at-bats (37 percent of his big-league total) after Mazeroski entered the majors. But, under the 1945/46 cutoff imposed by the VC's current eligibility structure, Hodges is defined for selection purposes as Harder's contemporary not Mazeroski's.

So Hodges and every other ten-year player who entered the majors before 1946 gets treated preferentially relative to those who didn't. As a result, at Cooperstown's two most under-represented positions, ten-year guys like catchers Moe Berg (441 career hits, 6 home runs, and a .243 batting average) and Lou Criger (709 hits, 11 taters and .221) plus third basemen Eddie Grant (844 hits, 5 homers, .249) and Charlie Irwin (981 hits, 16 dingers, .267) are still eligible for VC election. But backstops Bob Boone (second-most games ever played at the position), Thurman Munson (one-time MVP), Ted Simmons (more hits than any man who was primarily a catcher), Jim Sundberg (six Gold Gloves) and Joe Torre (who now can be eligible only as a manager), plus third sackers Buddy Bell (six Gold Gloves, more than any hot-corner hero except Brooks Robinson and Mike Schmidt), Darrell Evans (414 taters), Bill Madlock (four batting titles) and Graig Nettles (390 four baggers) can never be placed on the panel's ballot. If that is justice, then Charlie Manson would love to get a piece of it, and maybe California should parole every mass murderer born before 1946.

Clearly, both the 60 percent restriction and the 1945/46 cutoff date must be repealed for the Veterans Committee process to function appropriately. But, even if they are (which seems unlikely in the short-term future), that will not solve all of the panel's problems.

The well-intended but misguided impulse to honor the living over the dead has been evident in the VC process since the panel was formed in 1953 and — although there were no published quotes to that effect after the fact — may have been integral to Bill Mazeroski's lead over Gil Hodges in the committee's 2000 election. Everyone can fathom the emotional and economic influences that motivate the Hall of Fame's institutional preference for living inductees. But, by making the families of qualified dead men wait even longer, that mindset only exacerbates the injustices among HOF voting; and, if it must be tolerated at all, should only be acceptable in years when the BBWAA has failed to elect anyone. The only thing that can eliminate this flaw in approach is a conscious change in the attitudes of the Cooperstown trustees and VC members.

The VC's image and performance also have been damaged by the rampant politicking evident throughout the committee's history. Despite the best intentions of some of them, the presence of Hall of Fame players on the panel (notably Frankie Frisch) has led to frequent cronyism and the despicable practice of individual members blocking the candidacies of men who they do (or did) not like for some personal reason. Unfortunately, such behavior has not been limited to the era when Frisch was on the panel, as— from rumors which spread among the baseball community during the months following the 2000 VC voting — it apparently has persisted into the 1990s.

Surely, the Veterans Committee should be something more than a "good-ol'-boy" network of men electing their buddies or scuttling the prospects of someone else who once pissed them off for some reason. But none of that is likely to change unless VC members are prohibited from voting for their former teammates, and even that reform would not prevent them from abusing the hopes of any other player(s) for whom they might hold a grudge.

The degree to which politics influences VC elections is also increased by the existence of ad hoc committees—several of which operate at present — whose sole purpose is to lobby the panelists in favor of various candidates. On one level, the existence of such groups is attributable to nothing more nefarious than the sincere desire of certain fans to see their favorite player honored at a level they feel is appropriate to his deeds. But the Phil Rizzuto case, perhaps the most extreme example of this type of lobbying, demonstrates that the ultimate success of such efforts depends far more on the level of influence possessed by the specific lobbyists than it does on the actual merits of the candidate in question. There is no way short of violating freedom of speech to prevent influential sportswriters or anyone else from advocating the election of specific players. The elimination of lobby groups is also impossible and would only assure that the fans who do not write newspaper columns have no hope of any influence at all. But the VC members can, and should make a concerted effort to ignore such lobbying in the future, regardless of its source.

Beyond all that, regardless of its membership and whether infected by cronyism or not at any given time, the committee has tended over the years to conduct itself as though it is some kind of secret politburo with ultimate power. By tradition, its complete voting tallies are never formally made public, and its members are far too secretive (or, perhaps, justifiably defensive) about the content of their deliberations. At various times in its history, whether for good cause or not, the committee has also proved all too willing to circumvent its own rules in favor of some candidates, while denying equal treatment to others with similar credentials. And, whether by design or mere bumbling, the panel — and or the Hall of Fame trustees — has also done a poor job of publicizing its eligibility regulations. It may be specious as an economic argument, but from an emotional viewpoint, Cooperstown — like baseball itself — should belong as much or more to the game's fans as it does to those who control the museum and its processes. In that light, fans should have the right to be just as informed about the rules governing the VC's selection procedures as they are about a given player's batting average.

None of these conditions are conducive to securing respect for the Veterans Committee, and they are all contrary to the long-term best interests of the Hall of Fame as a whole. With that in mind, the VC process should also be reformed as follows.

- The committee's relative balance between former players, executives and sportswriters should be retained as is (with a minimum of twelve, and a maximum of sixteen members), but the panel should also include an equal ratio of baseball historians and or statisticians (i.e., three or four panelists from each of the four subgroups). Each of these new members should possess some academic or authorial credential that demonstrates appropriate qualification for membership. Equally important, in order to assure their maximum objectivity, they should have no direct personal or professional relationship with the baseball establishment as a whole (this would disqualify broadcasters, official scorers, Elias Sports Bureau statisticians, or anyone else with a potential obligation of gratitude to anyone in baseball).

- The committee should be freed from its traditional domination by elderly men, as the infusion of some younger members would broaden the panel's perspective. Age is not a prerequisite for wisdom, and neither the qualified historians and authors selected nor any of the other panelists need to average sixty-six years or older in order to be sufficiently knowledgeable of the game's history to serve as credible electors — especially with regard to men whose careers ended long before the panelists were born.

- Although it is the Hall of Fame's court of last resort, the VC itself is not the Supreme Court, and membership on the committee should be limited to a specific term of office. The six-year limit established in the 1990s, but ignored since then, would be adequate; or, if a longer duration is desired, anything up to about eight years would suffice. But the terms should also be staggered among each subset of panel members (i.e. players, executives, sportwriters and historians), so that the committee always includes a balanced blend of veteran members and relatively new ones in each subset. This constant, scheduled turnover would hinder the formation of long-term voting alliances based on personality conflicts or allegiances between intimates.

- The panel's voting should, of course, be done by secret ballot, but the full numerical results of each VC election should be made public. No good reason has ever been provided why the full tally of the committee's voting is kept from public knowledge, and there is no justifiable excuse for such secrecy within a Hall of Fame process that simultaneously publicizes the complete vote totals for the BBWAA balloting. Publication of the panel's voting results would make the committee more accountable and increase the overall level of public interest in the HOF selection process as a whole, thereby enhancing the panel's sagging credibility, lending added publicity for the museum itself, and providing baseball fans with a greater level of oversight of the entire selection process.

- With regard to the selection of managers and former Negro leaguers, the VC should also take whatever steps are required to assure that both groups are represented in Cooperstown in a ratio that is proportional to the enshrined major-league players. For managers, who are currently over-represented in relative terms, that means a temporary hiatus on any new selections. For Negro leaguers, justice demands—at absolute minimum — the rapid (but well-reasoned) elections of over two-dozen new members.

Relative to the Veterans Committee process, the problems which plague the BBWAA's selection procedure may prove far more difficult to fix. As indicated earlier, the writers as a group conduct themselves as if the Hall of Fame voting privilege is their birthright; and it's obvious that they believe their own brand of subjective wisdom is greater than that of Cooperstown's other elective organ.

But, throughout its sixty-five-year history, the writers' process has been far too susceptible to the individual and subjective whims and fallacies which have allowed clearly unqualified players like Jewel Ens and Moe Berg to earn votes, while George Davis, Vern Stephens and other far better qualified men slipped through the process without ever receiving an iota of BBWAA recognition. Some might argue that because many of those injustices occurred prior to existence of the Screening Committee, that aspect of the selection process has eliminated (or at least reduced) them. But the short shrift given to Darrell and Dwight Evans, Bobby Grich, Al Oliver, Ted Simmons and many other recent players as a result of the 5 percent support currently required to remain on the BBWAA ballot offers ample evidence that the scribes' voting process is seriously flawed by its retention of a wholly subjective foundation and by its excessive focus upon methods to improve or assure the likelihood of at least one new inductee per year.

Also, as evidenced by the BBWAA balloting of 1999, a 75 percent majority (or much more) of the scribes has obviously become permanent captive of the rigid, one-dimensional thinking that accompanies application of the Hall's current de facto standards for admission. Eleven of the fifteen players elected by the writers during the years 1991–2000 were de facto qualifiers, and the fact that three of them required multiple ballots to gain election offers no credible argument that the standards are not in force or paramount. With the possible exception of pitcher Mickey Welch (who, to be fair, was elected by the VC), de facto standards may not have produced any flagrant errors of selection to date, but their continued use must inevitably lead to one or more such errors in the future, perhaps as early as Jose Canseco's eligibility around the end of this decade.

Whether such a mistake ensues or not, there is no doubt that application of de facto standards unfairly demeans the credentials of every player who has not achieved at least one of them. In the long run, coupled with the current regulations governing BBWAA voting, it must also make it far more difficult for the Cooperstown roster to approach anything resembling proportional balance by era or position.

Proof of that is manifest among the third basemen recently eligible. With only nine third sackers in the Hall, the position has fewer representatives than any other among the HOF roster. But three of the last four hot-corner candidates elected by the scribes (Eddie Mathews in 1978 plus Mike Schmidt and George Brett in the nineties) were de facto qualifiers, as will be the next two (Paul Molitor and Wade Boggs). As a whole, and in the future, their elections can only reinforce the impression that for a modern (i.e., post–1945) third baseman to be a legitimate Hall of Famer he must have achieved at least one of the de facto criteria. That type of thinking has already derailed the prospects of Darrell Evans, Graig Nettles, Bill Madlock, Ron Cey and Buddy Bell — each of whom, relative to the norms for their eras, may be far better qualified for Cooperstown than the already enshrined Fred Lindstrom and (perhaps) George Kell. The same approach will also make it far more difficult to elect subsequent candidates (the still-active Matt Williams, for example) if, by the end of their careers, they have also failed to meet at least one of those standards. As a result, the only means left by which third sackers may ever reach their appropriate proportional share of the Cooperstown roster will be for the Veterans Committee to add Ron Santo and or Ken Boyer or pre–1945 candidates like Stan Hack and Harlond Clift. But, although all four men are eligible for VC consideration (and the first two are certainly better qualified than Lindstrom), doing so will only add to the controversy over the panel's anointment of BBWAA rejects and — in Hack and Clift's cases — would also add to the marginal over-representation of the Live-Ball Era.

In turn, all of that injustice will apply in spades to catchers, who — with a dozen current Hall of Famers — are ten men shy of their proportional share and (due to the defensive rigors of their position) have no real chance of meeting either de facto standard for batters. So, in the long run, continued application of de facto criteria can and will only exacerbate the Hall's representational imbalances to the detriment of justice for everyone.

With all of that in mind, several changes in the current BBWAA election procedure would be prudent, including — but not limited to — the following.

- Although the candidate Screening Committee should be retained, the number of names allowed on each ballot should be increased. The current limitation of forty candidates or less is inadequate to the increased number of men with ten-year major-league service produced by baseball's multiple expansions. There were twenty major-league teams at the time this rule was enacted (1968) compared to the thirty in operation in 2000. So a fifty- or even sixty-man limit would be more appropriate to the number of viable candidates likely to ensue from any subsequent expansions.

- The traditional restriction that electors can vote for a maximum of ten candidates per year should be liberalized. As demonstrated in Chapter 10, the growing predilection of many electors to vote for less than the maximum number of candidates allowed must and will (as long as it persists) counterbalance those few who might vote for twelve, fifteen or even twenty men per year. But, assuming the current VC eligibility requirements for post–1945 players are not changed, relaxation of this rule might gradually enlarge the number of Expansion- and Free-Agent-Era candidates that panel may consider.

- The current rule by which players who earn less than 5 percent support in a given year are dropped from the ballot must be liberalized. As noted earlier in the text, given existence of the Screening Committee, the 5 percent-support rule is both unnecessary and redundant. Historically, many candidates who received little support in their early years on the ballot have been elected later, after their individual credentials acquired increased luster over time, and modern players should be afforded the same (or relatively equal) opportunity to achieve that result. Any man who passes the Screening Committee process should be given at least half of his fifteen-year, maximum consideration by the scribes. Then, if he has not achieved 5 percent support after eight years on the ballot, it can more reasonably (and fairly) be argued that he will never gain election from the writers. This change would create a brief period in which the number of names on the ballot increased each year; but, as noted earlier in the text, by the ninth year of its application, the ballot-limiting effects of the rule would be identical as today.

Implementation of all of these changes might help to prevent the Hall of Fame from becoming Blooperstown in the eyes of its most ardent followers. But, realistically, it's doubtful that any of these suggestions will ever be followed. The baseball establishment has a long, consistent history of failure to take actions that were in the best interest of its sport, and — as demonstrated throughout this text — the Hall of Fame trustees and electors have never been immune to that myopia.

But the biggest flaw in the selection process as a whole remains the stubborn, institutional reliance upon a wholly subjective method which, as it has in the past, can only compound the frequency and degree of injustices that occur among the Cooperstown voting. Until the process is replaced (or augmented) by a numerically objective systemization, the long-term prognosis can only include ever more errors of selection and (especially) omission and increased loss of respect for baseball's highest honor among the fans who — like the members of SABR advocating establishment of an alternative Hall of Fame — hold the sport and its Shrine in highest reverence.

As indicated in the introduction, objective statistical standards for Cooperstown membership can be relative rather than absolute, and there is no doubt that adoption of a totally or partially objective method to measure Hall of Fame credentials is feasible within the structures of the BBWAA and VC processes. But, unfortunately, the format and establishment of such a procedure is a subject that requires a separate book.

Appendix:
The Hall of Fame Roster

The lists below include the full Hall of Fame membership through the 2000 BBWAA and Veterans Committee voting. To provide a complete but easily comparative voting history for each member and elective organ, the roster is divided into four separate listings.

The first list includes the ninety-three men elected by the BBWAA, arranged in the sequence of their selection. The first five columns after each man's name include his playing position as cited by the Hall of Fame (Pos), his year of election (Year Elect), his age at the time of election (Age, followed by one letter to designate whether he was living or dead at the time he was selected), the number of years after his retirement as a player that his election occurred (Yrs Ret), and the number of ballots he had received votes on at the time of his election (Num Bal, including all runoff elections and the OTC1 voting of 1936). Following that are four more columns which encapsulate each man's HOF voting history including the support percentage he received in the year of his election (Elect Pct, representing the highest percentage each man ever received), the support percentage earned in the first year he received votes (Yr1 Pct), the lowest support percentage earned on any ballot he received votes (Low Pct), and the average support percentage for all ballots with votes (Avg Pct). For men who were elected in their first year on the ballot (names boldfaced), the figures in the last three columns would be identical to those in the Elect Pct column, so a dashed line has been inserted to avoid confusion.

BBWAA Selections

Player	Pos	Year Elect	Age	Yrs Ret	Num Bal	Elect Pct	Yr1 Pct	Low Pct	Avg Pct
Ty Cobb	of	1936	50L	8	1	98.2	—	—	—
Babe Ruth	of	1936	41L	1	1	95.1	—	—	—
Honus Wagner	ss	1936	62L	19	1	95.1	—	—	—
Christy Mathewson	sp	1936	56D	20	1	90.7	—	—	—
Walter Johnson	sp	1936	49L	9	1	83.6	—	—	—
Nap Lajoie	2b	1937	62L	21	3	83.6	60.2	2.6	50.3
Tris Speaker	of	1937	49L	9	2	82.1	58.8	58.5	70.3
Cy Young	sp	1937	70L	26	3	76.1	49.1	41.0	55.4
Grover Alexander	sp	1938	51L	8	3	80.9	24.3	24.3	55.8
George Sisler	1b	1939	46L	9	4	85.5	34.1	34.1	60.2
Eddie Collins	2b	1939	52L	9	4	77.5	26.5	26.5	57.0
Willie Keeler	of	1939	67D	29	5	75.3	42.3	17.7	52.0
Lou Gehrig	1b	1939	36L	0	2	—	22.6	—	—
Rogers Hornsby	2b	1942	46L	5	5	78.1	46.5	17.6	30.9
Carl Hubbell	sp	1947	44L	4	4	87.0	9.8	9.8	43.8
Frankie Frisch	2b	1947	49L	10	7	84.5	6.2	6.2	36.3
Mickey Cochrane	c	1947	44L	10	7	79.5	35.4	10.2	39.6
Lefty Grove	sp	1947	47L	6	5	76.4	5.3	5.3	25.6
Herb Pennock	sp	1948	54D	14	9	77.7	7.5	7.5	27.0
Pie Traynor	3b	1948	49L	11	9	76.9	7.1	1.1	29.7
Charlie Gehringer	2b	1949	46L	7	7	85.5	4.1	4.1	42.1
Mel Ott	of	1951	42L	4	4	87.2	61.4	61.4	71.7
Jimmie Foxx	1b	1951	44L	6	8	79.2	9.3	6.2	39.3
Harry Heilmann	of	1952	58D	20	13	86.8	5.0	1.7	28.9
Paul Waner	of	1952	49L	7	7	83.3	2.0	2.0	48.3
Dizzy Dean	sp	1953	42L	6	11	79.2	6.9	6.9	44.8
Al Simmons	of	1953	51L	9	10	75.4	1.8	0.5	39.6
Rabbit Maranville	ss	1954	63D	19	16	82.9	12.4	12.4	37.4
Bill Dickey	c	1954	47L	8	11	80.2	6.9	6.9	40.1
Bill Terry	1b	1954	56L	18	15	77.4	4.0	2.7	36.8
Joe DiMaggio	of	1955	41L	4	4	88.8	0.4	0.4	50.7
Ted Lyons	sp	1955	55L	9	11	86.5	1.6	1.5	31.3
Dazzy Vance	sp	1955	64L	20	17	81.7	0.4	0.4	26.5
Gabby Hartnett	c	1955	55L	14	12	77.7	0.8	0.8	27.5
Hank Greenberg	1b	1956	45L	9	10	85.0	1.2	1.2	38.5
Joe Cronin	ss	1956	50L	11	11	78.8	3.7	3.7	28.3
Bob Feller	sp	1962	44L	6	1	93.8	—	—	—
Jackie Robinson	2b	1962	43L	6	1	77.5	—	—	—
Luke Appling	ss	1964	57L	14	8	83.6	0.8	0.8	31.2

Player	Pos	Year Elect	Age	Yrs Ret	Num Bal	Elect Pct	Yr1 Pct	Low Pct	Avg Pct
Ted Williams	of	1966	48L	6	1	93.4	—	—	—
Red Ruffing	sp	1967	62L	20	18	86.9	3.3	2.2	34.7
Joe Medwick	of	1968	57L	20	11	85.1	0.8	0.8	43.9
Stan Musial	of	1969	49L	6	1	93.0	—	—	—
Roy Campanella	c	1969	48L	12	7	79.2	57.2	57.2	65.8
Lou Boudreau	ss	1970	53L	18	12	77.3	1.0	1.0	33.4
Sandy Koufax	sp	1972	37L	6	1	96.9	—	—	—
Yogi Berra	c	1972	47L	7	2	85.6	67.2	67.2	76.4
Early Wynn	sp	1972	52L	9	4	76.0	27.9	27.9	54.3
Warren Spahn	sp	1973	52L	8	1	83.2	—	—	—
Roberto Clemente	of	1973	39D	0	1	—	—	—	—
Mickey Mantle	of	1974	43L	6	1	88.2	—	—	—
Whitey Ford	sp	1974	46L	7	2	77.8	67.1	67.1	72.5
Ralph Kiner	of	1975	53L	20	14	75.4	3.1	1.3	39.4
Robin Roberts	sp	1976	50L	10	4	86.9	56.1	56.1	69.3
Bob Lemon	sp	1976	56L	18	14	78.6	11.9	1.3	27.7
Ernie Banks	ss	1977	46L	6	1	84.0	—	—	—
Eddie Mathews	3b	1978	47L	10	5	79.6	32.3	32.3	52.8
Willie Mays	of	1979	48L	6	1	94.7	—	—	—
Al Kaline	of	1980	46L	6	1	88.3	—	—	—
Duke Snider	of	1980	54L	16	11	86.5	17.0	17.0	43.4
Bob Gibson	sp	1981	46L	6	1	84.0	—	—	—
Hank Aaron	of	1982	46L	6	1	98.1	—	—	—
Frank Robinson	of	1982	47L	6	1	89.4	—	—	—
Brooks Robinson	3b	1983	46L	6	1	92.0	—	—	—
Juan Marichal	sp	1983	45L	8	3	83.7	58.1	58.1	71.8
Luis Aparicio	ss	1984	50L	11	6	84.8	27.8	12.0	44.4
Harmon Killebrew	1b	1984	48L	9	4	83.3	59.6	59.4	68.6
Don Drysdale	sp	1984	48L	15	10	78.6	21.0	21.0	53.6
Hoyt Wilhelm	rp	1985	62L	13	8	83.6	41.8	38.9	59.0
Lou Brock	of	1985	46L	6	1	79.5	—	—	—
Willie McCovey	1b	1986	48L	6	1	81.4	—	—	—
Billy Williams	of	1987	49L	9	6	85.7	23.4	23.4	56.3
Catfish Hunter	sp	1987	41L	8	3	76.3	53.5	53.5	65.9
Willie Stargell	of	1988	47L	6	1	82.6	—	—	—
Johnny Bench	c	1989	42L	6	1	96.2	—	—	—
Carl Yastrzemski	of	1989	50L	6	1	94.4	—	—	—
Jim Palmer	sp	1990	45L	6	1	92.6	—	—	—
Joe Morgan	2b	1990	47L	6	1	81.8	—	—	—
Rod Carew	2b	1991	46L	6	1	90.3	—	—	—
Gaylord Perry	sp	1991	53L	8	3	77.0	67.9	67.9	72.3

Player	Pos	Year Elect	Age	Yrs Ret	Num Bal	Elect Pct	Yr1 Pct	Low Pct	Avg Pct
Ferguson Jenkins	sp	1991	48L	8	3	75.2	52.2	52.2	64.7
Tom Seaver	sp	1992	48L	6	1	98.8	—	—	—
Rollie Fingers	rp	1992	46L	7	2	81.2	65.5	65.5	73.4
Reggie Jackson	of	1993	47L	6	1	93.6	—	—	—
Steve Carlton	sp	1994	50L	6	1	95.8	—	—	—
Mike Schmidt	3b	1995	45L	6	1	96.5	—	—	—
Phil Niekro	sp	1997	57L	9	5	80.3	65.7	60.0	67.3
Don Sutton	sp	1998	53L	10	5	81.6	56.9	56.9	66.6
Nolan Ryan	sp	1999	51L	6	1	98.8	—	—	—
George Brett	3b	1999	45L	6	1	98.2	—	—	—
Robin Yount	ss	1999	43L	6	1	77.5	—	—	—
Carlton Fisk	c	2000	52L	7	2	79.6	66.4	66.4	73.0
Tony Perez	1b	2000	57L	14	9	77.2	50.0	50.0	62.1

The second list includes the ninety-two men who have been elected by the various veterans committees for their performance as major-league players, also arranged in sequence of selection. The information in the first six columns is identical in form and content to that given above for the BBWAA electees. The last four columns are also the same, except that — because these men were never elected by the writers — there is no support percentage given for their year of election. Instead, that column has been replaced by one that lists the highest support percentage received by that player on any BBWAA ballot (High Pct); and — relative to the previous listing — this information has been transposed, sequentially, with the support percentage for each man's first year with votes. The eight players chosen by veterans committees who never received a BBWAA vote are included on this list, with dashed lines indicating the absence of data for the last four columns.

SELECTIONS BY VETERANS COMMITTEES

Player	Pos	Year Elect	Age	Yrs Ret	Num Bal	Yr1 Pct	High Pct	Low Pct	Avg Pct
Cap Anson	1b	1939	87D	42	1	51.3	51.3	51.3	51.3
Buck Ewing	c	1939	87D	42	2	51.3	51.3	0.7	26.0
Charles Radbourn	sp	1939	86D	48	1	20.5	20.5	20.5	20.5
Roger Bresnahan	c	1945	76D	30	6	20.8	53.6	20.8	28.4
Dan Brouthers	1b	1945	87D	41	1	2.6	2.6	2.6	2.6
Fred Clarke	of	1945	72L	30	7	11.5	24.9	0.4	16.4

Player	Pos	Year Elect	Age	Yrs Ret	Num Bal	Yr1 Pct	High Pct	Low Pct	Avg Pct
Jimmy Collins	3b	1945	72D	37	7	10.3	40.8	10.3	29.0
Ed Delahanty	of	1945	78D	42	7	28.2	52.7	7.5	37.6
Hugh Duffy	of	1945	79L	39	6	5.1	33.0	3.5	14.9
Hughie Jennings	ss	1945	75D	27	6	14.1	37.1	2.0	16.9
Mike 'Kin' Kelly	of	1945	88D	52	1	19.2	19.2	19.2	19.2
Jim O'Rourke	of	1945	93D	41	0	—	—	—	—
Jesse Burkett	of	1946	76L	41	6	1.3	1.7	0.5	1.0
Frank Chance	1b	1946	69D	32	8	2.2	72.2	2.2	49.3
Jack Chesbro	sp	1946	72D	37	4	0.5	2.2	0.5	1.0
Johnny Evers	2b	1946	58L	17	8	2.7	64.4	2.7	37.2
Tommy McCarthy	of	1946	86D	50	1	1.3	1.3	1.3	1.3
Joe McGinnity	sp	1946	75D	38	7	6.0	25.3	6.0	16.9
Eddie Plank	sp	1946	71D	29	6	11.4	27.0	10.2	15.5
Joe Tinker	ss	1946	66L	30	7	7.5	27.2	4.4	14.0
Rube Waddell	sp	1946	70D	36	8	14.6	65.1	14.6	47.4
Ed Walsh	sp	1946	65L	29	8	8.8	56.9	8.8	41.0
Mordecai Brown	sp	1949	73D	33	8	2.7	27.7	2.7	18.7
Kid Nichols	sp	1949	80L	43	6	3.8	3.8	0.5	2.0
Charley Bender	sp	1953	69L	28	15	0.9	39.4	0.9	16.5
Bobby Wallace	ss	1953	79L	35	6	1.3	2.7	0.5	1.4
Frank Baker	3b	1955	69L	33	12	0.4	30.4	0.4	10.8
Ray Schalk	c	1955	63L	36	17	1.8	45.0	1.8	16.6
Sam Crawford	of	1957	77L	40	7	0.4	4.2	0.4	2.3
Zach Wheat	of	1959	71L	32	16	2.5	23.0	0.8	9.2
Max Carey	of	1961	71L	32	14	3.0	51.1	0.5	16.7
Billy Hamilton	of	1961	95D	60	2	2.6	2.6	0.4	1.5
Edd Roush	of	1962	69L	31	19	0.9	54.3	0.4	16.5
John Clarkson	sp	1963	102D	69	2	6.4	6.4	0.4	3.5
Elmer Flick	of	1963	87L	53	1	0.4	0.4	0.4	0.4
Sam Rice	of	1963	73L	29	13	0.4	53.2	0.4	14.0
Eppa Rixey	sp	1963	72D	30	16	0.5	52.8	0.4	8.3
Red Faber	sp	1964	76L	31	16	1.5	30.9	0.4	8.4
Burleigh Grimes	sp	1964	71L	30	14	0.5	34.2	0.4	9.1
Tim Keefe	sp	1964	107D	71	1	1.3	1.3	1.3	1.3
Heinie Manush	of	1964	63L	25	6	0.8	9.4	0.7	5.6
Monte Ward	ss	1964	104D	70	1	3.8	3.8	3.8	3.8
Pud Galvin	sp	1965	109D	73	0	—	—	—	—
Lloyd Waner	of	1967	61L	22	10	2.0	23.4	0.4	6.8
Kiki Cuyler	of	1968	69D	30	12	2.5	33.8	2.5	13.1
Goose Goslin	of	1968	68L	30	9	0.8	13.5	0.4	5.6
Stan Coveleski	sp	1969	79L	41	5	0.4	12.8	0.4	3.5

Player	Pos	Year Elect	Age	Yrs Ret	Num Bal	Yr1 Pct	High Pct	Low Pct	Avg Pct
Waite Hoyt	sp	1969	70L	31	15	0.4	19.2	0.4	7.3
Earle Combs	of	1970	71L	35	14	2.0	16.0	0.4	4.2
Jesse Haines	sp	1970	77L	33	12	0.4	8.3	0.4	3.6
Dave Bancroft	ss	1971	79L	41	15	1.5	16.2	0.4	5.0
Jake Beckley	1b	1971	104D	64	2	1.3	1.3	0.4	0.9
Chick Hafey	of	1971	67L	34	12	0.8	10.8	0.4	3.1
Harry Hooper	of	1971	84L	46	6	3.0	3.0	1.2	1.8
Joe Kelley	of	1971	100D	63	2	0.4	0.4	0.4	0.4
Rube Marquard	sp	1971	82L	46	13	0.4	13.9	0.4	5.1
Lefty Gomez	sp	1972	64L	29	15	2.8	46.1	0.6	15.1
Ross Youngs	of	1972	75D	46	18	4.4	19.1	4.4	12.8
George Kelly	1b	1973	77L	41	7	0.6	1.9	0.6	1.0
Mickey Welch	sp	1973	114D	81	0	—	—	—	—
Jim Bottomley	1b	1974	74D	37	12	3.3	33.1	2.7	10.7
Sam Thompson	of	1974	114D	68	0	—	—	—	—
Earl Averill	of	1975	73L	34	7	0.7	5.3	0.7	2.2
Billy Herman	2b	1975	66L	28	9	0.8	20.2	0.8	6.4
Roger Connor	1b	1976	119D	79	0	—	—	—	—
Fred Lindstrom	3b	1976	71L	40	5	0.7	4.4	0.7	2.2
Amos Rusie	sp	1977	106D	76	6	15.4	15.4	0.4	3.7
Joe Sewell	ss	1977	79L	44	7	0.5	8.6	0.4	1.8
Addie Joss	sp	1978	98D	68	7	5.5	14.2	0.4	7.6
Hack Wilson	of	1979	79D	45	16	0.5	38.3	0.4	15.3
Chuck Klein	of	1980	75D	36	13	2.5	27.9	2.0	11.0
Johnny Mize	1b	1981	68L	28	13	16.7	43.6	4.8	27.5
Travis Jackson	ss	1982	79L	46	12	4.1	7.3	0.4	2.8
George Kell	3b	1983	61L	26	15	16.4	36.9	3.5	21.8
Rick Ferrell	c	1984	79L	37	3	0.5	0.5	0.4	0.4
Pee Wee Reese	ss	1984	66L	26	16	36.3	47.9	5.2	33.1
Enos Slaughter	of	1985	69L	26	15	33.1	68.8	15.7	45.0
Arky Vaughan	ss	1985	73D	36	13	0.4	29.1	0.4	7.0
Bobby Doerr	2b	1986	68L	35	14	0.8	25.0	0.8	10.5
Ernie Lombardi	c	1986	78D	39	11	1.8	16.4	1.3	7.9
Red Schoendienst	2b	1989	66L	26	15	19.1	42.6	19.1	32.1
Tony Lazzeri	2b	1991	88D	52	15	0.4	33.2	0.4	14.0
Hal Newhouser	sp	1992	71L	37	14	2.5	42.8	1.3	18.6
Phil Rizzuto	ss	1994	77L	38	16	0.5	38.4	0.5	22.5
Richie Ashburn	of	1995	68L	33	15	2.1	41.8	2.1	19.2
Vic Willis	sp	1995	119D	85	0	—	—	—	—
Jim Bunning	sp	1996	64L	25	15	38.2	74.4	33.3	51.7
Nellie Fox	2b	1997	70D	31	15	10.8	74.5	10.8	36.6

Player	Pos	Year Elect	Age	Yrs Ret	Num Bal	Yr1 Pct	High Pct	Low Pct	Avg Pct
George Davis	ss	1998	127D	87	0	—	—	—	—
Larry Doby	of	1998	73L	39	3	2.3	3.4	0.3	2.0
Orlando Cepeda	1b	1999	61L	25	15	12.5	73.6	10.1	37.6
Bid McPhee	2b	2000	140D	101	0	—	—	—	—

The third list, also arranged sequentially, includes sixteen men chosen by veterans committees for non-playing capacities but who also received votes at some time from the BBWAA. The information provided is identical in form and description to that of the VC players selections above.

NON-PLAYER SELECTIONS BY VETERANS COMMITTEES

Player	Pos	Year Elect	Age	Yrs Ret	Num Bal	Yr1 Pct	High Pct	Low Pct	Avg Pct
Connie Mack	mgr	1937	74L	-13	1	0.4	0.4	0.4	0.4
John McGraw	mgr	1937	64D	5	3	21.8	21.8	1.8	13.7
George Wright	cont	1937	90L	55	1	7.7	7.7	7.7	7.7
Charles Comiskey	exec	1939	77D	8	1	7.7	7.7	7.7	7.7
Albert Spalding	cont	1939	89D	48	1	5.1	5.1	5.1	5.1
Wilbert Robinson	mgr	1945	82D	14	6	7.7	38.2	2.5	17.4
Clark Griffith	exec	1946	76L	-9	7	2.0	43.5	2.0	22.1
Joe McCarthy	mgr	1957	70L	7	5	1.1	1.2	0.4	0.8
Bill McKechnie	mgr	1962	76L	16	4	0.8	3.5	0.6	1.5
Miller Huggins	mgr	1964	85D	35	9	2.5	63.9	1.2	29.6
Casey Stengel	mgr	1966	76L	1	9	0.8	23.1	0.8	5.2
Branch Rickey	exec	1967	85D	12	2	1.3	1.3	0.8	1.1
Satchel Paige	sp	1971	65L	6	1	0.4	0.4	0.4	0.4
Bucky Harris	mgr	1975	78L	19	10	0.4	16.9	0.4	5.8
Al Lopez	mgr	1977	68L	8	12	0.7	39.0	0.5	13.9
Leo Durocher	mgr	1994	89D	21	9	0.8	10.5	0.4	2.8

Note: Negative numbers for Mack and Griffith indicate induction before they had retired from that capacity. Paige is included on this list, but was enshrined by the Negro League Committee, and not the VC.

Through the 2000 voting, there were also forty-eight other men enshrined at Cooperstown who never received votes in any BBWAA election. They are listed alphabetically below, along with their year of election, and grouped by whether they were chosen as managers, executives, pioneer contributors, umpires, or representatives of the Negro leagues. The umpire list also indicates each man's primary league of service, and the Negro-league list identifies each inductee's primary playing position(s).

Managers: Walter Alston (1983), Sparky Anderson (2000), Ned Hanlon (1996), Tom Lasorda (1997), Frank Selee (1999), Earl Weaver (1996).

Executives: Ed Barrow (1953), Morgan Bulkeley (1937), Happy Chandler (1982), Ford Frick (1970), Warren Giles (1970), Will Harridge (1972), William Hulbert (1995), Ban Johnson (1937), Kenesaw Mountain Landis (1944), Larry MacPhail (1978), Lee MacPhail (1998), Bill Veeck, Jr. (1991), George Weiss (1971), Tom Yawkey (1980).

Pioneer Contributors: Alexander Cartwright (1938), Henry Chadwick (1938), Candy Cummings (1939), Harry Wright (1953).

Umpires: Al Barlick (NL, 1989), Nestor Chylak (AL, 1999), Jocko Conlan (NL, 1974), Tom Connolly (AL, 1953), Billy Evans (AL, 1973), Cal Hubbard (AL, 1976), Bill Klem (NL, 1953), Bill McGowan (AL, 1992).

Negro leaguers: Cool Papa Bell (of, 1974), Oscar Charleston (of, 1976), Ray Dandridge (3b, 1987), Leon Day (p, 1995), Martin Dihigo (of-p, 1977), Bill Foster (p, 1996), Rube Foster (p-exec, 1981), Josh Gibson (c, 1972), Monte Irvin (of, 1973), Judy Johnson (3b, 1975), Buck Leonard (1b, 1972), John 'Pop' Lloyd (ss, 1977), Bullet Joe Rogan (p, 1998), Norman 'Turkey' Stearnes (of, 2000), Willie Wells (ss, 1997), Smokey Joe Williams (p, 1999).

Index

Aaron, Hank 10, 13, 30, 75, 226; de facto achievement by 182, 184, 186; HOF elective history of 78, 80, 231, 253–254, 265; as VC member 106–107, 113, 132, 251

active players, BBWAA votes for 56, 78

Acosta, Jose 240

Adams, Franklin Pierce 96

Adcock, Joe 14, 75

Agee, Tommie 68

alcohol, use of 18, 49–50, 62, 68, 76–77, 131

Alexander, Grover 93, 122; de facto achievement by 179; HOF elective history of 79–81, 90, 152–153, 264; use of alcohol by 50, 68, 131

Allen, Dick 136, 138, 146

Alley, Gene 68

Allison, Bob 68

all-star selection, effects on HOF prospects of players 26–27, 225–227

Almeida, Rafael 240

Alou, Felipe 62

Alou, Jesus 62–63

Alou, Matty 62

Alston, Walter 43, 234–236, 270

Altrock, Nick 233

American Association (major league, 1882–91) 3, 92, 227, 238

American Association (minor league) 90

Anderson, Dave 251–252

Anderson, George "Sparky" 1, 4, 43, 234–235, 270

Anson, Cap 93; de-facto achievement by 100–101, 181–184, 204; HOF elective history of 22–23, 89, 92, 97, 134, 266; role in baseball's segregation 239–240

Aparicio, Luis 19, 22, 116, 167–168; HOF elective history of 152–153, 265

Appling, Luke 23–27, 29, 34–41, 47–49, 82, 204, 232; HOF elective history of 44–45, 59, 82, 264

Ashburn, Richie 167–168, 251–252, 268

Averill, Earl 107, 268

Baines, Harold 192–193

Baker, Frank 98, 267

Bancroft, Dave 20, 105–108, 116, 133, 167–168, 268

Banks, Ernie 32–33, 49–50, 116, 167, 203, 211, 229; de facto achievement by 182–184; HOF elective history of 45, 78, 80, 231, 265

Barlick, Al 270

Barnes, Ross 49

Barrow, Ed 94, 97, 270

The Baseball Encyclopedia (Macmillan) 8, 51, 74, 170, 192

Baseball Writers Association of America (BBWAA) 1, 8, 11, 18–20, 64, 93, 96, 130, 132; Alphonse-Gaston tendancies of 53–67, 78, 87; average age of inductees 114; big-city voting block of 18, 200; Candidate Screening Committee of 70, 85, 155, 258–260; compositional changes of 37, 41–42, 200, 202; disputes of, with veterans committees 21, 94–99, 116–118, 132–144; eligibility of players for ballot 40–41, 56–60, 63–70, 81–86, 94–97, 114–115, 127–131, 154–155, 161, 231–233, 260; errors of selection or omission by 22–23, 88–89, 118; fallibility of 19–23, 40, 44–45, 51–52, 56–86, 88–89, 94–96, 115–116; fickleness of 151–156, 175, 207; first-ballot electees of 22, 78–82, 155, 181, 184, 186, 202, 217, 220, 231;

271

DEC X 2001

106–108, 131, 268
Winfield, Dave 140,
  186–187, 192–193
womanizing, by players 50,
  130
Wood, Smoky Joe 123–127,
  138
World Series *see* postseason play
World War II: effect on
  HOF credentials of players 48–49; player short-

ages during 24, 49
Wright, George 90, 269
Wright, Harry 270
Wynn, Early 179–180, 265

Yastrzemski, Carl 2, 78, 80,
  182, 226, 229, 265
Yawkey, Tom 270
Young, Cy 57, 93, 97, 99,
  153; de facto achievement
  of 80, 179; HOF elective
  history of 56, 79–80,

89–90, 114, 264
Youngs, Ross 105–108, 133,
  250, 268
Yount, Robin 32–33, 230;
  de facto achievement
  of 2, 15, 175, 177, 182,
  193, 197, 204; HOF elective history of 78, 198,
  266

Zimmernan, Heinie 121